Crusader Without Violence
A Biography of Martin Luther King, Jr.

Men say I am a saint losing myself in politics. The fact is I am a politician trying my hardest to be a saint.

—GANDHI

L. D. Reddick

Crusader Without Violence

A BIOGRAPHY OF MARTIN LUTHER KING, Jr.

HARPER & BROTHERS, PUBLISHERS, NEW YORK

For My Mother

Contents

(Picture section follows page 86)

Crusader Without Violence
A Biography of Martin Luther King, Jr.

I - The Man

MARTIN LUTHER KING *has attracted world-wide attention by his leadership of the Montgomery bus boycott in 1956 and the projection then and afterward of his philosophy of nonviolent social change. He has shown a rare combination of courage, wisdom and compassion. Perhaps more than any other American he has reminded us of the practical usefulness of the ideals of Henry David Thoreau and the techniques of Mohandas K. Gandhi.*

He has undergone tests which were not merely theoretical: He has been caricatured in cartoons and abused in editorials by those who oppose the cause he serves; his home has been bombed and he himself has been maltreated by police and convicted in Southern courts; and in September, 1958, he was almost assassinated in New York City by a woman who appeared to be demented.

On the other hand, Martin Luther King is a hero to the Negro people of the South and to others elsewhere. He has been honored beyond his years by universities and ethical societies. His name has been carried to many lands and nations by the written and spoken word.

But the image of the hero or monster or saint scarcely reveals the man. Or satisfies the human heart that asks how the man came to be

1

as he is—and may become. Quite naturally, people want to know what kind of person Martin Luther King really is and how it happens that one so young could achieve, apparently, such poise and moderation in the face of danger and fame. Above all, they search his life as they search their own, seeking after that which is real and rejecting that which is false.

Physical and Social

Martin Luther King is not tall. You may not be aware of this when he is up in the pulpit or on the rostrum. But when he comes down to shake hands with the audience, you realize, with him on the same level, that he is a little below the medium height. He has a well-formed, brown-skinned body, with good muscle and bone, strong shoulders and arms. His torso, firm and broad, is worthy of a larger man. King's shortness is in his legs, which are quick and fleet. Until September 1958 he was unscarred but for a slight nick below the knuckles of his left hand.

At that time, Dr. King was stabbed almost to death by a Negro woman as he sat autographing copies of his book in a Harlem store. Whether this was the senseless act of an unfortunate psychopath or part of a plot to destroy the leader of a movement is still in question. The wound and subsequent operation left him with a surgical mark on his chest, a few inches to the right of his heart, and minus his second rib and part of his breastbone.

King's face is boyish. His features are soft and rounded, except for his eyes, which have a slight Oriental slant. His lips and nose are full and well formed; his forehead is rather high with a receding hairline. His clear brown eyes sparkle. He wears a small mustache. He shaves daily with an old-fashioned English razor, a gift from his father, who also shaves with an open-faced blade. King keeps his crinkly black hair close cut and well trimmed.

He is in excellent health and has seldom known sickness. Yet on the few occasions when he has fallen ill, as during his visit to Ghana, King has wondered if he would pull through.

King sleeps well. In general, he relaxes easily and once in bed does not worry about the affairs of the day, unless there is some especially pressing problem. He usually gets to bed early and rises at about 5 or 6 A.M. He would like seven or eight hours of sleep but seldom gets that much. During the crises of the boycott he was averaging about four hours in bed a night. Fortunately, he could take a fifteen- or twenty-minute catnap during the day and bounce up from it feeling refreshed. When he is lounging informally, he habitually stretches himself, placing his feet on a stool or a second chair or his desk.

King's favorite exercises are walking, tennis and swimming. As a youth, he loved basketball, football and baseball. Although he did quite a bit of walking while in the seminary and graduate school, he cannot walk very far in Montgomery without having somebody stop him for a conversation. There it is also difficult to find a tennis court open to Negroes. But it is King's own fault that he does not make more use of the splendid swimming pool at Alabama State College— just seven blocks away, on his own street, South Jackson.

As a sports spectator, King keeps up fairly well with big-time football, baseball and boxing, although most of the games and bouts that he sees now are by way of television. His long-time ring heroes are Joe Louis and Sugar Ray Robinson. He admires Jack Johnson, who won the heavyweight crown when race feeling in sports was much more intense than it is today. He also likes Gene Tunney; Henry Armstrong, who held three world championships at the same time; and Tiger Flowers, the great middleweight from King's home town, Atlanta.

King loves food. "Eating," he says, "is my great sin." His tastes are wide and varied—steaks, chops, chicken, sauces, gravies, vegetables, fruits, cakes, pies, ice cream . . . He is especially fond of collard greens and black-eyed peas. But like almost everybody else, King has to watch his diet. He restricts himself on starches and denies himself that second helping—most of the time. When the scales tell him that he needs to do it, he will drop one meal, eating a late breakfast and an early dinner. Occasionally he takes vitamin pills.

In a word, Martin Luther King is an attractive, healthy, physical type, easy-going, with good motor control and all of his senses active. His robust health is perhaps part of the basis for his energy and poise.

In matters of dress, King is impeccable. Those who have seen him on his lecture tours may have noticed that the shades of his suits, ties, shirts and shoes blend harmoniously and that he wears a handkerchief—often an embroidered one—in his upper coat pocket. His clothes are of good quality, and his wife, Coretta, helps him select them. He likes suits that have a dressy sheen. The habit of giving attention to personal appearance goes back to his youth. In high school he was addicted to tweed suits. At college he was a fancy dresser, leaning heavily toward sports clothes.

Today he is more reserved. Wayne Phillips of the New York *Times* has remarked that King dresses in "conservative good taste." He favors gray or brown suits. He does not care for formal attire, has no tails, but does have a tuxedo and a light summer tux jacket.

He wears the standard, string-up footgear, not caring for "casuals" or loafers. His shoes are always shined; he brushes them up each morning himself. His socks do not hang down over the upper edges of his shoes in the collegiate fashion but have elastic tops or supporters. He prefers silk and hand-painted ties, and wears hats winter and summer. His nails are kept closely trimmed but he does not have them manicured.

During the height of the Montgomery boycott, the rumor was circulated by the opposition that King had taken the people's money to buy himself a Cadillac. Those who knew him laughed at this, because for one thing he does not care at all for big, flashy automobiles. He owns a 1954 Pontiac, and his church has a station wagon.

King finds little time for social life and attends formal functions only out of a sense of obligation. As a youth, he liked to dance and was considered quite a good jitterbug. But as he moved toward the ministry, he gave up these pleasures. He was never interested in card playing but believes that he is still good at billiards.

King is a member of a college fraternity—Alpha Phi Alpha—which he did not get around to joining until he had finished college. He is also an honorary Elk and a duly initiated member of Sigma Pi Phi—a sort of super fraternity of mostly elderly and distinguished Negro men.

He enjoys weekend visits with a small party of friends in the mountains, on the seashore or at a suburban home. He likes to fish and someday hopes to go yachting in pursuit of the prizes of the deep sea. Recently, he has taken up golf.

He enjoys movies if he can pick and choose. On TV he prefers the quiz programs, where he tries to beat the contestants to the answers.

Whenever he is in New York for several days, King tries to get in at least one Broadway or little theater show. He has seen *Mr. Wonderful, South Pacific* and *Damn Yankees.*

He does not read detective stories, the pulps or novels in general, nor does he know the great imaginative works of modern literature. He has not read Kafka or Proust and little even of Hemingway and Faulkner. Having fallen into social action as soon as he completed his education, he has not had the time for general reading. But he likes to quote the more communicable poets in his speeches and sermons. He reads Negro writers—especially James Weldon Johnson, Richard Wright and Langston Hughes.

King enjoys getting about and seeing America and the world, although most of his traveling thus far has been in connection with his speaking engagements. When flying, which he does frequently, he insures himself heavily: $50,000 when he is flying north and south; $100,000 on east and west flights, when he has to cross over the mountains. His wife and children, he says, deserve to be well taken care of.

Family

As that remark suggests, King is very much a family man. From both a personal and a theoretical standpoint he believes in the monogamous family. Two persons absolutely devoted to each other, he maintains, bring out the best in marriage by attaining a high standard of mutual understanding and self-fulfillment.

What is wrong with the American family, he insists, is not monogamy. Much of the blame for unhappy and broken homes he places on the strains that arise out of our struggle for material possessions and prestige. It is good that economic development permits more women to work—and they should have equal pay for equal work. But somebody should be at home, he feels. Biologically and aesthetically women are more suitable than men for keeping house. And for the children, there is no substitute for an attentive mother. If the economic grind to stay ahead of the Joneses were not so great both husband and wife could spend more time at home.

Children should be neither drastically inhibited nor permitted to run wild. King emphasizes that children are not young adults. Accordingly, they should be given freedom to express their innocent inclinations. They need guidance, not suppression. Physical punishment of any sort should be necessary only rarely. He favors spanking children "whenever necessary," for sometimes there is no other way. "Whippings must not be so bad, for I received them until I was fifteen," he says with a laugh.

King looks upon divorce as the "court of last resort." A family should prayerfully exhaust all other possible remedies before breaking up. But separation is better than prolonged and fundamental unhappiness.

In his column in *Ebony* magazine, "Advice for Living," King has said: "In advising anyone on marital problems I usually begin by urging each person to do an honest job of self-analysis. . . . People fail to get along with each other because they fear each other. They fear each other because they don't know each other. They don't know each other because they have not properly communicated with each other. . . . A marriage that is based only on external beauty lacks the solid rock of permanence and stability. One must discover the meaning of soul beauty before he has really discovered the meaning of love."

King's home life fits the theoretical picture he paints. The atmosphere is positive, co-operative and informal. A moderate number of receptions are held there for visiting personalities. Church members and other friends come in at almost any time.

Coretta Scott King is attractive and intelligent. She has no job of her own outside the home, but maintains an active interest in whatever her husband does and wherever he goes. She attends quite a few meetings of various women's groups and represents him now and then when he is out of town. For her own career, she takes on a few singing engagements each year. She is a soprano.

King and his wife talk over major problems together. When his life was threatened almost daily, she chose to remain in Montgomery with him even though both her parents and his felt that she should retire to a safer location. She and the baby were in the home the night of January 30, 1956, when a bomb exploded on their front porch. Luckily, no one was hurt.

The Kings have two children—Yolanda Denise King, better known as Yoki, born November 17, 1955, and Martin Luther King III, born October 23, 1957. Yolanda is thus a pre-boycott and Martin a post-boycott child. In his son's loud cry, King professes to detect the voice of a future preacher.

King describes himself as an "ambivert"—a cross between an extrovert and an introvert—and this is about right. He is outgoing, direct and not at all a worrier or brooder. At the same time, he does live an inner, contemplative life. Martin Luther King may be "striking" or "different" and his point of view may be considered "unusual" or even "odd," but he himself is not internally complicated. Neither is he "all balled up inside" by inhibitions or torn apart by deep-seated frustrations. As much as any ordinary human being, King is normal and his behavior is predictable.

No matter what people have heard about him or the mental picture they have formed of him, King's naturalness is felt by everyone who comes face to face with him. To meet him is to enter an atmosphere of simplicity, free of pretense or posing. He smiles and shakes hands easily. He is unhurried. He never seems to respond impulsively or impatiently. This delayed and calm reaction has helped him out of many an explosive situation.

He enjoys conversation, is a big talker himself and a patient listener —at times too patient for those who have appointments with him and who often have to wait while he is still accommodating somebody who "just dropped in."

Obviously, King likes people. He is the opposite of an egotist. One Southern white woman was impressed by his "almost touching modesty." A cynical New Yorker, who came all the way to Montgomery to look him over, said afterward: "There are few men like him in public life today. He's like the old-timers—really sincere."

King listens well but makes his own decisions. He is not argumentative but he has will and direction. He does not quibble over details but constantly advances his main point. He is so persuasive that almost everybody is happy to let him have his way.

For all his amiability, he has a touch of suspicion in his nature. In high school and college he thought at times that the big boys who elected him to student committees were not so interested in honoring him as in pushing him up to do jobs that they found to be a little risky, as, for example, negotiating with the faculty.

King also has a quiet shrewdness underneath his kindliness. Usually he can see through the motives of men, though this discernment may be difficult at the first meeting, when the atmosphere is friendly and positive. Along with this sagacity there is also a strong sense of responsibility for the material security of his wife and children. All his life the value of the dollar has been pounded into him, though his natural predisposition may have been otherwise.

He takes special pains with public moneys. During the height of the bus boycott, contributions came to him in every conceivable shape and form—check, money order, currency, silver. Some of it came to his home; much of it was addressed to him personally. He was careful to have it counted and taken to the office of the organization the day that it arrived. One of his secretaries, who worked very closely with him in those days, has said privately that "the Reverend King is the most honest man I ever knew; unnecessarily so."

Thus Martin Luther King, as much as the next one, likes good clothes, a suite at the Waldorf, dinner at Sardi's, plane trips, long-distance telephone calls and money in the bank. But all of these things must come to him by way of the straight and narrow path. His father before him always believed that the Church should give its pastor the best living that it could afford but that the pastor was not to help himself to one penny from the collection plate.

When relaxing among close friends, King is full of fun. He has a great zest for life. You feel it when you are with him. "Oh yes!" is a favorite expression of his enthusiasm. And he can tease, with a dry, erupting humor that reminds his mother of her father. King characterizes statements that have little intellectual content as "pretty light" and a person who makes them as "a light sister" or "a light brother."

Never given to clowning in public, King will regale his friends at private parties with his imitations of religious entertainers and fellow preachers. At a birthday celebration that his wife gave for him and about a dozen guests, King and his close friend, the Rev. Ralph Abernathy, "carried on." Pretending to be two semiliterate gospel singers doing a TV program, they began by "dericating" the number to Miss Coretta King, "a dear sister over there in Montgomery, Alabama." Then followed off-key, off-beat singing, slurring, grimacing, and prancing that kept the party howling for half an hour.

King's voice is possibly his most magnetic power. It is a rich, natural baritone with a wide range. His brother says that he can sing bass in a chorus and then double with a second tenor solo. Art Carter of the *Afro-American* once wrote that King has "a soft musical voice which he uses without oratorical tricks." Mrs. Almena Lomax of the Los Angeles *Tribune* is more lyrical when she writes: "His voice has great power, passion, great depths of tenderness and an overlay of gentleness to charm your heart out of your body."

Perhaps it was this overlay of gentleness that caused a long-distance operator to let her enthusiasm override her company's regulations. While King was "holding on," waiting for the other party to come to the telephone, she gushed out: "Oh, Reverend King, I've just got to tell you how wonderful you are!" It was his voice over the telephone that first fascinated Miss Coretta Scott, even before she laid eyes on him.

Thus, Martin Luther King is healthy, winsome, quite normal and enlightened in most of his tastes and in his family life. He is easy to meet and good company.

II - The Ideology

MARTIN LUTHER KING's home address in Montgomery is 309 South Jackson Street, a large, white frame house. About four blocks toward the southwest is the office of the Montgomery Improvement Association at 530 South Union Street, a two-story, red, new-brick building. About seven blocks northwest, at the corner of Decatur Street, stands Dexter Avenue Baptist Church—high steps, steep roof and old, red brick.

Home-office-church, this is the regular "beat" of the Rev. Dr. King. But during the year-long boycott of buses all of Montgomery was more or less his route. He was covering the whole city, so to speak—in and out of conferences, mass meetings, courthouses, the city hall and the state capitol. Since the boycott, the outside world has called on him more and more; thus his speaking and conferring have taken him into many parts of the nation and as far away as Ghana, West Africa and India. Nevertheless, the round of home-office-church describes his working orbit.

At home King has a den to which he can retreat from household activities and the stream of casual callers. It is a room about twelve by eighteen feet, lined with book shelves, outfitted with a desk, several chairs, an air conditioner and a gas-jet heater. It has the scholarly disorder that one would expect to find in the study of a man who likes to read but receives books, magazines, and pamphlets much faster than he can consume them.

Here in this den the Rev. Dr. King often begins his day at 6 or

7 A.M. by meditation. He usually ends it here also, doing his after-hours reading and dictating to a portable transcriber that he will take along with him to the office the next morning. Like many other people, King does some of his thinking in bed, just before dozing off to sleep or upon awakening in the morning. He believes that he is at his best, mentally, before ten o'clock in the morning.

The Montgomery Improvement Association, in the course of its history, had several office locations but finally landed at the Bricklayers' Hall on Union Street. Here the MIA rented a suite of four rooms, including a couple of closets and a lavatory. One of the small, eight-by-eight back rooms was reserved for the president. Like the other offices, this one had yellow walls, a black and gray tile floor, a steel gray desk and green filing cabinets. There was just space enough left in it for several chairs.

But it was here that President King read most of his mail, kept his confidential correspondence and dictated answers either to his transscriber or directly to his secretary, Mrs. Maude L. Ballou. A great many of King's public statements were composed or reworked in this little office; also it could accommodate interviews and small conferences. But the large meetings of the MIA board (some thirty-odd members) took place in the assembly hall on the second floor of the building.

MIA headquarters during and just after the boycott were bursting with activity—often both telephones ringing at once, some committee or subcommittee always in session or officers putting their heads together in a huddle, telegram and special delivery messengers darting in and out, and the secretary and her assistants pounding away at the typewriters, answering the phones and receiving visitors, all at the same time.

Normally King would get to the office about ten o'clock in the morning, greeting everyone upon arrival, and work through until his lunch hour at one-thirty. He often remained at home for an hour or so, returning to the office and remaining there until five or six.

This routine, of course, was often interrupted by callers and out-of-the-office conferences. Moreover, Saturday (and sometimes Friday) was spent at the church office, deciding upon and arranging the schedule of religious events for the week and preparing for sermons and other ministerial duties. The church had a secretary who cared for most of its clerical details. As pastor, King himself preached at Dexter about three Sundays out of each month.

The office staff agreed that "Reverend King is a very busy man, a hard worker, but pleasant to work with." King's secretaries all testify that he dictates easily, without much hesitation or impatience. They say he works them long and hard, frequently extra hours, but not nearly so hard as he works himself. Many a time during the boycott crisis he became so fatigued that he had to stop dictating for a while, excuse his secretary and lay his head down on his desk for a few minutes of rest or curl up on two large chairs pulled together.

Despite his oral mastery of words, King is the first to admit his weaknesses in the technical aspects of composition. "I can't spell a lick," he says. All the way through public school and college, his sister had to help him out, looking over his essays before he passed them in to his teachers. One of the chief qualities that he looks for in a secretary is the ability to spell "twice as well as I can." King says that "somewhere I missed learning all of the elements of grammar. My punctuation as well as my spelling is horrible. I always need somebody to go over my work for that." Obviously, King can handle ideas much better than the written word. Yet his Ph.D. dissertation in theology is well written for its specialized readers. Currently he is developing a more popular style for the general public.

Perhaps it is a general characteristic that King is more at home with a conception than he is with the details of its application. For example, though he made excellent grades in mathematics, he is not much interested in business administration—or administration in general.

The Orator

His great delight is in speaking and preaching. Essentially Martin Luther King is an orator. He himself admits that the eloquent statement of ideas is his greatest talent, strongest tradition, and most constant interest. It is his first love. King has been rated among the top public speakers of the nation. As Louis Martin of the Chicago *Defender* has noted, King may come after a long series of addresses and addressers; yet his effect is fresh and moving. "He's a real charmer," says Martin.

King is methodical in the preparation of his sermons and lectures. He likes to read up on his topic for a couple of days; outline it, then write out what he wants to say. He will then lay his manuscript aside, going back to it a few hours before it is to be delivered. When he has gone through this process, he does not need either script or notes when he stands up to make his speech.

Unfortunately, the luxury of such orderly preparation could seldom be afforded during and after the boycott.

He delights in talking over or debating what he is going to say with somebody beforehand. His wife is often helpful in these preparations, and when the pressure is really on him, she knows his pattern of thought so well that she can suggest connecting ideas or construct transitional passages. But Mrs. King does not write her husband's speeches. As a matter of fact, it is remarkable that King himself composed so many of the statements, press releases and letters that have been issued under his name and through the Montgomery Improvement Association. Perhaps it would have been better if he had been helped a bit more. However, when it comes to magazine or book writing, King more readily accepts assistance and advice.

King feels a little nervous just before he is about to begin speaking. But once he hears his own voice and senses the response of his listeners, he becomes completely at ease in a moment or two. Often the applause of the audience after he has been introduced and before he has uttered a single word is sufficiently assuring.

King uses his voice as an instrument, fitting its inflections to the tempo of his sentences and to the mood and thought that they are meant to convey. He enunciates clearly. He is probably at his best when he is "just talking" to an audience, saying what he has to say in a conversational tone. But he can rise to heights of emotion and climax, reminding us that he is, after all, a Southern Baptist preacher, though a highly educated and cultivated one. Mrs. Almena Lomax has written that "the impact of Martin Luther King is in his delivery, which is all of a piece, like a narrative poem. . . . His elocution has the beauty and polish of Roland Hayes singing a spiritual. . . ."

As a speaker he gesticulates only moderately—using both arms and hands and a slight wave or bow of the head. His right hand, of course, is utilized more than his left. He does not move about on the platform very much—this would be fatal with microphones. Usually he stands up straight and, viewed from behind by his colleagues on the platform, is seen to place his short legs firmly apart, giving him a good stance. He shifts his weight from foot to foot easily and naturally. Now and then he will raise himself up on the balls of his feet for emphasis. Being a short man, he does not find it necessary to drape himself over the lectern. This gives the audience a direct, clear frontal view of him.

Art Carter of the *Afro-American,* after watching King intently, remarked that "for emphasis he occasionally utilizes his fingers in little illustrative gestures, but mostly talks straight-wordly, unhesitantingly and with a command of the English language."

King likes mouth-filling phrases and colorful figures of speech. While yet a youngster in the first grade, he told his mother that he would get himself some big words. Apparently, he made good on this promise, for many of his speeches and sermons are punctuated with expressions such as "the iron feet of oppression," "crippling passivity and stagnant complacency," "incarcerated within the walls of inactivity" and "clouds of sorrow floating in our mental skies."

King is particularly fond of contrasting images—of color, sound, temperature, space. He has a special attachment to the darkness-versus-light analogy, as "from bass black to treble white," "from the midnight of Egyptian captivity to the glittering light of Canaan freedom," "from the black night of segregation to the bright daybreak of joy." "The stone of separate-but-equal had been rolled away, and justice rose up from dark and gloomy graves," "leaving the dark chambers of the subconscious and moving toward the bright parlor of conscious action."

These are, obviously, the metaphors of a public speaker, rather than of a writer. The requirement is immediate communication with an audience. All allusions and anecdotes must be understood when they are heard. A page in a book or magazine can be reread. The writer can be more subtle and his editor will help him catch and discard the inept and hurried phrase.

King's great theme, of course, is race relations in the modern world. But in a larger sense, his main thesis is the power of brotherly love to redeem a world that will otherwise destroy itself. "Only love can bring brotherhood on earth," he constantly repeats.

These grand conceptions allow for innumerable subthemes, variations and counterpoint. Usually, King applies his broad approach to Negro-white relations in the American South and nonviolent resistance to social change. As he puts it: "The strong man is the man who can stand up for his rights and not hit back."

Because of circumstances and history, since December, 1955, King has been speaking mostly on what happened in Montgomery, the implications of this experience, and his philosophy for racial desegregation in general. This is, of course, what he himself symbolizes to everyone and is what audiences want to hear from him.

On the other hand, his church members may feel that they get rather frequent doses of the "love your white enemies" purgative. One of the more vocal Dexter Avenue Baptist Church matrons has said, "Oh yes, I know the words by heart now—though I need not *like* Engelhardt [a local segregationist], I must *love* him."

In time the preoccupation with racial integration will presumably ease and the Rev. Dr. King will be allowed to address himself to some of the other great problems of life.

Heroes and Ideals

King will tell you that Socrates is his hero above all men of ancient times. "Socrates," he says, "had the courage to live, standing up for truth, even if it meant death. To the old philosopher, truth was greater than life."

Naturally Martin Luther King would be curious about Martin Luther. He was delighted when, after extensive study, he was sure that he admired his historical name bearer. He liked Luther's courage of his convictions, when he said, "Here I stand; I cannot do otherwise." King feels that this is "a grand statement." He was disappointed when he read of Luther's small sympathy for the common man. He does not approve of Luther's turning against the peasants. Nor does he altogether agree with Luther's theological system. But King reminds himself that "few men, great or small, have complete consistency of character or views." To him, despite any blemishes, Martin Luther is "a great force, a great soul, one who influenced history."

It has been said that the statement of the *Encyclopaedia Britannica* on Martin Luther as a climax to his contemporaries might be applied to Martin Luther King: "His courage and self-assertion precipitated the crystallization of a thousand thoughts and impulses with which society had gradually become saturated, but which had remained in solution until now."

King agrees with the common verdict that Lincoln is the greatest American. He holds Lincoln in the highest esteem for his steadfast devotion to duty, "his projecting morality beyond political expediency."

Among Negroes, King's hero is Frederick Douglass. He also thinks highly of Nat Turner and Denmark Vesey, the slave revolutionaries, whom he calls "freedom fighters." He sees much in the dream of Marcus Garvey, who led the "back to Africa" movement among Negroes just after the First World War. But it was Frederick Douglass who, unlike Booker T. Washington, stood up for the full equality of man as written into the Declaration of Independence and the Constitution of the United States. "Douglass," King says, "lived ahead of his time in that the American nation has not yet accorded Negroes the rights and privileges that are set forth in our organic law and about which Frederick Douglass spoke so movingly."

Jesus

Three of King's heroes—Jesus, Thoreau and Gandhi—supply the philosophical roots for his own theory of nonviolent social change. This is the concept that pervaded the Montgomery mass movement and that has subsequently spread far and wide over the South and elsewhere.

King is reluctant to list Jesus Christ as a hero, for he thinks of him not only as a natural, that is, historical, personality but also as supernatural. The appeal of Jesus for King is best expressed in the "Sermon on the Mount." "This is," King declares, "a wonderful statement of the practical solution of the major problems that man must face in any generation. In it, answers to life's great questions are given in terms of the love ethic."

This relatively short sermon (St. Matthew, Chapters 5-7) is the classic summary of the philosophy of Jesus, the very essence of Christianity. Though it is perhaps departed from more often than adhered to in our acquisitive society, it is the conscience of Western man. It contains the Beatitudes, the Golden Rule and the Lord's Prayer—all in support of humility, self-criticism, forgiveness and the renunciation of material gain. These are all prime elements of King's nonviolent movement:

> Blessed are the meek . . . the merciful . . . the peacemakers . . . they which are persecuted. . . . Ye are the salt of the earth . . . the light of the world. . . . Whosoever is angry with his brother . . . shall be in danger of the judgment . . . Agree with thine adversary quickly. . . . If thy right hand offend thee . . . Whosoever shall smite thee on thy right cheek, turn to him the other also. . . . Love your enemies, bless them that curse you, do good to them that hate you, and pray for them which despitefully use you, and persecute you. . . . Seek ye first the kingdom of God, and his righteousness; and all these things shall be added unto you. . . . Judge not, that ye be not judged. . . . And why beholdest thou the mote that is in thy brother's eye, but considerest not the beam that is in thine own eye? . . . Beware of false prophets, which come to you in sheep's clothing, but inwardly they are ravening wolves. . . . every good tree bringeth forth good fruit. . . . Thy kingdom come. Thy will be done in earth, as it is in heaven.

These were living truths for the Montgomery bus boycotters.

Thoreau

Henry David Thoreau, in King's opinion, is one of the most neglected of American idealists. He lived out most of his life (1817-1862) in or near his native Concord, Massachusetts. Yet his influence went around the world and Gandhi paid homage to him as the guide to his own thought and campaigns of civil disobedience.

Thoreau was not a reformer. His great concern was not in changing the conduct of other men but in freeing himself from the obligations and conventions of the social order so that he could do what he really wanted to do and what he thought was right. Of himself he said, "I wished to live deliberately, to front only the essential facts of life and see if I could learn what it had to teach and not, when I came to die, discover that I had not lived."

So, Thoreau withdrew to the fringes of the community. He never married and worked only enough to support his bare physical needs. He saved his time and energy for himself. He loved nature, spending hours in the fields and forests and streams. Most of his writings are those of an inspired amateur naturalist. Thoreau labored to bring man into harmony with nature.

But Thoreau did not withdraw from human society altogether and thus found himself involved in the great Negro question of his day. He was not an Abolitionist in the sense that he sought to influence other men mainly by his individual example. Nevertheless, his essays on "Slavery and Massachusetts" and "John Brown's Body" rank among the best thinking—and feeling—of his time on what we would call today "race relations." His essay "On Civil Disobedience" has been a textbook for many others besides Gandhi.

In "Slavery and Massachusetts," written in 1854, at the height of the antislavery controversy, Thoreau made it plain that a Northern, nonslaveholding state was guilty along with the slaveholding South for this crime of human bondage. That is to say, Massachusetts was passive; it tacitly assented and even actively returned fugitive slaves to the South. If a judge in Massachusetts ruled against a runaway bondsman who sought haven in the "free North," Thoreau contended that "only they are guiltless who commit the crime of contempt of such a court."

"The law will never make men free," he went on; "it is men who have got to make the law free." Sadly he concluded, "The majority of men of the North and the South and East and West are not men of principle."

Five years later, when John Brown electrified the nation with his attempt at Harpers Ferry to lead slaves in an insurrection for their freedom, Thoreau came out of retirement, as it were, and spoke on the burning issue at Concord's Town Hall, October 30, 1859. Henry S. Canby, a Thoreau biographer who does not altogether approve of the speech, concedes that it "belongs among the great orations in the history of the Republic."

Thoreau said: "Many, no doubt, are well disposed, but sluggish by constitution and by habit, and they cannot conceive of a man who is actuated by higher motives than they are. Accordingly, they pronounced this man insane, for they know that *they* could never act as he does, as long as they are themselves."

And

[John Brown] did not recognize unjust human laws, but resisted them as he was bid. No man in America has ever stood up so persistently and effectively for the dignity of human nature, knowing himself for a man, and the equal of any and all governments. In that sense he was the most American of us all.

✓ Thoreau endorsed John Brown's use of force against "evil": "It was his peculiar doctrine that a man has a perfect right to interfere by force with the slaveholder, in order to rescue the slave. I agree with him." Again Thoreau says, if government "requires you to be an agent of injustice to another, then, I say, break the law." He recalls John Brown's statement:

I want you to understand that I respect the rights of the poorest and weakest of colored people, oppressed by the slave power, just as much as I do those of the most wealthy and powerful.

Thoreau then goes on to quote one of John Brown's most famous lines:

You may dispose of me very easily. I am nearly disposed of now; but this question is still to be settled—this Negro question, I mean; the end of that is not yet.

Thoreau was arrested and jailed for not paying the annual poll tax for six years. He remained in prison for just one night, his aunt paying his fine and tax without his consent. On his brief stay there, Thoreau wrote:

I did not for a moment feel confined, and the walls seemed a great waste of stone and mortar. . . . They plainly did not know how to treat me, but behaved like persons who are underbred. In every threat and in every compliment there was a blunder; for they thought that my chief desire was to stand the other side of that stone wall. I could not but smile to see how industriously they locked the door on my meditations, which followed them out again without let or hindrance, and *they* were really all that was dangerous.

Mrs. Rosa Parks, who initiated the Montgomery bus boycott, could understand this when she was in jail.

Thoreau, for all his well-known gentleness with birds and flowers and children, did not disapprove of violence when it came to what he felt was injustice. The nonviolent principle in Gandhi and King does not come from Thoreau, only the element of *non-co-operation with evil*. This is clearly set forth in Thoreau's most famous essay of all, "On Civil Disobedience."

Thoreau agreed with Thomas Jefferson that "that government is best which governs least." He really preferred, ideally, no government at all but was practical about it. "I asked for, not at once no government, but *at once* a better government."

Thoreau placed individual conscience at the summit of social duty. "The only obligation which I have a right to assume is to do at any time what I think right." Or again, "O for a man, who is a *man,* and, as my neighbor says, has a bone in his back which you cannot pass your hand through!"

One passage that the leaders of the Montgomery boycott seemed to take literally was the observation that "Under a government which imprisons any unjustly, the true place for a just man is also prison." When some ninety-odd leaders of Montgomery were indicted for their part in the boycott, instead of running and hiding, they willingly came forth and submitted themselves to arrest.

Logically, there was always a contradiction in Thoreau for King and his followers, because if they could disregard Jim Crow laws that they thought were wrong, could not white Southerners also defy federal laws that they thought were wrong?

So the boycotters had to adapt Thoreau to their own conditions. They accepted federal laws—and the United States Supreme Court's interpretation of these laws; but resisted state and local laws that were contrary to federal laws. Negroes in the Montgomery movement applied civil disobedience to what was actually a Southern defiance of the highest law of the nation. In contrast, Thoreau placed individual conscience above *any* man-made law. On this ground a conscientious white segregationist, who challenged the United States Supreme Court, was as right in Thoreau's principle as Martin Luther King.

But would a sincere segregationist dare quote Thoreau? How far would he get? Even the reading of Thoreau, if done with an open mind, would bring segregationists and anti-segregationists together at many points.

Gandhi

Mohandas K. Gandhi, unlike Thoreau, was a mass leader. He read "Civil Disobedience" in the midst of the struggle of East Indians in South Africa against discrimination and segregation. Thoreau never made use of his own theories, save in his individual rebellion, while Gandhi devoted his life to the liberation of multitudes, first in South Africa, then in his native India.

Under Gandhi's leadership—and following his example—the Indian masses would deliberately break laws they considered unjust, invite arrest and accept blows from the police or military without fleeing or striking back.

More than any other personality, Gandhi mobilized India for its struggle against imperialism, and he used methods that were certain of victory in world opinion. His was the appeal to conscience. Accordingly, the motives as well as the devices of the foreign rulers were exposed. Imperialist Britain lost her moral prestige during the Indian struggle for independence.

Gandhi appealed to the ordinary people with symbols that they understood: prayer, fasting, the famous salt march to the sea in 1930, and the boycott of British goods and British honors. With such methods, the nonviolent resisters required more self-discipline than the military force and more courage than those who would fight back. Gandhi made it plain that nonviolence is not a refuge for the fearful: "Where there is a choice between cowardice and violence, I would choose violence."

In the large, Gandhi was interested in something more than merely putting his opponent in a morally weak position. The Mahatma's main point was to activate his own followers to higher standards of conduct and living. "Desirelessness" was the core of his teachings—renunciation of the world's materialism and vanity. "Satyagraha"—soul force—Gandhi said, "is the vindication of truth not by infliction of suffering on the opponent but on one's self." "Turn the searchlight inward," he urged, "perhaps the fault is partly yours. Adjudicate, negotiate, arbitrate, otherwise one interreligious brawl or one race riot will immediately create fuel for another, and one war will generate the venoms, fears and military designs which make a second and third more likely."

In all of his gentle directness Gandhi drove the point home: the impulses to anger and retaliation, the appetites to indulgence and false pride must be conquered. Plain living, personal kindness, sacrifice—love—these are the essentials of the good life.

The only cause for which Gandhi would ask men to lay down their lives was the cause of brotherhood.

Withal, Gandhi alone did not free India. He worked concurrently with other leaders and, above all, in harmony with the progressive historical forces of his day. Gandhi did not try to do everything himself. He was aware of his limitations and was most pleased when he could inspire or encourage others to do what he personally might be unable to do well.

Gandhi was a man of great determination, despite his soft spokenness. He threatened to fast himself to death when it appeared that drastic measures had to be taken, forcing certain of the Indian leaders to accept the untouchables. Gandhi knew that this agreement was but a start toward wiping out India's great internal problem of caste. This, he reminded his countrymen, could not be blamed on the British. He felt certain that once a start had been made by removing the religious and social sanctions to caste segregation that the subsequent industrialization and urbanization of India would complete the job of social integration.

For all of his influence and sagacity, Gandhi could not prevent the partition of India. When the day of freedom came in 1947, two "nations"—Pakistan and India—were born.

And so likewise, Martin Luther King knows that nonviolence is not the only element in the struggle of Southern Negroes for equality. Neither is the American South of the mid-1950's Southern Asia. Nor are American Negroes a majority ruled by outsiders. All this is to say that the situation in Martin Luther King's South is vastly different from that of Gandhi's India. Nevertheless, the Gandhian philosophy and technique have a great application to the needs of the Negro masses, making America's nonconformist tradition as symbolized by Thoreau socially useful. Moreover, Gandhianism fits in with the strong Christian traditions of the Negro people and mobilizes them to social action under self-discipline. Above all, in not being vindictive, they leave a way open for the opponent to stop being the opponent.

As Chester Bowles has written of the Montgomery movement:

> It is difficult to judge prospects for this program on a nation-wide scale. Gandhi was not only a spiritual leader of depth, dedication and courage but also a political genius. In America much will depend on the ability of Negro leaders to develop similar conviction and skill under pressure. Even more will depend on the number, raw courage and dedication of their followers.

Gandhi himself once said that perhaps through American Negroes the message of nonviolence might be delivered to America and the world. "This," Bowles adds, "will take a miracle of greatness. . . . But we Americans are living in an age of miracles and we are capable of greatness."

The teachings of the Great Three—Jesus, Thoreau and Gandhi—have been brought together by the Montgomery movement. This new synthesis is known simply as a "philosophy of love." It is not just a theory; for almost a year, despite the sharpest provocation, the bus strikers demonstrated in practice that there is an alternative to the conflict and killing that we usually associate with social progress.

The boycotters withstood assaults by the state (local), the press (local), racist organizations, gangs and terrorists. At the same time, the boycotters were supported—often fitfully but supported nonetheless—by the state (national), the press (national) and various equalitarian and humanitarian organizations and groups and individual idealists (but no terrorists).

Without the help of the "outside world" the boycotters never would have won. But it was the philosophy of love that gave the Negro masses their inner strength to endure their travail and the compassion for their "enemies." Symbolically, they did learn to love Engelhardt while hating what he stood for.

"Love" is a much-used and abused word. King has attempted to clarify its meaning for the Montgomery movement:

We must distinguish between levels of love. . . . *Eros* is a very interesting type of love. *Plato* talks about it a great deal in his dialogue. It is romantic love, and we must admit that there is something selfish about romantic love. You love your lover because there is something about your lover that attracts you. That is *Eros*. . . . Then there is *Philia*, another kind of love that we have for personal friends. That is not the type of love we talk about when we say "love your oppressor and love your enemy." . . . *Agape* is understanding good will for all men. It is the love of God working in man. It is a type of love that loves a person that does an evil deed while hating the deed that the person does. That is the love that we are talking about—a transforming, creative sort of love—and that is the love that we place at the center of our movement.

Communism or Love

The philosophy of social progress through nonviolent resistance is considered by some to be an oblique challenge to the characteristic methods of democratic capitalism and a direct challenge to Marxism. Colonial peoples seeking freedom may look to India or China as contrasting models. India became independent by way of Gandhianism, China by way of communism.

Minority peoples within nations also seek freedom. They may find any number of examples—some successful, some failures—by way of violent rebellion, assassination, arson and guerrilla warfare. Perhaps the Negroes of the South, if they persist in their nonviolence and if they succeed in becoming free and equal, may furnish a model for peaceful minority struggle *within a nation* that will be comparable to the national struggle of India against an external power.

King sees Africa as the current battleground of colonialism and the American South as the battleground of racialism, with communism and democracy both holding out a hand of friendship to the subjected peoples.

Which hand should colonials and minorities grasp?

King has a warm feeling for Africa much like the feeling some Americans of Old World ancestry have for Europe. With him this feeling is stronger since he has visited the erstwhile "Dark Continent" and seen for himself something of its possible future. He says that his trip to Ghana, on the occasion of its birth as virtually a self-governing nation, was one of the most vivid experiences of his adult life. It was a nonviolent rebirth.

Democracy, King feels, "is one of the grandest forms of government ever conceived by the minds of men." And when realized, that is, "transferred from thin paper to thick action [another favorite expression of King's], is unsurpassed." King is convinced that democracy will finally overcome race prejudice. "Senator Eastland's day is about over."

King says that he has both positive and negative reactions to Karl Marx. "Marx does have an appeal—his dialectic, his critique of monopoly capitalism, and his regard for social and economic justice in part at least explain the attraction that Marx has for his followers." Although he realizes that capitalism, too, has its evils, King unequivocally rejects communism. "I am not a materialist. I do not believe that all history is guided and shaped by economic determinism. Marx was wrong in this and in his contention that the economic sub-structure of society determined the superstructure."

King admits that "Hegel greatly influenced my study of philosophy, but he was an absolute idealist, a pantheist. Hegel said that growth comes through struggle. I agree with that, but not when Marx makes it necessarily a class struggle. There is such a thing as ethical relativism—the ends justify the means. This I reject absolutely."

One feature of communism King was sure to oppose. He put it this way. "I cannot accept at all the theory of the necessity of violence. It is surprising that many with power and wealth can be persuaded to share their possessions or even give them up." King admits that the American Revolution and the French Revolution brought about progress and improvement, but he feels that after all violent social change the heritage of violence persists.

The American South is regarded by King as a land of terror and painful anxiety today but a land of prosperity and peace for tomorrow. "It has within itself resources for becoming one of the great sections of our country if it would but throw off its provincialism and its racial segregation and move on into economic and political maturity."

In response to the question as to when this would happen, he answered, "In the not too distant future." When pressed further and reminded that the National Association for the Advancement of Colored People has made 1963 the target date for the complete abolition of segregation from the United States, King added that this was a bright hope. Surely, he agreed, one hundred years after the Emancipation Proclamation abolished slavery (later confirmed by the Union victory and the Thirteenth Amendment to the Constitution) should be time enough for the next step to be made toward equality and democracy, that is, the end to discrimination and segregation on the basis of race, color or creed.

Federal law, yes, indeed! But it is almost too much to hope, he continued, that all local and state laws will be wiped from the books by that date. It may take the Negro and white people of the South a few years more to work out a real integration of the South. Perhaps the process will not be completed before the year 2000. Such dates, of course, are mere speculations, for some unforeseen event or force could speed up—or slow down—the rate of change. However, he feels sure the final results are inevitable.

King listed four forces that would greatly help in removing racial segregation and discrimination from American life:

1. World opinion. As America plays the role of world leader, it necessarily becomes more responsive to world opinion and world opinion is overwhelmingly against segregation.

2. Industrialization of the South. Business and modern living will have little place for the inefficiencies of antiquated Jim Crow.

3. The aroused moral conscience of the church. National church organizations are, though belatedly, taking a moral position on the question of civil rights and school integration. It is particularly encouraging that many Southern religious bodies are doing likewise.

4. Social action led by Negroes. The Negro himself inescapably will play a decisive role in bringing the new day to the South. Negroes will not let threats and difficulties swerve them from the path of leadership in this crusade for citizenship through nonviolent social action.

These, of course, are mundane forces. King does not leave God out of account. King is a theist. He looks upon God not merely as an abstract force, as a deist would, but as a personality, though one not bound by body, time or space. "He is perfect selfhood; will; not finite but infinite. He performs miracles, not in the sense of tearing up the laws of nature; rather in bringing us closer to his law and in working out new creations through his law. A miracle is working today in the South—a miracle of emergent brotherhood. And it is the will of God."

This, then, is the picture—in broad strokes—of what Martin Luther King is like and how he thinks.

How did he come by these views and these qualities of mind and heart? What are his roots? Where are the sources of his strengths and weaknesses?

Perhaps we will find some of the answers if we look more deeply into his life.

III - M. L. K.'s Atlanta

MARTIN LUTHER KING was born in Atlanta, Georgia, on January 15, 1929, at 501 Auburn Avenue Northeast. To be born in Atlanta was very different from being born in New York City or on a Mississippi plantation; 1929, we recall, was the year of the stock market crash; Auburn Avenue was one of Negro America's famous streets.

To King, Atlanta was more than a birthplace. He grew up, went to school and finished college there. This took up the first nineteen years of his life. After that, even when he went away from Atlanta, he always came back to it. Chester, Pennsylvania; Boston, Massachusetts; Montgomery, Alabama, seem always to turn out to be more or less temporary addresses.

Any environment in which a person spends virtually the first two decades of his life would leave an indelible impression on him. But Atlanta must have been especially influential for a Negro child and youth with the sensitive personality and family background of Martin Luther King. Perhaps it is not possible to understand him at all without first understanding something of the world which bore and reared him: its tempo and vitality; its culture and contradictions.

When you say the word "Atlanta" to the average American, the image conjured up in his mind may be that of a wide, dreamy street named "Peachtree" somewhere down in Georgia. It is, of course, lined with dogwood in bloom. On one square is a giant factory turn-

24

ing out millions of bottles of Coca-Cola. On the opposite square, "the Rambling Wreck from Georgia Tech" is practicing football. A few blocks on, at the steps of the Confederate Memorial, a Talmadge politician is haranguing a cluster of "Rednecks." At the far end of the street, Bobby Jones is sinking a twenty-five-foot putt on the green. The big house in the background could be none other than Scarlett O'Hara's Tara. The children on the lawn are listening to a Br'er Rabbit tale from the lips of Uncle Remus. . . .

This romantic stereotype, of course, suggests the city's reputation rather than her character. But for the people who live in Atlanta and those who would understand her, both character and reputation are interesting and important.

Urban

In King's youth Atlanta was the South but even then not the rural South. It definitely had a Southern exposure but it was, first of all, a city—bustling and expanding and roomy, despite some of its crowded, crooked streets. It surprised New Englanders, when they visited Georgia, to discover that Atlanta was more modern than Boston in hustle and growth. Atlanta's 270,000 people in 1930 had grown to 900,000 by 1957. Every third Atlantan was a Negro.

Some of these near-million people were recruited from the farms and hills of rural Georgia. They came into town with traditional folk beliefs about Negroes—and much else. But the city at least partly "citified" (civilized) them. After a while they found it a little hard to continue to look at life through the same old country knothole. There was so much that one saw or heard during the passing day; so many different kinds of people, including all kinds of Negroes—some with fine cars, fine clothes and fine homes; some who might work in the same plant with you and could read and write better than you could.

There were Yankees in Atlanta, too, and some Southerners who chased dollars just like Yankees. Most of the time they didn't seem to give a dang about race relations one way or the other. And the newspapers, radio and, later, TV brought in the whole world.

Politics, naturally, reflected the paradoxes and divergencies. The biggest city in the state was also the state capital. The Georgia counties ran the statehouse but the big cities ran their own city halls. Whenever a governor was inaugurated, Atlanta would be crowded by the "wool hat" boys who came in to cheer their champion—who often forgot about them until the next election.

But the Atlanta crowd was different—more educated, more prosperous, more sophisticated. It often looked at a Talmadge with more curiosity than enthusiasm. Their own man was a city man,

William B. Hartsfield, a native conveniently born about five blocks from Peachtree Street at Five Points. Beginning in 1937, Hartsfield remained Mayor of Atlanta for more than two decades, with only one interruption (1940-42). Under him Atlanta made "progress." As cities go, it was efficient, free of organized crime and generally free of the political bigot. Hartsfield was once adjudged to be among the nine best mayors of the nation. In 1953 his fellow mayors elected him President of the American Municipal Association.

In Atlanta, as in most places of the South, the police had a bad name among Negroes—and others; however, the chief of police was said to have told his men to deal less harshly with "those educated colored people from the colleges and the businessmen from Auburn Avenue."

Atlanta was big and varied, so that organizations of opposite faiths coexisted there. It was once the headquarters of the Imperial Wizard of the Ku Klux Klan and for a while had a branch of the Communist party, U.S.A. In between these extremes could be found the NAACP, the Commission on Interracial Cooperation, and B'nai B'rith.

The Communist party never had much of a following in Atlanta, although Marxist pamphlets and the *Daily Worker* did have considerable circulation around town when times were hard. But the Klan had its hordes. KKK masked parades and demonstrations were fashionable until, in the 1940's, masking was outlawed. Klanlike violence, however, continued to erupt from time to time. Bombs would be thrown, dynamite set off and threats made by telephone and letter whenever Negroes moved into neighborhoods of whites. In time Mayor Hartsfield and Negro real estate dealers would work out a plan of orderly expansion that kept such housing friction down to the minimum.

Atlanta, like most Southern towns, had been drenched in Southern history. The difference was that Atlanta's industrialism and commercialism pushed up through it. For example, the banks stopped closing down for Confederate Memorial Day.

The great historical experience, of course, was the War Between the States. Atlanta has never forgiven General William T. Sherman for seizing and burning the city in 1864. His was a left-handed compliment to the town's strategic and economic importance. Sherman said: "Atlanta was like my hand. The palm was the city, or hub. The fingers were its spokes—in this case, the railroads. I knew that if I could destroy those railroads, the last link of the Confederacy would be broken."

In one of the parks is a cyclorama of the Battle of Atlanta and on the state capital grounds are the usual Confederate statues.

The big emotional reliving of the war was, of course, *Gone With the Wind*. Published in 1936, it sold a million copies in six months; in twenty years, six million. In 1939 when the film was released, the première, of course, was held in Atlanta. This was perhaps the most stirring spectacle the city had known since Sherman himself rode into town.

Atlanta, the South and the nation responded tremendously to this ceremonial pageantry. The psychological impact of *Gone With the Wind* upon the public mind has been incalculable.

As one item in the monumental celebration, the United Daughters of the Confederacy lit what they called "The Eternal Light of the Confederacy." It was, they said, to burn day and night, forever, at Alabama and Whitehall streets.

The divided public reaction to this light is a good example of the way symbols may have opposite meanings for groups with opposite orientations. This gas-jet lamp of the UDC was originally one of twenty-one such street lights that the city installed in 1855. When General Sherman advanced on Atlanta in the summer of 1864, this particular lamp at Alabama and Whitehall streets was shattered by the first blast that struck downtown Atlanta from the Union artillery. (Subsequently the city's streets were lighted by electricity.)

When the UDC restored the single gas-jet lamp in 1939 and made it "eternal" they did so to commemorate the "wrong," the "humiliation," the suffering and destruction of Atlanta in particular and in general to keep vivid to the younger generation the sad beauty of the "Lost Cause."

On the other hand, to Atlanta Negroes, General Sherman was—and remains—a conquering hero; the leader of an army of liberation. His gun shot that destroyed the lamp was a joyous sound. *Gone With the Wind* to Negro Atlantans meant literally what it said: gone with the wind, finished! They looked upon the "Eternal Light" as a reminder of a cause that *should have been* lost; of a psychological hangover that even today gets in the way of the acceptance of the equality of man. Thus, different men, looking through different spectacles, see life differently.

Liberals

Atlanta's colleges were Jim Crow, but from them came a small but active group of liberals. The city's best-educated people, Negro and white, often got together at concerts, book reviews, forums and teas —usually, but not always, on a Negro campus.

The college-bred liberals were matched and sometimes joined by the labor liberals. Atlanta had a strong organized labor movement that had some progressive tendencies. Despite the usual Jim Crow pattern, there were a few racially mixed unions that quietly treated everybody as "brother and sister." The high officials of the CIO could be counted on usually for "advanced" views on race matters.

There were religious liberals, too. Atlanta's churches, like her schools and most of her other public institutions, operated by the Jim Crow rule. Almost never did Negro and white congregations worship together. Even on Race Relations Sunday that came in February, few Negro and white pastors followed the suggestion made by the Federal Council of Churches of Christ and exchanged pulpits with each other.

And yet within such limitations there were many expressions of the needs and responsibilities of brotherhood. A favorite Sunday sermon was "Am I My Brother's Keeper?" Now and then such homilies were specific and included recommendations for action.

Moreover, almost every denomination had some committee for "interracial fellowship" or "improving race relations." White Christians did visit Negro churches occasionally, and if some very special speaker came to town for just one engagement, or if some special conference had to be arranged for a national church representative, Negro Christians might be invited to a white church or meeting place. Individual Negroes were infrequently invited to Jewish synagogues.

The religious liberals joined with the college liberals to form good will and moderate social action organizations. Atlanta was the home of the Commission on Interracial Cooperation, later renamed the Southern Regional Council. The Association of Southern Women Against Lynching was also of local origin and was remarkably successful in its campaign. The League of Women Voters, though oriented toward more than just civil rights, opposed race-baiting politicians and restrictions on any legitimate voter.

These interracial contacts—tenuous and fleeting as they often were —sometimes developed into real friendships. Individuals got to know other individuals as such and discovered mutual interests and began visiting with each other informally. A door would thus open to a joyous new world, hitherto unknown and scarcely imagined. Doubts and inhibitions faded, hope was fulfilled and faith in man confirmed. There were some disappointments and disillusionments, too.

Almost everywhere Southern newspapers serve as an index of community race relations. The daily press has been—and still is— the most constant reflector and molder of public attitudes on this and many other questions. That the daily paper as a mirror may be convex or concave has not always been realized by the average reader.

Through the years Atlanta has had its share of yellow journalism on the race issue—and on other subjects, too. The riot of 1906 was in part the result of inflammatory newspaper stories about Negro men and white women. But by the 1930's the Atlanta press had matured. The morning Atlanta *Constitution,* representing traditional local interests, was "conservative" and "reasonable" and stood for quiet "progress" in race relations. The afternoon Atlanta *Journal,* following an up-and-down career, was purchased by ex-governor James Cox of Ohio in 1939 and added to his string of newspapers. The *Journal*'s policy remained "Southern," but less so, and the reporting became less provincial.

In 1950 the Cox interests purchased the *Constitution* also. It was permitted to continue its format and staff but in time both papers—morning and afternoon—resembled each other, differing slightly in particular writers, columnists and type style.

Ralph McGill came of a long line of Atlanta editors and journalists that included names recognizable anywhere. The permanent fame of reporter Joel Chandler Harris came from the Negro folktales of Uncle Remus that he wrote down. Editor Henry W. Grady was famous in the eighties and nineties as an apostle of the "New South" of industrialism. Today Atlantans know Henry Grady as a big statue athwart the middle of downtown Marietta Street. Motorists curse him daily as a traffic hazard. And there are numerous vulgar jokes about the imaginary doings of Henry Grady in the dark of night.

Margaret Mitchell, too, was an Atlanta journalist before she wrote *Gone With the Wind.* And so was Erskine Caldwell, whose *God's Little Acre* and *Tobacco Road* have somewhat balanced Miss Mitchell's romance. But nobody bragged about Caldwell's unflattering realism. Nobody believed you when you told them that *God's Little Acre* outsold *Gone With the Wind;* that since publication in 1933, its sales by 1957 exceeded seven million copies.

For a decade Editor McGill of the *Constitution* was a Southern liberal with a national reputation. Almost every month he wrote some magazine article or appeared on some national radio roundtable.

McGill tried hard to keep evenly balanced the three corners of liberalism—Northern, Southern and Negro. The task proved greater than his strength. The Negroes—and often the North—demanded more and faster concessions to equality than the Southerners would or could yield. McGill himself was almost torn to shreds when Negro intellectuals got him at closer range, face to face, in an Atlanta forum.

In the mid-thirties the United States Supreme Court began cutting the ground from under the Jim Crow liberals, that is, from under those white Southerners who were against racial *discrimination* but who would not or could not afford to come out against racial *segregation* itself.

After the May 17, 1954, court ruling on public schools, Jim Crow liberalism disappeared almost completely. Nobody would "buy" it any more. Some Southerners who felt that they could not make any additional advances lapsed into silence. In 1958 McGill re-emerged, fighting rigid segregation.

This in general was the Atlanta of Martin Luther King's day. It was a dynamic city. It was Southern and Jim Crow but not absolutely or rudely so. It manifested liberal as well as reactionary tendencies. No Atlanta Negro with eyes and ears could conclude that all white people were the same, and vice versa. There was much interracial good will and some real interracial friendships, though most of these had to remain inconspicuous.

Sweet Auburn

There was yet another part of the forest in which Martin Luther King grew. This was his neighborhood; the part of Atlanta that was very close to him; the places he frequented and the people he knew personally, who talked to him and exchanged visits with him; his playmates and schoolmates; his childhood heroes and idols. This, with his family, was his intimate world.

To be born on Auburn Avenue was to come alive on one of Negro America's famous streets. Almost every metropolitan Negro community had a well-known street or corner where people met and where the spirit of Negro life unfolded itself. In Los Angeles it was Central Avenue; in Washington, D.C., U Street; in New Orleans, Rampart Street; in Jacksonville, Ashley Street; in Memphis, Beale Street; in Chicago, 47th and South Parkway; in Harlem there were several such streets—125th, 135th and 7th Avenue, for example.

Auburn Avenue was such a street—alive and proud. It was a street with a great past, a prosperous present and a doubtful future. It had grown up with the city and now some of its businesses were worth millions, but the City Fathers were not sure that they wanted Auburn Avenue to live forever.

It was also a street of many faces. In the daylight its Negro-owned banks, newspapers and insurance companies were busy and crowded and its churches stood as symbols of respectability. In the evening, its night clubs and hideouts lifted their veils.

The latest news on Auburn Avenue was always interesting but history frequently crowded in on current happenings. One could recognize well-known personalities moving about, but always behind them were the shadows of the legendary men who had built Auburn Avenue or had torn themselves apart trying to build it. Still others had lost their way, ensnared by the twin temptresses, ambition and vice.

Auburn Avenue was a short street, just seventeen blocks long. At noon a Negro youth walking down it for five or six blocks could see all that he would ever need to inspire him; at midnight, the pleasures of the "after hours" world would beckon to him.

If the wanderer could tarry long enough he would hear true tales —and tall tales—of men who made and lost fortunes, who left their initials in the concrete pavement or otherwise stamped their personalities on the street. Some men came to violent ends there.

That Auburn Avenue ran into Peachtree Street suggested all of the limitations of the ghetto, however beautiful and comfortable it might be at times.

Auburn Avenue had its chroniclers and oral historians. No man loved it more than I. P. Reynolds, better known as "Ike" or "Sam." It was his mail route for forty-one years. He knew everybody on the avenue and everybody knew him. His family said that Ike spent more time on Auburn than he spent at home. Ike took up journalism mainly to tell the world about the avenue. For years he was a columnist for the Atlanta *Independent,* then the Atlanta *Daily World* and finally the Pittsburgh *Courier.* In a sort of rude Damon Runyon style he told of the "characters" who inhabited the avenue and the moving stories of young men who came there looking for the success ladder. Ike was also interested in all of the charities, civil rights campaigns and church rallies. Thus, on the afternoon of his funeral some businesses closed their doors for him. Though he was nonsectarian, every church claimed him as an honorary member.

Auburn's other historian was John Wesley Dobbs. He was a big fraternal man—Grand Master of the Masons—and a big Republican —a member of the state executive committee of the party, and it was interracial, too. He was also a Negro History Week orator. And above all, he was the father of Mattiwilda Dobbs, the operatic soprano.

Dobbs had a famous speech that he delivered in the old grand manner. He called it "Sweet Auburn." It usually ended with this flourish:

It takes sugar to sweeten things, and, as you know, it takes money to buy sugar. The acquisition of this kind of wealth along Auburn Avenue has caused us to call it "Sweet Auburn," a name now known among Negroes throughout America as a symbol of the development of Negro Business in Atlanta, Georgia.

"Sweet" Auburn Avenue, ladies and gentlemen, is not a slum street; is not over behind the railroad tracks. It runs straight into Peachtree Street. When you go up "Sweet Auburn," you are going to town, that's all.

Both Reynolds and Dobbs were family friends of the Kings, who lived east of Boulevard Street, in the few blocks of Auburn Avenue that were strictly residential. The main part of Auburn, the business district, was west of this. Here, in the eight blocks between Boulevard and Courtland Street, Negroes owned about 90 per cent of the property and operated a variety of concerns.

Perhaps the most formidable of these was the Atlanta Life Insurance Company, established in 1905, incorporated in 1916. It had assets of some $20,000,000 by the 1940's. It was located near Courtland Street, at the beginning of the Negro business area, in a yellow brick building renovated and enlarged with giant front columns that bespoke the conservatism of the institution. Though extremely careful in its investments, Atlanta Life did use some of its accumulated capital to assist other enterprises.

A block further along on the avenue was the Citizens Trust Company. This was "the Negro bank" though it had some white customers, too. It won a good reputation by standing up during the Great Depression while other banks in Atlanta and throughout the country were failing. In appearance, the bank, unlike the insurance company, was quite modern. Its building, fixtures and furniture were neat and up-to-date. Soft music in the background added to the tranquillity of the businesslike atmosphere. It was a member of the Federal Reserve Bank system.

The Mutual Federal Savings and Loan Association, just across the street from the bank, was also modern; at least it became so in 1952. It was perhaps the chief credit facility that accounted for the great number of homes that Atlanta Negroes owned. In 1954 its resources were more than $10,000,000.

There were any number of real estate firms on the avenue that worked closely with the bank and the loan association. These "realtors" competed with each other, of course, but organized themselves for mutual assistance in the Empire Real Estate Board. This body, with the help of the Mayor's office, planned and negotiated large-scale transactions so that the expansion of Negro residential areas would generate the least friction with white property owners.

Next door to Atlanta Life was the Rucker building, office of the biggest Negro construction firm in town. It was a miracle that this company—W. H. Aiken's—could get materials during the scarcities of World War II. It put up more homes during that period than all the other Negro builders combined and more than most of the city's white contractors. After the war, Aiken put up for himself "Waluhaje." This was possibly the most impressive Negro-owned apartment hotel in America. It cost $5,000,000.

Next door to the bank was the Atlanta *Daily World*. Founded in 1929, it was the only Negro daily in the United States that had lasted for several years. It owned its printing press and published weekly *Worlds* for some dozen other Southern localities. The *Daily World* gave Atlanta Negroes one of their two organs of rapid mass communication. The other was radio station WERD, owned by Negroes and beamed to the interests of Negro listeners. Whenever there was need for a quick message to the Negro community—as in a political crisis—the *World* and WERD could do the job.

On one of the busiest corners of the avenue was Yates & Milton pharmacy. This was one of a chain of such drugstores that were located in different Negro neighborhoods of the city.

Above Yates & Milton, on the second floor, were offices for Negro professional men and women, mainly physicians and dentists. But the largest office building on the street was the six-story Odd Fellows hall at the other end of the square from Yates & Milton. The Masons and Elks had their structures, too.

Within the two blocks from the Atlanta Life to the Odd Fellows hall there was more than $80,000,000 in business resources. Since these and other Negro enterprises of the city were not admitted to the Atlanta Chamber of Commerce, they organized themselves into the Atlanta Business League.

In addition to the big commercial houses, there were numerous smaller shops: a job printing plant, a jewelry store, restaurants, barber shops, beauty salons, grocery stores, service stations, cleaning and pressing places, liquor stores, beer taverns and the Hopkins Book Concern.

There was a branch of the public library, but it was little used.

Both the NAACP for civil rights and the Urban League for job placement and social welfare had offices on Auburn Avenue.

Three of the street's churches were famous: Big Bethel A.M.E., Wheat Street Baptist and Ebenezer Baptist. They all had large congregations, were well run financially, and during weekdays served as rallying points for the campaigns of social justice and civic improvement.

Night clubs came and went on Auburn Avenue, but the Royal Peacock seemed to withstand the years. There were two hotels, rated "B"; still they were much used. The movie house was white-owned but the funeral parlors were not. Until the 1930's, when it burned, the roof garden of the Odd Fellows hall was *the* place for the "high society" dances.

Just off the avenue was the Butler Street YMCA. In addition to the usual programs, this Y supplied the meeting place for the Atlanta

Negro Voters League, the political voice of the Negro community. After 1944 when Negroes won the right to participate in the Democratic primary, which was the decisive election in Georgia and most of the Deep South, they built themselves into a balance of power, locally. Some twenty thousand votes could swing almost any municipal election.

The Y was also the locale of the weekly Hungry Club luncheons that came each Wednesday. This interracial group, open to the public, brought in after-luncheon speakers, who led lively forums on local and national issues of the day.

Various personalities were associated with these Auburn Avenue institutions. The leaders knew each other professionally and socially, not only meeting across their desks and business counters but at their clubs, at fraternity affairs, and in their fine homes, which were usually on the west side. The public knew these men as they passed to and fro on the avenue or as they headed this or that community or charitable drive.

Notables

N. B. Herndon, the president and treasurer of the Atlanta Life, was an "invisible" man. He was seldom seen publicly; apparently, E. M. Martin, vice president and secretary, was the "big wheel" that ran the company. Martin looked like a middle-aged white man, with a square chin, firmly set lips, kindly eyes and an even pace. He was a cautious businessman but would lash out at racial discrimination. His indignation, ordinarily, would appear strange but he was the brother-in-law of deceased Walter White, the well-known NAACP leader. Their views on racial injustice appeared to be identical.

L. D. Milton was short and light-brown-skinned. As president of the bank, he tried hard to be one of those cold-blooded, "business is business" executives. He knew the principles of money management and applied them, but underneath this exterior was a sympathetic man. Moreover, he enjoyed his connections with cultural and idealistic institutions and causes.

Milton's partner in the Yates & Milton drugstores was a different sort. His employees spoke of him as both a "clock-watcher watcher" and a "nickel-nurser." His response to the humanistic and artistic side of life appeared to be slight. C. R. Yates was short, white-haired and white-faced, with eyes that tended to congeal in a cold, inflexible stare.

The Mutual Federal Savings and Loan Association was the "child" of John P. Whittaker. He nursed it through the years, dividing his time between the Association and his job as college registrar. Whittaker was another product of the schooling that the New England humanitarians brought to the South. He was not out for profit; he wanted to help Negroes build and purchase homes. He, too, was light-skinned.

After Whittaker retired from school work, he devoted full time to the Association. Even so, the weight of his responsibilities was too much for his declining energies. After his death, J. B. Blayton took over the executive directorship. Whittaker was affectionately remembered by all who knew him.

Some people said that Blayton was worth a quarter of a million dollars. J. B., as everybody called him, would never admit this, but his denials were unconvincing. He was a certified public accountant, a bank director, had set his wife up with a school of commerce and his son with radio station WERD. J. B.'s modesty was matched by his genius with figures. Yet he forgot about half of the small personal loans that he made to youngsters who were trying to get a start on the avenue. J. B. was brown skinned and of medium height. He was a member of Ebenezer Baptist Church.

The fellows spoke of T. M. Alexander as "Pierre," meaning the fabulous Frenchman. T. M. was a little fellow, slim, tireless, olive-skinned, well-dressed, preferring a felt hat with a crimped-down brim. He knew how to chase the dollar and would try anything once. He made his money in real estate and insurance, built himself one of the most beautiful houses on the west side and in 1957 ran for the City Council. He almost won, losing out in the run-off only after the Governor intervened in the city election and made a white supremacy appeal. T. M. said that he would run again—and win!

W. H. "Chief" Aiken was a man with several distinct careers. He looked like a big yellow Indian, a kind of Jim Thorpe athlete. The Chief coached championship college football teams and married into the aristocratic Rucker family.

Chief then turned his force and ingenuity to the building and construction industry. Everything he touched seemed to turn to gold. He ran the modest Rucker wealth into millions. "Waluhaje" was his crowning glory. This name was not Indian but a compound of letters taken from the names of members of Aiken's family. The well-bred Rucker girls—Hazel, Ann and Lucy (Mrs. Aiken)—joined with the Chief in managing their "baby"—Waluhaje.

The Chief did not believe in the color line and did as much as anyone to erase it from the big-time jazz entertainment that came to Waluhaje; also, he was an ardent supporter of Moral Rearmament.

To anyone who did not know him, Warren Cochrane, walking down Peachtree Street, would pass for just another white businessman of medium height and weight and straight black hair. But on Auburn Avenue everybody knew that Cochrane was colored and quite race conscious. He had always associated freely with white people and was not fazed by them at all. He was a man of ideas, which he sometimes projected with autocratic impatience. He had respect for intellect but only scorn for pretense.

Cochrane ran the Butler Street YMCA but otherwise operated over the whole city in the interest of the Negro community. He was known among the rich and powerful as well as in every office of City Hall, from the Mayor's on down.

Cochrane stayed in the South by choice. He had lived and worked in New York. His wife, who did college teaching, would go with him anywhere but patiently awaited the day when her husband would conclude that his Southern mission had been completed.

The Atlanta *Daily World* was a family enterprise in every sense of the word. The Scotts owned all of the stock and held a large share of the jobs. C. A. Scott was editor-in-chief and general manager. His wife was his private secretary; his sister-in-law, the accountant; his mother, the cashier. When the last was presented by one of the sororities for consideration as "Woman of the Year," the *World* printed the positions that some of her children and grandchildren held on the paper:

One son was editor in chief
Another son, circulation manager for the weekly Birmingham *World*
Another son, head pressman
Another son, plant foreman
One daughter, assistant cashier
Another daughter, proof reader
One grandson, city circulation manager
Two other grandsons, mechanical helpers in the print shop
Two granddaughters did the teen-age column.

Two of the editor's sisters-in-law were at various times linotypists for the paper. A brother-in-law was advertising manager. And perhaps there were a few others kindred by blood or marriage who also helped out in the *World*'s operations.

At the same time, the *World,* over the years, had served as a training school for a long list of well-known journalists: Ric Roberts and R. M. Ratcliffe for the Pittsburgh *Courier*; Bob Johnson and Lerone Bennett of *Jet* and *Ebony*; Miss Lucile Bluford of the Kansas City *Call*; Cliff McKay of the *Afro-American*; Frank Marshall Davis, poet, who worked with the Associated Negro Press in Chicago before retiring from journalism to Hawaii, and William Gordon, whose

Nieman fellowship took him to Harvard and whose Reid award took him to Africa.

Editor C. A. Scott, slightly below average height, of medium weight and light-brown-skinned, was cautious in his business dealings; forthright in his politics. For a while he backed the New Deal and the Fair Deal but shifted to the Republicans when Eisenhower came along. Scott began to plead that politically the South's greatest need was a two-party system; also, he added, the Negro would make his greatest gains when there was a real contest between these parties. Scott refused to print scandal in his papers. He, too, was a member of Ebenezer Baptist Church.

Of the Auburn Avenue clergymen, the Baptists were better known than the Methodists. The tenure of the latter was usually shorter and altogether unpredictable, being subject to the will of the church hierarchy. The word was "The Bishop appoints—and disappoints." The Rev. D. T. Babcock and the Rev. H. I. Bearden successively were among the prominent religious leaders of Big Bethel A.M.E. Church.

William Holmes Borders of the Wheat Street Baptist Church was one of the most dramatic and outspoken of Atlanta's Negro leaders. He was the type of speaker whose words came easily and who gave free expression to his feelings. He had a touch of the theatrical about him. He made some of his sermons melodramatic with gestures and his own sound effects. But he was also forthright in criticizing city officials or state house politicians who opposed equal rights for "all the people." Some felt that the Rev. Mr. Borders, on occasion, was too harsh. But his followers believed in him without qualification. Borders was a big man, brown-skinned, with gray spotting his black hair. When Atlanta's buses were desegregated in January, 1959, the Rev. Mr. Borders exclaimed, "Thank you Montgomery; thank you Martin Luther King, Jr."

The Avenue's other outstanding Baptist minister was Martin Luther King, Sr., whose life would unfold further with that of his son.

Colonel A. T. Walden was the most prominent—and venerable— of the Negro lawyers. He was short and wore a bulldog look upon his face that could melt into a genial smile. He had two daughters, both of whom were artists. The colonel had fought in World War I, had subsequently made money, built the Walden building next door to the Y, and owned a big, roomy west side home. But he probably devoted more time to charity court cases and the campaigns to get Negroes to vote "wisely" than to his profitable law practice. For years he was the chief counsel for the Georgia NAACP and participated in most of the big civil rights suits.

Walden and Dobbs were co-chairmen of the Negro Voters League.

A Democrat and a Republican respectively, they were paired so that the organization could speak with a bipartisan voice.

Formerly a Republican, Walden convinced other Negroes, after convincing himself, that they should force themselves into the Democratic party. He argued that since the Democratic primary was the decisive election in Atlanta—and most of the South for that matter —Negroes had to vote in it if they were to influence the selection of those who would be holding office.

Herman Talmadge and Walden once were co-defenders of the same parties when Talmadge was getting his start as a young lawyer. The two were personal and legal friends. But the road to power is many-forked. When Walden began to mobilize Negro voters, Talmadge attacked him as a "bloc vote" manipulator and accused Mayor Harts-field and other Atlanta city officials of being under the thumb of "Boss Walden."

Walden, like many another Southerner, was an honorary colonel. Even this did not escape Talmadge. He would say that Walden was "Colonel of *Nothing*." Walden himself would simply smile but his friends would reply that "Colonel Walden is more than a *Colonel*; he's the best political *general* we've ever had." In 1953 the colonel and druggist Miles Amos were the first Negroes ever elected to the Executive Committee of Atlanta. This was a victory of prime importance, for this committee actually set up and operated the election machinery for the city.

Of the medical men, probably the most versatile was Dr. R. A. Billings. Successful as a physician and surgeon, he invested his earnings in enterprises ranging from a housing project to a dance hall and bowling alley. Tall and well-built, he was at one time considered Atlanta's most eligible Negro bachelor before he met Miss Celestine Taylor of Americus, Georgia.

Billings headed the local medical association for a while, was national president of his fraternity, and led his neighborhood political organization. He was active and influential in these endeavors until a mild stroke forced him to slow down. His declining health in later years considerably reduced his activities as a prominent leader in the Negro community.

One of Dr. Billings' office neighbors was the "dean" of Atlanta's Negro medical men. This was James Porter, Doctor of Dental Surgery, a short brown-skinned man gifted with a remarkable memory of his childhood. Born in 1860, the son of a one-time member of the Georgia Legislature, he could vividly recall the days when Negro militia marched up and down the streets of Atlanta, Augusta, Savannah, Macon and Albany.

These, then, were some of the personalities that moved about Auburn Avenue. They were men of different types and manifested or betrayed qualities as varied as generosity, public spirit, selfishness and vanity. Any young boy who wanted an idol to adore or a demon to frighten him could find his model here.

The names and faces of these men appeared often in the newspapers. They spoke at banquets, commencements and during Negro History Week. But on the stage that was the avenue these current actors were often crowded by the ghosts of a past that was also immediate and real.

Almost every long-time, successful Auburn Avenue institution had its patron saint. And there were the devils, too. These latter were not deliberately enshrined, of course, but they were as much talked about and argued about as those whose portraits hung in the company president's office or whose busts rested on pedestals in the hall near the time clock where the workers checked in.

Titans

No man did more for Auburn Avenue than A. F. Herndon, N. B.'s father. He ran the most palatial barbershop in town, exclusively for the white carriage trade, and used his profits to build the Atlanta Life Insurance Company for Negroes.

While Herndon was careful and conservative, Heman Perry was daring. Some called him a "financial genius"; others, a "crook." When the "empire" that he built on insurance, banking and a catch-all holding company collapsed in 1929, the crash was heard—and felt—in Negro homes and businesses throughout the nation. Soon afterward Perry himself was found dead, probably a suicide.

Another man who tore himself apart building Auburn Avenue was W. A. Scott, C. A.'s brother. Like Perry, W. A. was a man of originality, vigor and nerve. He founded the Atlanta *World* on a shoe string and had scattered little *Worlds* across the Southland when death struck him down. Scott was a magnetic personality. As to be expected, women were also drawn to him. He was slain by an unknown assailant under obscure conditions.

Bishop Henry McNeil Turner, one of the most striking figures in Georgia history, often preached and presided at Auburn Avenue's Big Bethel Church. He had been at one time or another chaplain in the Union Army—probably the first Negro as such—member of the State Legislature, magazine editor, author and advocate of the Back to Africa Movement.

Turner fought Jim Crow all the way, going so far as to say of the American flag: "Not a star in it can the colored man claim, for it is

no longer the symbol of our manhood, rights and liberty." So deep
was his hurt that he did not wish to die on the American soil that
had rejected him as a native son and first-class citizen. So, when he
felt that death was upon him, he dragged himself to Canada, dying
in Windsor, a little town just across the border from Detroit.

Chief Aiken's father-in-law, H. A. Rucker, from 1897 to 1910
held the juiciest political plum in the state. He was Collector of
Internal Revenue at Atlanta, appointed by President William McKin-
ley and reappointed by Theodore Roosevelt. About ninety of the one
hundred men who worked under Rucker at the Customs House were
white.

Rucker's deadliest enemy was his fellow Negro Republican, Benjamin J. Davis, Sr. Rucker was light-skinned and a "gentleman."
Davis was dark brown and had come up in the rough-and-tumble
back alleys of politics. He was adept at scuffling and gouging.

Davis could make friends but found it hard to keep them. A
mercurial personality, he would like you in the morning, but by
afternoon might think differently about you.

Yet it was Davis who built the entire block of buildings on the
north side of Auburn Avenue from Bell Street to Butler Street. This
was "Odd Fellows Block." Also, Davis ruled the state Republican
party organization, whites and Negroes alike, with the same iron
hand that he used with the Odd Fellows fraternal order that he headed.

Davis' son rebelled against the forces that he felt made his father
what he was. Benjamin J. Davis, Jr.—trained at Morehouse and
Harvard—joined the Communist party, rose high in its councils and
won a seat on New York's City Council.

Ben Davis, Sr., died a broken and defeated man. In his last days,
his power, money, influence and friendships ebbed away from him.

There were other names that were wrapped in fables: such as
William Finch and George Graham, only Negroes to serve in the
City Council; and Dr. Miles Amos, Atlanta's first Negro druggist,
whose generous heart brought him to bankruptcy but whose brilliant
niece and nephew restored the family name and fortune.

Some of the avenue's heroes were nameless. For example, the man
who is given credit for banishing Ku Klux Klan parades from Auburn
Avenue. The Klan, in its heyday, was bold and terrifying. It would
burn a cross before a Negro home or school or church and always
demonstrated its strength so that the Negro community could see it.

In a later and leaner period, the Klan declined in prestige and
came to be regarded by many whites as well as Negroes with a mixture
of amusement and curiosity. This happened even before masking by
the organization had been outlawed. Yet, almost by habit, whenever

the local klansmen paraded, they made a swing down Auburn Avenue to Peachtree Street.

On one such occasion, Negro spectators were out in great numbers. As the hooded and sheeted kleagles and klops trudged down the Avenue, loud guffaws and catcalls greeted them all along the way. Any oddity was pointed to; any misstep was ridiculed.

One tiring parader fell a few yards behind his brigade. As he passed near the sidewalk, the mask from his face was jerked off by an impish Negro bystander. Obviously embarrassed, the middle-aged white man smiled apologetically, then trotted to catch up with his fellows.

After that, the Klan never again paraded on Auburn Avenue.

The avenue also had its jesters. Two men made a bet by which the loser was to commit suicide by jumping from the top of the Odd Fellows hall. At the appointed hour for the settlement, the losing bettor, with a few of his friends, went up to the roof. A crowd gathered below. He peered down and then seemed to hurl his body over the ledge. Men yelled and women fainted. But it was only a dummy that fell to the street.

Auburn Avenue was like that. Something was always going on. People liked to stand on the corners just to see what was happening and who was passing by.

It was an interesting street, in an interesting town. It was a privilege and a challenge to grow up in such an environment.

IV - Family Circle

MARTIN LUTHER KING, SR., was not a native Atlantan. He was born at Stockbridge, a little hamlet about twenty miles down the road from Atlanta on the way to Macon. Some of his Auburn Avenue friends have a joke that whenever they drive down that road their cars will automatically stop and refuse to move when they reach the clergyman's home town.

The Rev. Mr. King, Sr., remembers his days in Stockbridge vividly. He spent the first sixteen years of his life there when it was even less of a whistlestop than it is now. It was then just another Southern village surrounded by farmland on which his father, James Albert King, was a sharecropper. Life was hard, work and children plentiful, material rewards slight.

James Albert King was part Irish, part Negro, a hard worker and a hard drinker. He also fitted into the pattern of the typical sharecropper overwhelmed by the forces that moved against him. Somewhere during the years of suffering he gave up trying to become an independent farmer, a landowner who worked for himself. He resigned himself to his fate, drowning his pride in weekend binges.

His wife, Delia, was apparently all Negro; she was a dark, well-built woman of great physical and spiritual strength.

There were ten children—five girls and five boys, eight of whom reached maturity: Woodie Clara, Martin Luther, Lucius, who died in infancy, Lenora, Cleo, Lucille, James Albert, Jr., Ruby, who died at age fifteen, Henry Lincoln and Joel Lawrence.

The children grew up strong and healthy but largely uneducated. There were but three months of school each year, and often the teacher was a "pickup," who knew little more than her brightest pupils.

A girl, Woodie Clara, was the oldest child. "Michael" was the name that the mother wanted for her second child, her first boy; but the father wanted him to be "Martin." They agreed on "Luther" for his middle name. The debate on the first name continued through the years. The mother had her way with the children—at least most of the time. Out of deference to her, the boy called himself Michael as long as she lived. This is why he was known by the friends and acquaintances of his early years as "Mike." Some of them, years later, quite naturally began calling his son, Martin Luther King, Jr., "Mike," too. Thus, for a long while there were "Big Mike" and "Little Mike."

There was not much of a legal question about this, for in rural Georgia in those days nobody was greatly bothered about the formality of a birth certificate. As we shall see, later a change of name was made and, by necessity, it was formalized and legalized.

Martin or Michael of Stockbridge was born December 19, 1899. He grew big and strong and was physically and psychologically mature beyond his years. As a youngster he was aware of the brutality of local race relations. Dramatic incidents added emphasis to the folkways and day-to-day routines and race etiquette. He noticed differences between the way Negroes spoke to each other and the way they spoke to white people—and the way they spoke *about* white people "behind their backs."

He also heard white people speak to each other quite differently from the way they spoke to Negroes. He wondered, too, what they said about Negroes "behind their backs."

When he was a youngster of about seven or eight, his mother sent him on an errand to a neighbor's house, a short distance down the road. While playfully walking along the way, he was commanded by a white man to take a bucket and bring back some water from the nearby spring. The boy replied that he could not do this because his mother had told him to do something else—and kept on walking. The man slapped him.

The blow dazed him for a few moments; recovering, he made his way back home.

His mother returned with him. She confronted the man. "Did you slap my child?" she asked. He said, "Yes." She grabbed him, threw him down and tore most of his clothes from him, striking him several sharp blows.

On the way back home, she made her son promise never to mention this to his father or anybody else. She knew that her husband, if he heard about it, would "take it up" with that white man. Maybe somebody would get hurt or the family would have to leave the place. She did not expect the white man to say anything or do anything about the incident on his own initiative. He would be ashamed to face the fact that he had been beaten by a woman. But for a white man to be challenged or assaulted by a Negro man— that would be different! White supremacy would have to be maintained! All this was bewildering to the boy, and made him admire and love his mother more than ever.

As young Michael (Martin) grew up, one of his chores was to curry the mule in the morning. Some of the mule's hair would come off on him. After he had completed this job he had to rush off to school (during the school season). He did not always have time to do more than wash his face and hands before hurrying over the hill to his first class.

His schoolmates could tell by his odors whenever he had been cleaning up the mule. They teased him about it. This embarrassed him and, he says, gave him a "mule complex." He struck back. "I may *smell* like a mule but I don't *think* like a mule," he told them. He was the best student of the school in arithmetic.

Anger, though, was not his only schoolboy mood. He was generally mischievous and was full of good-natured pranks.

He was ambitious, too. He had a hunger for education. And what he read and heard about the world beyond Stockbridge made him want to possess things and go places.

He admired a horse and carriage. They looked "classy" to him. He saved up his profits from tending and raising hogs "on the side" and bought himself a colt. This was an event. It was the first horse —or mule—that anyone in his family had ever possessed. Even the mule his father plowed with belonged to the plantation owner.

As a growing boy he had often wondered why his father did not own things. He got his answer when he was old enough and had learned enough arithmetic to realize what happened at the end of the harvest, at "settling-up time."

On one such occasion he went into the commissary with his father. As a sharecropper, his father reported the number of bales of cotton that he was turning in. The owner noted this and then went over his account book, finally announcing that the value of the cotton and the debts accumulated by tenant James King balanced "even." This meant that neither party owed the other anything.

Michael then spoke up. "Papa, what about the seven and a half bags of cotton *seed*?" His father had forgotten to turn them in. If his cotton had paid up all of his debts, his cottonseed would be clear profit, about a thousand dollars.

Mr. King was happy. The plantation and commissary store owner was furious. He denounced "that smart boy" and would have struck him but the father intervened, saying that he would "take care" of his son's chastisement. Mr. King told Michael to go over to the other side of the store, where he would be out of the conversation.

Michael obeyed but as he walked away he said: "Papa, don't forget about the cottonseed." His father didn't.

Papa himself was a problem at home. Drink had fastened itself upon him permanently. The family hated to see the weekends come. Papa was sure to get "tight." His liquor made him vocal and aggressive. All of his suppressed resentments came to the surface but, as the psychiatrists tell us, they were displaced and misdirected. He vented his spleen on the very person who loved him most, his wife. She would not raise her hand to harm him.

On one of those terrible Saturday nights, Papa came home and began to abuse and beat his wife. Michael stood it as long as he could. Then he came to his mother's defense.

He was robust and powerful for his fifteen years. He grabbed his father, picked him up and threw him to one side of the house, slammed him down again, then jumped upon him and began choking him.

This was no mock fight. Papa was muscular and strong but the whiskey weakened him and made him slow and awkward. Perhaps the son, enraged as he was, would have strangled his father but for the cries and pleas of his mother and the other children. They pulled Michael up.

Now freed, Papa made for the boy, who shot out of the door. Papa reached for his gun on the wall. This time Mrs. King was pleading for her son's life.

Finally, tempers cooled. Michael did not come home that night. The next day, when father and son met, both were sobered. Papa apologized. He admitted that he was wrong, saying that he understood how Michael felt about the mistreatment of his mother by *anyone*.

After that James Albert King never again beat his wife.

To Town

Michael, though, had had enough. He was tired of it all, especially tired of working for others, "for nothing." "Why do *they* have things and *we* don't?" he wanted to know. He saw this question everywhere. He often looked at the red brick house of the village banker for whom his mother did housework and the laundry. When Michael delivered the clean clothes that his mother had washed for the banker's family or helped her sweep and dust, he got a chance to see the rich furnishings of the red brick house. He would run his fingers across the soft draperies and unnoticed try out the easy chairs.

All signs told him that he could never have such a home for himself, in Stockbridge.

So, restive under the deprivations, the cheating and bullying, Michael, in his sixteenth year, announced to his father that he would never hitch up a mule again that was not his own. This was one way of saying that he was quitting the farm and going to the city.

His father tried to persuade him not to leave, but his mother felt that perhaps it was "for the best."

Michael came to Atlanta in 1916. His sister, Woodie Clara, had preceded him there by a year or so. She had come to get more than the four years of schooling that Stockbridge had provided. She worked during the day and attended school at night.

When Michael reached town, he seemed just another oversized farm boy, eager and willing but unskilled and uneducated. He was dazzled by the fast-moving and strange life of the city but he was never swept away by it; never lost his bearings. He realized that his two big tasks were to get a good job and an education. He meant "to amount to something."

At first all that he could find were odd jobs and heavy common labor. At one time he was a mechanic's helper at an automobile repair shop. His duties included such dirty work as changing tires and tinkering with the oil pans while lying on his back underneath the cars. Some of the people who passed by the garage and saw Michael in the dirt and grime cracked jokes about him. Bystanders often joined in the laughter. Ever sensitive and proud, Michael fumed but held his peace. Instead of the mule's hair of the farm, it was now the car grease of the city.

After a while, Michael got a chance at a job that he really wanted. He was tested out for fireman on a railroad engine. This was thrilling. For to Michael, as to several generations of American youth, the locomotive was the most fascinating symbol of power and motion imaginable. With Thomas Wolfe, these youngsters all heard the thunder of the fast express and saw the road stretch westward with the moon shining on the rails. Planes, missiles and satellites would come later.

As a Negro boy, Michael could not aspire to become an engineer. Such a job was reserved for white men. But a fireman was the next best thing, for he was the one who made the power that made the engine go. He sat in the cab, opposite the engineer, who might be friendly and who might let the fireman handle the controls sometime —starting, stopping, speeding and slowing the great iron horse.

On his trial run, Michael fired so well that he made his engine "pop off" with surplus steam. The engineer was so satisfied that he gave Michael the highest recommendation. The job was for a man, but Michael could qualify by pushing his age up a few years. He was hired for the run from Atlanta to Macon. Overjoyed, Michael wrote home to his mother, telling her the day of his first run and that he would blow the whistle for her when his train came to Stockbridge. The letter alarmed his mother. She felt that this was a dangerous job. She took a train to Atlanta and reported her son's correct age to the railroad authorities. That settled that!

This, of course, was a keen disappointment that would not fade for quite a while. But the young man understood his mother's concern for him, though he was certain that this time it was entirely misplaced.

As the weeks and months went by Michael learned his way about the city. He found money rather plentiful after America joined the war against Germany. Prices and wages soared but the really good jobs that he heard about always seemed to require a little more education than he had.

At church Michael was deeply impressed by the way some of the preachers expressed themselves. The conviction grew that he, too, might someday talk eloquently to the people and lead them onward and upward.

Accordingly, he enrolled in Bryant's preparatory evening school, where his sister was already studying. Michael had had four years of schooling in Stockbridge, but in Atlanta they made him repeat the fourth grade. Nevertheless, he had great drive and determination. In a short time his reading and speaking improved. He had always been good in mathematics.

During the next few years he skipped grades. Still it was a slow climb. Finally, by the fall of 1925, he had completed his high school work. He was now ready for Morehouse College.

Meanwhile, he had begun to preach, and had become the pastor of two small churches, which he served on alternate Sundays. This was good, clean work—no hair, no grease—and the collections, reflecting the prosperous twenties, gave him a higher standard of living than he had ever had. He wore better clothes and now and then could let a schoolmate borrow a dollar or two. He had always helped support his sister Woodie Clara and he never forgot the folks back home.

Morehouse represented all that was highest and best in education to Michael but it posed difficulties for him. Most of the students were city boys who would comment in passing on the Rev. Michael King's size, age and rural characteristics. Then, too, some of the studies were exceedingly difficult for him, for example, biology. Miss Constance Crocker (later Mrs. Nabrit), young but stern, flunked him in English. Professor Lloyd O. Lewis doubted that he was college material.

But his will to succeed could not be denied. Many teachers went out of their way to help him. The college smoothed out many of his cultural kinks. He began to look and sound like a Morehouse man. Yet Stockbridge was still there and Michael never put on airs.

Romance

Having attained manhood, Michael began having thoughts about a wife and home of his own. This image became sharper upon the death of his mother in 1924. Without her, Stockbridge was no longer home. She had held the family together. Now all the Kings would leave the little town.

The children followed the general trek of Southern Negroes to the North, most of them settling in Detroit. The father finally gave up farming altogether, came to Atlanta and took a job at the railroad terminal. This was the way it was everywhere—people were leaving the farm. For Southern Negroes it was more than the farm problem that drove them from the land and to the crowded city streets.

With his mother gone, Michael began to use the name "Martin" that his father, now rather forlorn and lonely, had always preferred. Thus Martin Luther King, Sr., was "born" in 1924. Most of his friends habitually continued to call him Michael or Mike.

One year while Woodie Clara was attending night school, she boarded with the Rev. and Mrs. A. D. Williams. Their daughter Alberta and Woodie Clara were good friends. Alberta attended the high school of Spelman Seminary, a college for girls on the west side of the city. The Williamses decided that the two-way trip each day from their home on the east side to the college was too much streetcar traveling for their daughter. So they secured a room for her in the dormitory.

During the course of the frequent conversations between the girls, Woodie Clara often told Alberta about her brother. He was her main financial support in her struggle for an education. Eventually Alberta and Martin met. Although Martin began to think seriously about Alberta after a few weeks, the girl was much more interested in a teaching career than in marriage. Moreover, her picture of an ideal husband was not a Baptist preacher, even though her father was one.

The young Rev. Martin Luther King was likable, full of fun and sincere, but Alberta's friends were sure that she could "take him or leave him," and she herself would join in the friendly laughter about her "big, fat preacher-beau."

In 1923, Alberta left Atlanta to study at Hampton Normal and Industrial Institute in Virginia. While she was gone the romance waned. Not only did distance dim its glow but word got all the way up to Hampton that another girl had so comforted Michael at his mother's funeral that everyone was saying that this new girl must be the future Mrs. King. With her eye on a teaching post, Alberta was not greatly disturbed by the gossip. She completed the two-year normal course and came home with her mind set on teaching in the Atlanta public schools.

But the first day that Alberta was back in town, Martin appeared as she was sitting on her front porch, chatting with her father. Invited to have a seat, Martin remained in it for three hours. The Rev. Mr. Williams, quite aware of the situation, quietly excused himself. Thereupon, Martin and Alberta renewed old acquaintance and realized how much they both cared for each other.

And so on Thanksgiving Day in 1926 they were married. Even for the Ebenezer Baptist Church it was a big wedding. Alberta's father "gave the bride away" and the ceremony was performed by three of the city's most prominent ministers—the Rev. James M. Nabrit, Sr., the Rev. P. Q. Bryant and the Rev. R. A. Carter.

For Martin the marriage was a personal fulfillment and achievement. His life, he felt, was moving in the right direction. It was true that some things were not happening in the customary order. For example, Martin was a preacher and had acquired a wife but he was still a student at Morehouse. But this was no calamity. Withal, he was happy.

The newlyweds moved in with the bride's parents. This was to be a temporary arrangement which worked out so well that it was never changed. The house at 501 Auburn Avenue, Northeast, had a dozen rooms and was big enough for all.

The groom was still in school, having three more years of college work before him. Actually, two of his three children were born before he graduated, in June, 1930, and his third child was well on the way by that time, appearing in July. The coming of the children naturally cut short Mrs. King's teaching career.

The Rev. Adam Daniel Williams, though largely self-taught, had taken a course for ministers and was himself that much a Morehouse man. He was a strong character—tall, dark, full-featured, deliberate. Alberta got her sloe eyes and quiet humor from him. Her constant good spirits came from her mother, Jennie, who was extremely popular among church members and the ladies' civic endeavor clubs.

The Rev. Mr. Williams literally built Ebenezer, at Jackson Street and Auburn Avenue; he was also associated in several of the avenue's businesses and for a while was president of the local NAACP. He was in the forefront of the movement that brought a high school and a branch of the YMCA to Atlanta's Negro community. He helped organize the boycott by Negro readers that killed the inflammatory daily *Georgian*. He was a well-rounded leader in the days when integrity and a sense of responsibility counted most. The highly trained specialists and experts would come later.

The Rev. Mr. Williams was well pleased with the prospects of his son-in-law as a preacher. Sensing that time lay heavy upon his more than threescore years, he asked Martin to become the assistant pastor of Ebenezer. The Rev. Mr. King was loath to give up his own charges—he had two small but well-paying congregations—and he did not want people to say that he married to get a church. But after the family talked it over several times, the father-in-law's wish prevailed. Years later this move turned out to be most fortunate for the church. Then the young minister knew all about the affairs of Ebenezer when it became necessary for him to take the helm quickly.

Children and Grownups

On January 15, 1929, at high noon, Martin Luther King, Jr., was born. The new-born infant did not seem to breathe until the doctor beat life into him. It was a cold and cloudy day. And yet his mother became so warm that she had to be fanned. He had been a heavy child to carry. Years later he would tease her about this, saying, "I hear that I was a burden to you in the period before I was born. Was I worth it?" He knew that she would smile and assure him that she would go through it again for him.

There was once more a name mix-up. The father had told the physician who delivered the child that, if it was a boy, he would be a junior. Dr. Charles Johnson, knowing the father informally as "Mike," automatically entered the baby's name on the birth certificate as *Michael* Luther King, Jr. A few days afterward, when the father discovered this error, he went to the hospital and requested that "Martin" be substituted for "Michael" on the infant's record. He was told that this would be done. Years later, however, it was revealed that this request had been ignored or mislaid or forgotten, because the change had not been made.

Thus according to the record there was a *Michael* Luther King, Jr., until 1934. At that time the father needed to clear his own name in order to get a passport for a trip abroad. Accordingly, he had all the vital entries reviewed and had both his first name and that of his son legalized as *Martin*. Despite this formality, many friends of the Kings even today speak of "Big Mike" and "Little Mike."

Willie Christine, first child of the family, was born a year before Martin Luther. Alfred Daniel, the third and last child, is about a year younger. At home Willie Christine was known as "Christine" or "Chris"; Martin Luther as "M. L." and Alfred Daniel as "A. D." They called their father "Daddy," their mother, "Mother Dear," "Mama" being reserved for their grandmother. The Rev. Mr. Williams was "Granddaddy."

Their grandfather moved about the home quietly and unobtrusively. He was deferred to by all, as the patriarch. He would take time to play with the children or chat with his daughter and son-in-law but kept out of their personal affairs. He died suddenly at sixty-eight of an apoplectic stroke one Saturday morning in March, 1931, after preparing his sermon for the next day's services. A week before, the thirty-seventh anniversary of his pastorate at Ebenezer had been celebrated.

Grandmother, or "Mama" as she was called, blended in perfectly with the King family. A woman of health and spirits, she radiated cheerfulness wherever she went. She and Martin were each other's favorites. She did little things especially for him; she could never bear to see him cry. As we shall see, he was more concerned about her than about himself.

The closeness of their ages made the children more or less peers and associates, with a community of interests. Chris was never a *big* sister—just a sister; A. D. was never a *little* brother, for he outgrew M. L. slightly.

The Kings' was a father-centered household. Remembering the Stockbridge days, Martin Luther King, Sr., meant to be the kind of father he had wanted for himself. He was glad to assume the responsibilities of providing for and protecting his wife and children; but in the household, his word, considerate and benevolent as he tried to make it, was final.

The children were taught to love and respect their parents and elders. The old-fashioned verities of hard work, honesty, thrift, order and courtesy were adhered to faithfully. Education was looked upon as the path to competence and culture. The church was the path to morality and immortality.

Materially, the Kings lived a secure but plain life. There was plenty but there was nothing fancy, and nothing was to be wasted. The house, a rambling, two-story frame structure, with an attic and a front porch, was spacious and comfortable but not stylish. The furniture was appropriate for the house, strong and serviceable. All had good clothes and shoes for everyday wear and a dress-up suit or frock for Sunday.

Each child was given a weekly allowance for the Sunday school and church collection plates and for his individual coin bank and an extra ice-cream cone or soda. These were the first lessons in money management. Each had his chores about the house but could earn extra money by doing special chores.

The children responded wonderfully to this pattern of living. They were healthy, happy and well-behaved. It was a home of laughter but also of serious business. There was a time to play, a time to work, a time to talk and a time to be quiet—for study or prayer or out of consideration for others.

The family was thus basic to the environment in which the King children grew up. In its character-conditioning task it was aided by the school and the church. Most of the Kings' precepts of life came from these institutions, and most of their friends were selected from the boys and girls they met at school, at church or in the neighborhood.

Since their pastor was also their father, the King children looked upon Ebenezer as an extension of the home. It was just three blocks away. All day Sunday and parts of several afternoons or evenings of weekdays they spent there. If Daddy was not at home, he could usually be found in or about the church. Both Grandmother and Mother participated in church activities. Mrs. King often played the piano or organ and directed one of the choirs; Mrs. Williams was good at making little heart-to-heart talks.

The church members were like neighbors, always doing nice things for the pastor and his family. Almost everywhere one went on the east side there was some member of the congregation or somebody who otherwise knew the Rev. Mr. King and his children.

One of Martin's best friends was his neighbor Emmett Proctor, grandson of Professor C. L. Harper, a hero of the Negro community for his manly struggles against the city's reluctant Board of Education. Although Professor Harper was a school principal and could be demoted or transferred or fired, he conducted a firm and consistent campaign for equal pay for Negro teachers and equal facilities for Negro schoolchildren.

Another long-time friend was William Murphy, son of a neighbor, Mrs. Airrie Murphy. He used to ride with little Martin when Mrs. King took them over each morning to the nursery school.

One place where Mrs. King knew to look for Martin when she

missed him from the house and yard was down at Alfonzo Johnson's home. Alfonzo's mother was an excellent cook and may have been responsible for Martin's fondness for collard greens and black-eyed peas. Her husband was a leading deacon at Ebenezer. Another good neighbor was Mrs. Nannien Crawford, who welcomed the King children as her own and would come over "any time" to lend Mrs. King a helping hand. She was always there when the babies were born.

Martin loved bouncing rubber balls off the side of the house, a wall or a fence and playing sand-lot and street baseball. The children put up a home-made basketball court in the Kings' back yard. The open field behind the King property served as a baseball diamond. They made and flew kites and model planes. Martin almost always owned a bicycle.

Physically he was strong and sturdy and apparently indestructible. Several times he fell on his head, with no lasting ill effects. He once said that the Lord must have been preserving him for something by giving him a hard head.

Once when A. D. was batter-up, the bat got away from him and struck Martin, who was catching at the time. The blow knocked him down, but he bounced right up, reminding A. D. that he was "out," since he had missed that third strike when the bat flew out of his hands.

Twice Martin was knocked from his bike by automobiles. When he got home he complained more about the damage to his beloved vehicle than about his own hurt, though he landed on his head during one of the crashes. Once when a truck brushed his bike only hard enough to knock the rear tire flat, Martin kept on riding, coming in on the back rim.

The neighborhood boys sometimes threw rocks for distance, trying out their "arms." This occasionally degenerated into the rough sport of throwing rocks at each other. It was not gang war but a test of accuracy in "chunking" and agility in skipping about to avoid being hit.

Martin played with anybody and everybody who came along. The neighborhood was mostly lower middle class, and upper lower class. The few really palatial homes were overbalanced and outnumbered by shacks and double tenements. Neither the children nor their father and mother drew class lines but there was parental concern about the behavior pattern of playmates. Badly behaved children were to be avoided.

For a while two of Martin's playmates were white boys, sons of the neighborhood grocer. Although the children got on well together, the white mother informed Martin one day that her offspring would not be able to play with him any more. Mrs. King had the task of explaining why without shocking her children.

Books and People

The serious business away from home, of course, was going to school. When Chris started attending the Yonge Street elementary school, Martin, who was only five, but somewhat precocious and talkative, insisted on going, too. Accordingly, he was slipped in and enrolled by pushing his age up one year. But he forgot to keep his secret. Artlessly, he gave himself away to his teacher, by describing the details of his last birthday party. They put him out and made him wait a year.

From the first day Martin liked going to school. He was a good pupil and during the course of his elementary and secondary education skipped about three grades.

He remained at Yonge Street for a couple of years, then transferred to David T. Howard (then an elementary school, later a high school), completing the sixth grade there. From Howard he went to the Laboratory High School of Atlanta University. But this private institution, moderately patterned along "progressive education" lines, was discontinued after Martin had been there for two years, and he completed his high school education at the Booker T. Washington public high school, where he skipped both the ninth and the twelfth grades.

Meanwhile, Chris had transferred to Oglethorpe, the private elementary school of Atlanta University, going on to the Laboratory High School a year ahead of Martin. She spent one year at Washington High, afterward entered Spelman College.

When A. D. was ready for his high school training, the Lab School was closed. Feeling that the rougher Booker T. Washington High students would be too trying for his quick temper, he decided to do his college preparatory work at Palmer Memorial Institute, in Sedalia, North Carolina, a private school run by Mrs. Charlotte Hawkins Brown, whose pedagogical aims are reflected in her booklet: *The Correct Thing to Do, Say and Wear*. A. D. found the atmosphere a bit stifling.

At Laboratory High School Martin and Chris studied together. He helped her with math; she helped him with spelling. By national standards, public school education in Atlanta was "fair" but the training at Oglethorpe and Laboratory School was "superior."

Martin was a B-plus student. He enjoyed studying. He was moderately interested in extracurricular activities but was no interscholastic star. He recalls that he was president of some student organization or other at Booker T. Washington that he can no longer identify.

While Martin and Chris were drawing closer together, he and A. D. were drifting apart. By the time Martin completed his elementary school education, his younger brother ceased to be a regular companion. Martin was making new friends in high school. This shift did not upset A. D., for he was a forceful personality in his own right and had many "chums."

As Martin grew up, he paid increasing attention to dress. He began taking a look at his shoes and the mirror before dashing off to school. He had a taste for fine clothes, with such a predilection for tweeds that he was nicknamed "Tweed" by one of his boyhood chums, Emmett Proctor. When the gang—especially Rial "Rooster" Cash, Joe "Shag" Roberts, Oliver "Sack" Jones and Howard "Mole" Everett—would be talking about the new *suits* that they were expecting to get for Easter or Christmas, Martin invariably would say that he hoped his father would buy him a new *tweed*.

Rooster, Shag, Sack and Mole were the core of "the bunch" of high school days. The Bell brothers—William and Patrick—Billy Perry and Clarence Chandler were also members of the clique that played baseball, basketball, tag football and billiards, or went swimming at the Y and at times paired off to see the girls.

It was a jolly crew. Their affinity was largely athletic and social rather than intellectual. Some of the fellows never made it to college and some of them who made it did not remain long enough to get their degrees.

Naturally, Martin's interest in girls increased as he grew up. A. D. once said, "I can't remember when he began being interested in girls, neither can I remember when he wasn't." When he was in the third grade Martin had a crush on one of his classmates whose name he has since forgotten. Chris thinks that Emma Lyons was perhaps his first girl friend. They were both about seven.

In high school Martin would linger about whenever certain of Chris's classmates and associates appeared. There were, for example, June and her sister Mattiwilda, the singer, daughters of the Auburn Avenue politico and fraternal leader, John Wesley Dobbs; Rose Martin, daughter of E. M. Martin of the Atlanta Life Insurance Company; Rebecca Jackson, whose father was also in insurance; Juanita Sellers, the daughter of a prominent undertaker, and Betty Milton, daughter of the banker and Martin's classmate at the Lab School. The "best" families sent their daughters to the School and, of course, families "on the make" did so, too. It provided the best high school education in the city.

Most of these contacts, of course, were touch-and-go in the exciting swirl of first dates, first dances, parties and outings. Often Martin accompanied Chris as her escort; at times they double-dated.

While learning about girls, Martin was also learning about making money. As a four-year-old youngster he had already discovered that his singing voice could be exploited. He began appearing occasionally before churches and church conventions. His mother accompanied him at the piano and he sang out with a rollicking gospel beat or a slow, heart-rending sob. His favorite number was "I Want to Be More and More Like Jesus." Mr. and Mrs. Roger Anderson booked the little songster for various church programs. Often a special collection was taken up for him.

When he was seven, Martin thought that selling soft drinks during the summer vacation might be profitable. His sister and brother agreed with him and his father advanced the capital. And so the three children were in business with a stand in front of the home. They paid off all debts and had a grand time with the customers, but drank up most of the profits themselves.

At eight, Martin began selling the weekly Negro newspapers and at thirteen had a paper route for the Atlanta *Journal,* the city's afternoon daily. He worked himself up to become assistant manager of one of the paper's deposit stations, where the big trucks would unload the home editions for a whole section of the city. This meant that he helped the manager see to it that each of thirty-odd newsboys got his bundle of papers for his route, that complaints from customers were looked into, and that emergency arrangements were made whenever any newsboy, for one reason or another, failed to show up.

This was a position of some responsibility. If the station manager himself should unexpectedly become ill or otherwise not be available, his assistant was to take over and carry on. Martin was the youngest assistant manager the *Journal* had at the time, but he never became a station manager. Such a top post, even in Negro neighborhoods, was reserved for white men. It involved handling money and coming into the downtown office where the cashiers and clerks were mostly young white women.

No Defense

Martin was also learning about race relations more directly. He cannot recall his first encounter with the color question, but the experience of losing his white playmates from the grocery store was perhaps the first time that skin color became a definite problem requiring some explanation from his parents. It would not be the last.

Martin remembers quite vividly an incident that occurred when he was six years old. His father had taken him to a downtown shoe store in Atlanta. They took seats in the front of the store while waiting to be served. When the young white clerk appeared, he said, "I'll be happy to wait on you, if you'll just move back there to those seats in the rear."

"There's nothing wrong with these seats we have," the elder King said, bristling.

"Sorry," said the clerk, "but you'll have to go back there."

"We'll either buy shoes sitting right here or we won't buy any of your shoes at all," snorted the father. There was a brief, awkward pause. Then boy and father stalked out.

The elder King was always alert to discourtesy or condescension coming from white persons. There was a widespread Southernism of even poor whites addressing Negroes by their given names, calling adult Negro males "boy" and elderly Negroes "Uncle" and "Auntie." The Rev. Mr. King did not permit white agents to make collections at his home. He did not approve of his children working for white families for fear it might habituate the youngsters to subservience. He insisted on a modicum of courtesy in public offices and wherever he spent his money. He was thus always "straightening out the white folks." If it wasn't some clerk, it was a policeman.

A cop would call out, "Boy, what d'ya mean running over that stop sign?" The Rev. Mr. King would say back to him, deliberately, "That's a *boy* there," pointing to his son beside him. "I'm Reverend King."

The family admired Daddy for his courage but feared that some policeman would lose his temper in these verbal exchanges. Once in court, he even talked back to the judge. Everyone agreed that this was going too far.

At another time, a policeman harassed some young people who were meeting at Ebenezer. The Rev. Mr. King complained about this to City Hall. The policeman was suspended and moved to another beat. City Hall knew that the Reverend had a following that meant votes. But the family was apprehensive that the white policeman would retaliate in one way or another.

Like other Negro families, the Kings were disinclined to use the segregated buses of Atlanta. The family automobile was their chief means of getting about the city. But it was not always available when somebody had to go somewhere.

Atlanta had the "first come, first served" system of seating whereby white passengers took the frontmost seats first while Negroes took the backmost seats first, both groups filling in toward each other and the center of the bus. On the Auburn Avenue–West Hunter Street line, which served the city's chief Negro neighborhoods, there were few white riders. Accordingly, Negroes usually had the whole bus to themselves and sat wherever they wished. However, if a Negro passenger was sitting in the front seat and a white passenger boarded the bus, the Negro would be expected to "move back." Some did so silently; others fussed or cursed; occasionally they would not move back unless "made" to do so.

Atlanta, like other towns where segregated public transportation services were operated, had a history of verbal and physical conflicts, some between passengers, but more often between white drivers and Negro riders. Probably there would have been even more but for the flexibility of the "first come, first served" feature. In contrast, where the system was rigid as in Montgomery, and the front seats were reserved for white passengers even though no white passengers were on the bus, the unfairness and senselessness of the system were fully exposed. Resentment swelled to the bursting point in Negro standees, crowded against each other and hanging over empty seats that they could not sit in.

The Rev. Mr. King, Sr., because of some indignity, had adopted the personal policy of not riding Atlanta buses. Although Martin himself never had a personal encounter on Atlanta buses, he became involved in one on an intercity trip. When he was a senior at Booker T. Washington High School, Miss Sarah Grace Bradley, the speech teacher, took some of the students to Valdosta, Georgia, for an oratorical contest. The trip was made by bus. A girl from Savannah won first prize, Martin coming in second.

On the way back home, a change of buses had to be made at Macon. The Negro students took seats that were available. Later when additional passengers—mostly white—boarded the bus, some could not find seats. The bus driver directed the Negroes to stand up so that the whites could sit down. Some older Negroes gave up their seats, but the high school students ignored him. The driver, becoming abusive, referred to the students as "niggers" and threatened to call the police. The students continued to ignore him until Miss Bradley finally asked them to stand. They obeyed her reluctantly and had to remain standing for most of the trip to Atlanta. They did not forgive Miss Bradley for a long time, though she explained that she was only trying to keep the peace, to keep something from happening to the students in her care. Years later, Martin would feel that he already knew the bus problem even before he ever took a bus ride in Montgomery.

On the other hand, young Martin did have some pleasant contacts with whites who were friendly. One of these was Miss Beatrice Boley, his biology teacher at the A.U. Lab School. There each instructor was expected to write up a detailed report on each of her students, indicating scholastic strengths and weaknesses and recommending practical remedial measures. Miss Boley counseled with Martin and made such a thorough yet sympathetic analysis of his educational progress that she drew him to her. She was, he recalls, at once an excellent instructor and a strict disciplinarian.

Martin's antipathy to violence goes back to his youth. He never liked fighting. He would wrestle and tug and play football, but he was against striking others and would do so only as a final resort. This was a personal and individual reaction, for both his father and brother were stout counterattackers. His mother and sister were normally nonviolent, as mothers and sisters often are; but even they felt that, if somebody hits you first, you have the right—perhaps obligation—to hit back.

A. D. was a more usual product of American culture. He stood his ground wherever he went. At times, feeling somewhat aggressive, he would poke or slap Martin or even Chris. Once he was teasing and provoking his sister to the point of tears. Martin pleaded, then commanded that he leave Chris alone. But A. D. kept on. Unable to stand it longer, Martin picked up the telephone and slammed it down on his brother's head, knocking him senseless. Chris cried, "You've killed him!" But a dash of cold water revived A. D., who from that time thought twice before harassing Chris or Martin.

Once when the brothers were at the David T. Howard school, Martin was going up the stairs as Black Billy, the school bully, was coming down. When Martin did not move aside quickly enough, Black Billy beat and kicked him all the way down the steps. Martin did not strike a single blow.

Later someone told his parents about this encounter. When A. D. heard about it, he was furious and wanted to go after Black Billy, disregarding his size and reputation, but Martin talked him out of this reckless notion.

Again, at one of the chain grocery stores there was a little mix-up between Martin and another boy as to who came first to the turnstile. The boy jumped on Martin and beat him up. As usual, Martin did not fight back.

One day when Martin was about eleven years old, he accompanied his mother on a shopping trip downtown. As they began to accumulate packages, his mother asked him to wait in one of the stores while she went to another nearby to pick up one more item. While Martin was standing and waiting, a white woman came up to him and said, "You're the little nigger who stepped on my foot" and slapped him.

He was startled and dazed, yet neither said nor did anything in his own behalf. When his mother returned he told her what had happened, but the woman had gone. His mother consoled him.

The nonviolent tendency must have been quite pronounced, for Martin never wanted to strike the other children of the family, even when commanded to do so by his father. The Rev. Mr. King, in an effort to demonstrate that chastisement was impersonal—the rule of law—used to have the children give each other a stipulated number of licks in their hands or on their buttocks with a belt or rod as punishment for their little deeds of misconduct. Martin would accept such whippings from his brother and sister, but he would not want to whip them—especially Chris. He just could not bring himself to strike her. She was a girl; she was his sister; he loved her and he did not want to hit anybody, anyway.

This withdrawal from violence was not cowardice or timidity. Martin was, as we have seen, a person of force and energy, and most of the time he could talk himself out of a conflict situation. In high school, for example, a rowdy bunch "crashed" the class dance. The school boys confronted the street boys, who were known to be "rough." A clash appeared to be unavoidable. But Martin talked the intruders into leaving.

The only time A. D. remembers seeing his brother fight was in defense of A. D. when three boys had ganged him.

However considerate of others, Martin might nevertheless deal violently with himself. Twice he seems to have attempted suicide, each time because of his grandmother. Once A. D., while playfully sliding down the banister from upstairs in the home, accidentally knocked his grandmother down and unconscious. Martin thought that she was dead. He was so distraught and disorganized that he went to a second-story window and jumped out, falling some twelve feet below. Fortunately, he did not injure himself.

On May 18, 1941, his grandmother was at the Mt. Olive Baptist Church, about to speak on their Woman's Day program, when she suffered a heart attack. She was rushed to the hospital, but died before arrival. That day Martin had slipped away from home. He was down in the business section of Auburn Avenue, watching a big parade, when somebody told him what had happened to his grandmother.

He ran all the way home, where he found the whole family crying. Martin went to pieces. He was sad and remorseful for having slipped off. This was the first death of anyone close to him. He had been just a two-year-old baby when his grandfather died in 1931. His grandmother had been a second mother to him. Martin went up to the second floor of the house and again jumped out of a window. He was jarred and badly shaken up, but not injured.

Soon after Grandmother's death, the family moved away from 501 Auburn Avenue, Northeast. Such a change had been talked about for some time, since both the house and the neighborhood were running down. Grandmother's death made the family even more anxious to get away to a new location. A better house and neighborhood were found at 193 Boulevard, three blocks away. This was a yellow brick structure that sat upon a high terrace. It was well built like most of the other houses and was located in what had once been a fashionable residential area for bishops, doctors, politicians and fraternal leaders. This class was now gradually moving over to the west side of the city, retreating before the invasion of commercial enterprise.

Thus, the first fifteen, formative years of Martin's life had been fortunate. Diverse influences had helped shape and integrate his personality. One of his grandfathers had been a sharecropper; the other a college-bred minister. One grandmother he never knew personally, the other he loved dearly. His own mother was gentle; his father was fearless and protective. He and his brother and sister were bound together by a thousand common experiences. And yet each respected the individuality of the other. He had pals of his own and was recognized and accepted by countless friends of the family.

Physically, Martin was healthy. Intellectually, he was slightly ahead of his age group. Socially, he was enjoying the threshold years of self-discovery and the companionship of the opposite sex. He wore good clothes, had a little money in the bank—and was willing to work for more. Martin was aware of mean policemen and curt clerks but there were friendly white teachers at the Lab School. He was happy in his family, his neighborhood, his school and most of the time in his Atlanta. The church was almost a part of the home. Hostile forces did not come upon him often but, when they did, he would stand for what he believed was right and fair. At the same time, by nature and by choice he was opposed to physical violence as an instrument of dealing with fellow human beings.

Though but fifteen years old, he was ready for college.

V - Morehouse

IT WAS inevitable that Martin Luther King, Jr., would attend Morehouse College. In a sense, his grandfather had been a Morehouse man and his father never tired of talking about the transformation that Morehouse had wrought in him. Aside from these parental influences, Martin would probably still have chosen Morehouse because of its president, Dr. Benjamin Mays.

In the eyes of a young boy, Dr. Mays was a wonderful combination of the intellectual and the spiritual. Many of the preachers Martin saw as he grew up in the world of churches and conventions were poorly trained, old-fashioned, garrulous, florid. His distaste for what they represented became greater as he himself became more educated and, in his boyish way, urbane.

But in Dr. Mays Martin saw a man who could speak with force and effectiveness and then leave one with something to think about after he had finished talking. To the rock-bound orthodox, he was a "notorious modernist." Among religious liberals, this characterization was considered a compliment.

Dr. Mays could lecture or preach. He was popular with both the common people and the college crowd. Anybody could see that there was something to him. He stood tall and straight. His steel-gray hair seemed to crown his dark, even features. His voice, too, had a hypnotic quality. In the summer of 1950 at a huge meeting in Cleveland, after Dr. Mays had finished his speech, a white woman in the crowd was so moved that she threw her arms around his neck and kissed him.

62

Class of '48

Martin had often visited the Morehouse campus as a boy, but he had an entirely different feeling when he came to it as a freshman in the fall of 1944. He was part of it now. He himself was beginning to become a Morehouse man.

The college had the freshmen arrive a few days before the other students. This gave the slightly bewildering newcomers a chance to become oriented somewhat before the sophomores descended upon the campus—and upon them.

Of the 205 young men who were Martin's classmates, some from Atlanta were already known to him. He was a little smaller and a little younger than most of them. He had jumped ahead by taking —and passing—the college entrance examination while he was still in the eleventh grade. He came directly to Morehouse, skipping the twelfth year.

Quite a few of the freshmen were from other parts of Georgia and the South. There was a sprinkling of Easterners, a dozen or so from the Midwest, two or three from the Far West, one from the West Indies, and this time nobody from Africa. (Morehouse usually had a few students from Liberia, Nigeria or the Gold Coast [Ghana].)

The freshmen were of all sizes, shapes and colors and reflected their varied backgrounds in their speech, gait and dress. They were greeted by college officials, given a battery of informational, physical and psychological tests, and then, under student guides, sent on a tour of the campus. In a sense, there was not much to see. In 1944 all the buildings were old. But perhaps this added to the college atmosphere.

As the young men leisurely made their way down the walks that spread across the campus in easy geometrical patterns, they had a look at the dormitories, the science building, the assembly hall, the president's home and the wooden gym. These were all modest and unimposing structures. But there was a quiet dignity about them suggesting something more than the eye could see at first glance. They seemed to say: "This is a college."

Some of the buildings were vine covered. The trees and grass were green. There was a wide gate, gracefully arched and bricked. There was a tower atop one of the dormitories, so high that it could be seen from most parts of the city. It had a loft with a bell.

Moreover, Morehouse was helped out in appearance by the merging of its campus with that of Atlanta University. Here the quadrangles, lined with dogwood trees, were flanked by the massive library and the golden-domed administration hall. Just across the street from A.U. was Clark College, new and neat. And to the right of Clark was cloistered Spelman College. Two blocks beyond Clark was Morris Brown College, with its historic landmarks and bridge where the students lingered and looked down on the street below.

This cluster of colleges made each of the institutions look larger and less isolated than it would have appeared standing by itself. Also, the whole university center, as it was called, gave the freshmen a feeling of moving about in something that was considerable and worthy of further exploration.

Very quickly the young strangers got to know each other. Most of them lived on the campus, and that made it easy. Martin did not have this advantage; he was still spending his nights at home. Even so, he was better off than the out-of-town student, who, working his way, lived off campus, earning his keep by the chores he did for a family in town.

In a few days, the sophomores, juniors and seniors arrived. The freshmen wore the little maroon caps that set them apart. This was a concession that the administration had made to the sophomores long ago. The school colors were maroon and white.

Hazing was not rough or prolonged, if the freshmen were polite and if they learned the Morehouse Hymn "immediately, if not sooner." The sophomores insisted on respect. "Call us mister," they declared. If this was done, things were all right. Otherwise, a newcomer might get a part shaved down the center of his head or a few sharp belts on his buttocks or a cold drench under the shower.

Sometimes a big, strong farm boy or a potential football player would challenge the powers that be. The sophs would gang him and quickly smother his revolutionary impulses. However, most of the Morehouse fellows were city boys who came from middle-class families—or acted as though they did. They took things in stride, going along with any reasonable gag in the very best of humor.

After a week or so, college life settled down into its established pattern. This would be the hub of Martin's life for the next four years. He joined with others in the grand experience of becoming a Morehouse man. But you could start a cross-country debate by asking what that expression meant—what really was a Morehouse man? "I don't know," said one freshman, "but I know I want to be one."

M. Man

Perhaps nowhere on earth is there a typical Morehouse man any more than there is a typical Oxford or Harvard or Fisk man. But there seems to be a widespread belief in such institutional types. The folklore is often more interesting than the fact and frequently reveals attitudes toward the colleges more than actual traits that are fairly common to the students and graduates of the schools in question.

For example, Fisk men have a cigarette joke that involves Howard and Morehouse. Howard is the government-supported university at Washington that once described itself as "The Capstone of Negro Education." Fisk, at Nashville, Tennessee, takes pride in the "culture" of its students and claims to have produced more distinguished graduates than any other college for Negro youth. The *Afro-American* newspaper, published by a Howardite, ardently supports this claim —a claim that is otherwise hotly disputed.

According to the joke, three men were standing and talking. One was from Howard, one from Morehouse, one from Fisk. If the Fisk man would strike a match, he would light the cigarettes of the other two men, then light his own. If the Howard man would strike the match, he would light his own cigarette first, then light those of the other two men. But the Morehouse man would light his own cigarette and then absent-mindedly flick out the match and throw it away.

The joke has gone the rounds and the roles are reversed sometimes according to who is telling it. But it does suggest the truism that Morehouse men are supremely interested in what they themselves are doing.

Morehouse men say that in life one must be careful of the curve in the road ahead; that you can never tell what you may meet coming toward you around the mountain. "But the chances are," they add, "it will be another Morehouse man!"

In Atlanta, one joke is that a wise mother would not dare leave her pretty daughter alone in the company of a Morehouse man. Everybody laughs at this, for, while the townspeople may be thinking of the reputed aggressiveness of the Morehouse men, they, themselves, are thinking of the virility and magnetism that the anecdote suggests.

Howard men are not very conscious of Morehouse. Their orientation is toward the North and their ancient rival, Lincoln University in Pennsylvania. Morehouse is just another good school down South.

Fisk men are a bit more aware of Morehouse men and in jocular moments refer to them as members of a semibarbaric tribe, located in north Georgia. Many decades ago when the first football team from Morehouse visited the Fisk campus, the Fiskites were all eyes in the dining hall. They wanted to see if the rumor was true that Morehouse men ate peas with their knives.

The Morehouse men will complete that story by telling of the way the Fisk coeds were swept off their feet, finding the masculinity of

the Morehouse men irresistible. Upon leaving the campus, the Morehouse men sang to the Fisk men:

> Your girls are so sweet,
> but your boys can't compete
> with a Morehouse man. . . .

Both jokesters and sociologists seem to agree that ability and self-
confidence are characteristic qualities of the men of Morehouse.
Among them the will-to-achieve is strong. They have drive, daring
and a bit of brashness; they believe in themselves and do not mind
saying so. They command, but are individualists, often rather rugged.
Even the advancement of the common welfare they tend to regard
in terms of the decision and projection of leadership rather than as
the sharing of responsibility and the submergence of egos.

There is keen mentality behind the energy, push and optimism of
these men. Success is their goal. "A Morehouse man cannot fail" is
their long-standing slogan.

Such vitality, obviously, is but another manifestation of the
American spirit of the go-getter. In this sense, the spirit of Morehouse
is the spirit of the middle class, colored by the position of the Negro
in American society and enlightened by a good liberal arts education.

On the record, Morehouse has probably produced more college
presidents than any other Negro institution of higher learning and
more than its share of prominent doctors, lawyers and preachers. In
1958 some sixty-eight Morehouse men had earned the Ph.D. or
its equivalent, at American and European universities. The long list
of illustrious sons of the "Maroon and White" would have to include
Mordecai Johnson, John W. Davis and H. C. Trenholm as college
presidents; Benjamin Brawley, Ira De A. Reid and George Kelsey,
social scientists and humanists; John Wheeler, W. A. Scott and T.
M. Alexander, businessmen; John Lawlah, medical administrator;
James Nabrit, jurist; Louis Peterson, playwright; Charles Hubert, the
great-souled, and Howard Thurman, the mystic. As elsewhere, the
most prominent men were hardly typical.

Martin would hear much about all this, and had been hearing
about some of it even before he reached the campus. From time to
time, he would meet many of the Morehouse greats. They were fine
men, spirited and successful. They returned to inspire others and to
renew themselves.

And Spirit

Morehouse was a boys' school. As such, its life was relaxed and
informal. Speech could be direct and uncensored. There was no need
to dress up every day.

Morehouse was a small college. Its student body was usually about five hundred. Everybody got to know everybody else. This community of interest was greatly enhanced by the daily assembly. All the men were brought together each morning for a half hour, Mondays through Fridays. A brief devotional service was followed by the remarks of some local or national speaker on the issues of the day. In season, the students put on their own programs. On Tuesdays the president usually gave an informal talk.

Sale Hall chapel, where these assemblies were held, was a rather plain auditorium, seating about 400 on the main floor and another 150 in the balcony. The walls were bare except that a portrait of the president painted by a student was displayed occasionally. The low speaker's platform jutted out almost to the front-row seats. This placed the performers and their audience close together and made for directness and intimacy of communication.

Morehouse men, chafing somewhat under compulsory chapel attendance, demanded good speakers. Otherwise they would read books, papers or notes concealed on their knees. Whenever a performer spoke exceptionally well, the men would come to life, cheer and stamp their feet. When they were displeased, they would groan and almost boo.

Among themselves the students were equally exacting. When the clubs and fraternities put on their programs they had to be good to earn applause. Many a later-day spellbinder received his baptism of fire on the Sale Hall stage.

Morehouse practiced student government. The undergraduates ran their own affairs with a minimum of faculty supervision. The students on their own initiative put out their paper—the *Maroon Tiger*—wrote their own speeches, arranged their dances, ran contests among the Spelman girls for their homecoming queens, and staged rallies and election campaigns. The faculty was not there to tell them what to do, only what they could not do. When the student council met, only one member of the faculty—the advisor—would be present, and he might be asked to excuse himself. A joint faculty-student committee acted as a sort of supreme court on any disciplinary case when the penalty was suspension or expulsion of a student from the school.

As a private college, Morehouse was free of the pressures that were normally felt by state-supported institutions everywhere and the special pressures felt by Negro state schools in the South. There were, of course, other pressures, but whatever restraint there was at Morehouse was not based on the fear that a Talmadge might cut off the annual appropriation if he was denounced by some student or faculty member.

Being private also meant that the students could be selected—usually from the upper third of the secondary school senior classes. At the state colleges, anybody with the minimum number of high school credits had a legal right to demand admission. "Y'all come!" was often literally true, educationally.

Morehouse was a liberal arts college. This made it unlike Tuskegee and Hampton, which traditionally specialized in manual, industrial and agricultural education. Although these latter institutions had failed to follow their logical development by becoming scientific and technical universities and had quietly converted themselves into teacher-training institutions, they still symbolized the anti-intellectualism and social conservatism of the famous Booker T. Washington. The Negro liberal arts college, on the contrary, followed the equalitarianism and scholarship of W. E. B. DuBois, a Fisk graduate, who did most of his teaching and research next door to Morehouse, at Atlanta University.

The liberal arts, naturally, made for a liberal outlook. Academic freedom was a reality. There were comparatively few rows between administration and teachers, and student freedom was greater than at most schools.

This liberalism was not restricted to campus affairs. Martin has said that his teachers encouraged their students to explore and search for solutions to campus and world problems. Nobody on the faculty seemed to be afraid to think and speak out. The example for the faculty and students was set by President Mays, who was on the national board of the NAACP and a half-dozen other civil rights and human relations organizations. Locally as well as nationally he was willing to be counted.

If the Negro community of Atlanta had had its preference, Dr. Mays would have been on the city's Board of Education when the opportunity came to place a Negro there. But this position went to another educator, less popular and less known as a champion of Negro rights. Dr. Rufus E. Clement of Atlanta University was first to declare publicly that he would run for that office and filed his candidacy before anyone else did. There were some groans, but Dr. Mays would not consider running, since he knew very well, as everybody else did, that his candidacy would be a sure way of splitting the liberal white-Negro vote and thus destroy the chance of a symbolic victory.

Heritage

Morehouse had a vital tradition. It was founded by a Negro, supported and controlled by whites for years and then repossessed, so to speak, by the Negroes. The colored people themselves were largely responsible for creating and nurturing the Morehouse spirit.

The founder of Morehouse was the Rev. William Jefferson White. Yet, from its founding in 1879 until 1906 the institution was dominated by the American Baptist Home Mission Society that supplied the main financial support. During this period the Negro Baptists of Georgia even more than the Morehouse student body chafed under the benevolent despotism of the white administrators. So in 1906 the Mission Society recognized the unrest and gave the college its first Negro president.

John Hope, quite logically, was Morehouse's first Negro president. He was the outstanding member of the faculty, and generally admired and respected. He thoroughly identified himself with colored people although he looked white. Dr. W. E. B. DuBois, with his usual touch of irony, has described Hope as "an American of Scotch descent who had somewhere among his ancestors a black man."

Dr. Hope was handsome, temperate, a schoolmaster of the classics and a blend of a seventeenth-century Puritan, a nineteenth-century gentleman, and a twentieth-century businessman. He was born in Augusta, Georgia, and was educated at Worcester Academy in Massachusetts and Brown University in Rhode Island. His wide-sweeping moderation is suggested by the paradoxical circumstances that he was a warm admirer of DuBois and yet sought the aid of Booker T. Washington in securing funds for Morehouse. Dr. Hope was on intimate terms with wealthy men but he took a trip to Soviet Russia at a time (1932) when anyone who did so was suspect. At about this time, he was made president of the Southern Commission on Interracial Cooperation—the first Negro so honored.

Among those that John Hope drew to him were Samuel H. Archer and Benjamin G. Brawley. These three men made up the team that worked closely together for more than a half-dozen years and probably created the Morehouse spirit. As Professor Kemper Harreld, a living link between the old days and Martin Luther King's time, used to say, "Hope had the vision, Brawley supplied the tone and Archer gave the punch."

Samuel Howard Archer was a "lowbrow" in the better sense of that term. There were no poses about him. He could laugh or shout and would bloody the nose of any boy who displayed cowardice. In this physical directness, he was unlike Hope or Brawley, but he was very much like them in his devotion to scholarship and his faith in men. Archer's stammer gave rise to the legend that when a father once brought his son to Morehouse and said half casually that he wanted the college to make a lawyer out of the boy, Archer responded: "W-w-we'll f-f-first make a m-m-man out of him and th-th-th-then a l-l-lawyer c-c-can be m-m-made out of the m-m-man."

Professor Archer was a huge man and had a huge frown. "When you see that frown," the boys would say, "look out for the lightning." Afterward, that infectious laugh meant that the storm had passed.

Archer taught math but also knew Greek. He was an inspiring teacher but the full force of his personality was felt even more in the day-to-day affairs of campus life. He stood for honesty and integrity and would ferret out any violator of this code, sharply correct him and then send him on his way happy that there was such a fair-minded and good-natured fellow as "Big Boy," the nickname the students affectionately gave him.

Archer was successively teacher, athletic director, dean, acting president and president. He came to Morehouse in 1905, was made dean after Brawley left, and when John Hope moved over to Atlanta University to head up the new affiliation of Morehouse, Spelman and Atlanta University, Archer became president of Morehouse. His health failed a few years after this and he resigned in 1937. It was hard to believe that such a dynamo could run down. He died in 1941 at the age of seventy-one.

Benjamin Griffith Brawley was a Chesterfieldian scholar. No student ever caught him in a soiled shirt or in a grammatical error, however informal the occasion. He finished Morehouse in 1901, returning to his alma mater in 1902 as a teacher. After a few years, he studied with William E. Dodd at the University of Chicago and George Lyman Kittredge at Harvard, where he earned his master's degree. He stopped at Howard to teach for a while but came back to Morehouse in 1913 as its first dean.

Brawley was also professor of English. He was actually a great teacher, old-fashioned and thorough. One of his brightest students, Ira De A. Reid, has said that "Dean Brawley, more than anyone else, gave Morehouse efficiency and power of expression and habits of study." He initiated intercollegiate debating among Negro colleges and was the most prolific writer that Morehouse had produced. Brawley was the youngest as well as the most scholarly of the great triumvirate.

Like his father before him, Professor Brawley was also a minister. The students respected him as a living, though somewhat unattainable, standard of conduct and scholarship. Later, some of the more critical ones would see that Brawley's piety marred his literary judgment and turned him away from the realism of the Negro renaissance of the 1920's. Neither was he a bold thinker on broad social problems, nor did he care for what to him was the "new-fangled" pedagogy.

Brawley clearly articulated the precepts of bourgeois individualism in his brief history of Morehouse College. He characterized the major tendency of the John Hope administration (of which Hope, Archer and Brawley himself were the architects) as a faith that "the greatest success and the greatest expansion lie in the future . . . and in racial and community uplift." His words with the slightest translation could be used by any optimistic chamber of commerce.

Hope, Archer and Brawley moved as a unit for about seven years. And then came the break. Dr. Hope took a leave of absence from the college in order to help out in overseas work during the First World War. He left Archer as acting president.

Dean Brawley felt that he had been passed over. The pain was lasting. He decided to leave Morehouse and do the traveling and writing he had been planning to do for so long. He resigned and made a trip to Liberia. Upon his return to this country, he stopped at Shaw University for a while but finally ended up at Howard, where he finished out his career, teaching and writing a half-dozen books. And though his alma mater presented him with an honorary Doctor of Letters, at his death in 1939 he left his library to Howard.

Nobody could replace Brawley, but another influential personality moved to the front rank as Brawley departed. This was kindly Charles DuBois Hubert, who weighed about 250 pounds, and whose manner seemed to fit his size. He was deliberate, big-hearted and thoroughly sincere. Although not dynamic, he was real, and the Sale Hall assembly listened attentively and respectfully whenever he spoke there.

Hubert never put a boy out of school; he always had a suggestion for helping the indigents meet their financial obligations. He himself had come from a big and famous family that had sent scores of brothers, cousins and nephews to Morehouse. Hubert finished More-house in 1909 and received his B.D. from Rochester Theological Seminary in 1912. He returned to Morehouse as a teacher in 1914 and remained there the rest of his professional life. The Rev. C. K. Steele, of the class of '38 and leader of the Tallahassee bus boycott of 1956, has said that "For me, Dr. Hubert *was* Morehouse."

Hubert found it hard to say no. This normally good quality was perhaps his weakness as president. Morehouse alumni will tell you that he gave in too often to the other members of the tri-school affiliation.

Hubert was appointed dean of the School of Religion in 1924, and when Archer's health failed in 1937, Hubert became acting president. He was never made president but held the line until Dr. Mays was elected head of Morehouse in 1940.

Perhaps his dream of becoming president of his alma mater—

almost within his grasp but never realized—shortened Dr. Hubert's last years. He died in January, 1944. All of the great four were now gone—Hope in '36, Brawley in '39, Archer in '41 and Hubert in '44.

These, then, were the principal personalities who created the Morehouse spirit. They did their work so well that Morehouse men who have themselves become college presidents elsewhere send their own sons back to Morehouse for their college education.

The Morehouse spirit, like that of all other colleges, waxes and wanes. During Martin Luther King's time it waxed. It had waned somewhat in the years just after John Hope moved over to Atlanta University and for the three or four years following his death in 1936. Morehouse had budgetary problems and its ardent supporters felt that the college was putting more into the affiliation than it was getting out of it.

Dr. Hope, of the large vision, tired during the last years of his life. Increasingly, the hand of a white woman, Florence Read, could be seen behind most of the significant moves that the three related colleges made. Miss Read was only moderately trained academically, holding a bachelor's degree from Mount Holyoke College. Her source of power was her close connections with the big, philanthropic foundations and the Rockefeller family. A standard joke in Atlanta was that Miss Read had been sent South to look after the investment that the foundations had made in Negro education in Atlanta. She was executive secretary of the International Health Board of the Rockefeller Foundation when she was made president of Spelman in 1927. Also she became the treasurer of Atlanta University and a member of the board of Morehouse.

She was a woman of boundless energy. At Spelman she personally made every important decision. There was neither dean nor student government. She counseled with every student and decided upon the individual programs of studies. To Morehouse alumni Miss Read represented the kind of benevolent despotism that the college had escaped way back in 1906. To Morehouse undergraduates, she was the one who made it difficult to associate with the Spelman girls.

Miss Read was an ardent admirer of John Hope. She was doubtless sincere in lifting administrative burdens from his shoulders as a measure of helpfulness. His death in 1936 was a personal sorrow to her. She served as acting president of Atlanta University for a few years and ruled the three campuses with matronly directness. She had a master key to most of the buildings and would erupt unannounced almost anywhere. She signed the checks.

Dr. Mays, therefore, from the time he became President in 1940, began an uphill fight "to recover the integrity of Morehouse," to use the phrase of the alumni. That he was well on the road to victory in this cause gave an exhilaration to campus life while Martin Luther King was there as a student.

Schoolmates

Martin's closest friend was his classmate Walter McCall. McCall was from Marion, South Carolina, and worked his way by barbering. He was clear about his intention of going into the ministry, whereas Martin was slow in making up his mind. In his sophomore year Martin met a freshman, Philip Lenud, who would later turn up as a friend indeed in the far North.

One of Martin's lasting associations was made with Robert Williams of the class of '46. They came together mainly through a mutual interest in music. The King family attended almost all the campus concerts even before Martin entered college, and frequently waited a few moments after the performances were over to congratulate and chat with the singers.

Bob had a beautiful tenor voice. He was one of the soloists with the Morehouse Glee Club and the Atlanta University-Morehouse-Spelman Chorus. These were first-class aggregations under the direction of Kemper Harreld and his assistant Willis Laurence James.

Bob Williams was a nonpartisan type of upperclassman who did not look down on lower classmen. He was a nonfraternity man by choice. The horseplay of the Greek letter initiations appalled him. Martin was nonfraternity too. Another nonfraternity friend was Charles Evans Morton, who had his mind set on becoming a minister and was the intellectual, modern type that Martin admired. Williams and Morton took a personal interest in Martin. They looked upon him as "quite promising"—especially after he won second place in the Webb Oratorical Contest in his sophomore year.

For his first two years in Morehouse, Martin took the courses in general education that all lower classmen were expected to take. As yet, he was not sure in his own mind whether he wanted to be a doctor, lawyer or preacher. His father, of course, wanted him to be a minister but did not push the point. His mother sympathetically reasoned with her son as he toyed with first one, then another possible career.

But the example and suggestion of upperclassman Charles Morton and classmate Walter McCall were persuasive. And then there was the image of Dr. Mays and the profound influence of Professor George D. Kelsey, Director of the School of Religion. By his junior year Martin was steadily moving away from medicine and law, and by his senior year was quite sure that he was fitted for the ministry.

Martin's major was sociology, his minor, English. He had enough A's to win second-class honors but for a D that he received in French.

Martin was favorably impressed by many of his teachers, such as Claude B. Dansby, a remarkably clear mathematics professor; Samuel W. Williams, a young Socratic philosopher; Walter R. Chivers, a folksy sociologist; Gladstone L. Chandler, a precise grammarian. But his favorite teacher was George D. Kelsey, who struck Martin as having "vast resources of knowledge, depth of thinking and a winning personality."

In extracurricular activities, Martin was not so active as he might have been had he lived on the campus. He sang with the glee club and the chorus of the affiliated colleges. He was a member but not an officer of the Morehouse chapters of the YMCA and the NAACP. His only important post in student government was membership on the faculty-student discipline committee.

Some of the white and Negro colleges of Atlanta formed an inter-collegiate student association for the purpose of fellowship and discussion of common problems. Martin was a member of this association and later said of it that "The wholesome relations we had in this group convinced me that we have many white persons as allies, particularly among the younger generation. I had been ready to resent the whole white race, but as I got to see more of white people my resentment was softened and a spirit of co-operation took its place."

Father Knows Best

Martin spent his vacations earning some spending money. One summer he worked at an Atlanta mattress factory. At first he was with the loading gang but was soon spotted by the supervisor and made a "straw boss"—but without a pay increase. A little later, his ability with figures won him a real promotion that included a raise. He was made stockroom clerk—all paper work.

The workers at the factory were both white and Negro, and through this brief experience Martin felt subsequently that he came to see that the problems of workingmen were about the same, irrespective of superficial differences among them.

For a short while, Martin worked with a railway express company during its rush season but quit when the foreman called him "nigger." During the Christmas mail avalanches, he got on as an extra with the U.S. Post Office's sorting and delivery service. This was good, quick money and the college boys made a dash for such jobs.

One summer he traveled with other Morehouse men to the tobacco fields of Connecticut. The college maintained this contact for its students. During a good season, the boys got back home with $300 or

$400 clear. But it was hard work picking tobacco leaves in the broiling sun, day after day. When he returned to Atlanta, Martin announced that he was certain that he was "called" to preach the Gospel. Some of his friends smiled and said it was really the hot sun of the tobacco field that had "called" Martin to preach.

But the weekends in Connecticut were free. On their time off, the tobacco pickers went into Hartford, a real city though small. For most of them it was a wonderful experience to be free to enter restaurants, theaters and other public places. Their association with white persons, as tangential as it was, gave them a new feeling of freedom.

Martin's world was expanding in other ways, too. He began to look at Atlanta more steadily and more critically, noting its paradoxes and contradictions. He went to a downtown Jim Crow theater once, and only once! He began to meet the men of Auburn Avenue as a "young man" rather than a child. He began to have entrée to the Dobbses, Waldens, Cochranes, Alexanders, Miltons, Scotts and Blaytons for serious conversation. His father delighted in taking his sons around.

Martin studied his father and sought to avert what loomed ahead as a possible domestic collision. As we have seen, the elder King was a man of strong will, courage and great love for his children. But his was an austere love compounded of discipline and the resolve that his children must not fail. He would shield them from the world's evils and point out to them the path of righteousness—and success.

But as the children grew up, they developed wills of their own. They wanted to experiment, to try new paths, to do as they saw others doing. They wanted the right to make mistakes. And so, the age-old problem of youth versus maturity emerged.

Mrs. King was a moderating influence. She tried to soften and hold down her husband's powerful impulses. He himself tried hard to be fair and democratic, initiating discussions with the children as a group and individually. He let everybody talk. But the teenagers came to have little hope that their logic could ever win.

The three children had their individual reactions to their father's well-meant assumption that he knew what was best for them. Chris tended to debate less and less and usually let him have his way. A. D. held out firmly and in a sense revolted. He was not happy with himself during this time. Though possessed of a good mind, he was flunking in college. Eventually he quit school, married and set up a household of his own. His marriage was more than rebellion against his father. He had been keeping company with Naomi Barber since he was twelve years old.

Martin evolved the technique of listening patiently to what his father advised and then doing what he himself thought was best. He did not surrender; neither did he separate from his father. His strategy was to argue a little, yield a little where he had to, but quietly draw his own conclusion and, without announcing it, move forward deftly as far as he could go toward his goal. Perhaps as the middle child he was not as much under scrutiny as his sister and brother. Perhaps this diplomacy fitted in with his temperament and personality. On the other hand, when A. D. balked, the lightning almost struck, menacing the family circle and upsetting the procession of progress.

Everybody but A. D. was doing well. Chris and Martin were continuing their education. Mrs. King had gone back to school and completed the work at Morris Brown College for the bachelor's degree. (She had only a normal school certificate from Hampton.) For two years she did substitute teaching, but gave it up because of other duties. She had kept at her music and was appointed one of the official organists of the National Baptist Convention. She directed her church choir and assisted her husband in the management details of Ebenezer.

The Rev. Mr. King himself was receiving increasing recognition in business and civic affairs. He won a place on the board of directors of the Citizens Trust Company, Morehouse College, Atlanta University, the local NAACP and the National Baptist Convention. He himself was proof positive that his code of success worked. He had come a long way from the cotton fields and mule stables of Stockbridge. He wondered why the children did not see things his way.

In June, 1948, Martin Luther King, Jr., stood in the graduation line. He was finishing Morehouse. He was nineteen years old. He took a handsome picture. His health was good. His habits of study were methodical. Though not yet widely read, his interest in learning was large. He was articulate and optimistic.

How deeply the Morehouse experience had entered into his unconsciousness could only be guessed. The trials of future years would be the test of these new fortifications of mind and heart. Like other men, what came out of Martin in moments of crisis would be the real measure of what had gone into his making.

At any rate, he was a Morehouse man and was thus ready, he felt, for whatever he might chance to meet around the curve in the road ahead.

VI - Golden Day

CROZER THEOLOGICAL SEMINARY was Martin's choice for his professional training. It was among the top theological schools of the nation. Originally Baptist, it had long since forgotten about sectarianism. It was a liberal and intellectual rather than a denominational institution, in fact, too liberal for some of the Baptists. Historically, the fundamentalist brethren had split off from what they felt was the almost Godless modernism that was taught at the seminary.

When Martin left Atlanta for Crozer, he entered upon a new phase of his life: he would be living away from home, up North and in an interracial situation.

Crozer occupied a beautiful location on a slight hill in Chester, Pennsylvania. The trees and shrubs enclosing and softening the outline of the buildings gave the campus a cloistered look, connoting meditation and repose. It served a small, well-selected student body of about one hundred.

Martin was glad that at last he had both feet in school. His day was no longer divided between home and campus. These had become distinct worlds, each with its own rhythms.

At Crozer, Martin lived in the main dormitory, with classrooms, library, dining hall and tennis court all within a few steps.

Being away from home gave Martin a new, adult feeling of independence. He could do as he pleased. His father was six hundred miles away in Atlanta, and although his valuable advice was accessible through letters and the long-distance telephone, it was no longer ever-present. Martin could now make hundreds of minor decisions about himself.

Martin made a much better academic record at Crozer than at Morehouse. He was an A student throughout his three years at the seminary, and was chosen valedictorian. Having come to Crozer on a scholarship and remained in the top five of his class, he did not have to pay tuition during his stay.

The three-year course for the B.D. was designed to give a thorough grounding in the history of theology and philosophy as well as in the theory and practice of preparing and delivering sermons and offici-ating at religious ceremonies. Crozer's original charter of 1867 (the same year Morehouse was founded) stated its aims rather quaintly as:

> The preparation of candidates for the sacred ministry, by providing them with thorough instruction in biblical, theological and other religious learning, by cultivating moral and religious affections and habits, and by training them in the practice of the various duties which devolve upon them as preachers, pastors, and missionaries.

For his first year, Martin studied history and criticism of the Bible; for his second, he took church history and special phases of the lives and works of the major prophets; for his third, the psychology of religion, ethics and social philosophy. At the same time, there were courses on the techniques involved in performing the tasks of the ministry, including church administration. Practice preaching was done before critical classmates and in real-life situations provided by the regular services of neighboring churches.

Toward Gandhi

The seminary changed presidents while Martin was there; both were friendly to him. President Edwin E. Aubrey had tutored Dr. Mays of Morehouse College at the University of Chicago, and was favorably predisposed toward Morehouse men. His successor, Presi-dent Sankey L. Blanton, often had Martin in his home and at times would leave "this very bright young man" in charge of the class that the president taught.

Dean Charles E. Batten, too, had a favorable impression of Martin. In answer to an inquiry from President Mays of Morehouse, the Dean wrote: "We have just had a period of comprehensive examinations and only one man was granted honors in them; it was King . . . [who] seems to know where he wants to go and how to get there."

Dr. George W. Davis seems to have been the member of the faculty who most impressed Martin. Professor Davis taught Systematic Theology, and he taught it most systematically. "He was a marvelous teacher," says Martin, "conversant with the trends of modern culture and yet sincerely religious. He was warm and Christian. It was easy to get close to him."

Then there was Dr. Morton Scott Enslin. "He was one of those precise scholars and superb linguists, who had a rather iconoclastic manner of criticism," Martin recalls. Professor Enslin's course on the New Testament was so shocking that the fundamentalist beliefs of some of his students were completely uprooted. Enslin applied the higher criticism and the lower criticism to the basic dogma of the virgin birth and the resurrection of Christ. Some of Martin's classmates were so upset by the unanswerable evidence laid before them by their teacher that they withdrew from the course. Enslin was always the unperturbed scholar—accurate and relentlessly logical. He did for Martin what Kant said Hume did for him: "He knocked me out of my dogmatic slumber."

Professor Kenneth Lee Smith has been characterized by Martin as a teacher who "had a tremendous capacity to grapple with big ideas." Smith loved an intellectual quarrel with his students. He encouraged them to hold independent views. He and Martin would tangle over the social philosophy of the Rev. Walter Rauschenbusch, who once worked in New York's Hell's Kitchen, and the neo-orthodox views of Dr. Reinhold Niebuhr.

Rauschenbusch's book, *Christianity and the Social Crisis,* was a persuasive statement of the social implications of religion. Perhaps the author was somewhat too optimistic, too much attached to the idea of inevitable progress, overlooking man's capacity and tendency toward destructive, antisocial behavior.

Niebuhr in his *Moral Man and Immoral Society* (and elsewhere) makes the point that men in groups commit greater crimes and sins than they do as individuals; that collective evil is worse than that of a person acting alone. In contrast to Rauschenbusch, perhaps Niebuhr was too pessimistic, overly impressed by the power of "Satan" in society. As a pacifist, Niebuhr had favored nonresistance. He was frightened out of this negative position by the terror of totalitarianism. He then swung back to the orthodox stand of forcible, that is violent, resistance. Martin would have neither nonresistance nor violent resistance. He was searching for a philosophy of nonviolent resistance.

Further stimulation and enlightenment came from visiting lecturers. One of these was A. J. Muste, well-known long-time left-wing "Christian socialist." There was great appeal in what he said against war. Yet, again, his theoretical position terminated in what for Martin was negative pacifism.

A more positive and responsive chord was struck by the mellow oratory of Mordecai W. Johnson. Dr. Johnson was a public speaker in the great tradition of Daniel Webster, William Jennings Bryan and Winston Churchill. He was a Morehouse man of the class of 1911. He taught at his alma mater for two years, afterward going into the ministry.

While serving as a pastor in Charleston, West Virginia, Dr. Johnson was brought face to face with what he later described as a major dilemma of his life; that is to say, he believed in the gospel of brotherly love but found that exhortation of it had little effect on race prejudices. He faced the conclusion that a forcible fight for social justice had to be made because mere appeals did not seem to impress those whose vested interests or status would be endangered or dislodged by social change.

Dr. Johnson was never able to resolve this dilemma in Charleston. He still worried over it after he became president of Howard University in Washington, D.C. There he began to read about Gandhi and Gandhi's own words in young India. He also talked with Charles Andrews and others he chanced to meet who had been to Asia. The Gandhian way seemed to offer an answer to Dr. Johnson's question.

In 1950 Dr. Johnson himself got a chance to visit India when some of the descendants and disciples of Gandhi invited sixty-five religious leaders of Europe and America in the hope that, if these visitors could but see and feel the effect of the life and work of the Mahatma, they would subsequently spread the message abroad. This was a little more than two years after Gandhi's death. Dr. Johnson spent some fifty days in India, traveling widely and talking with thousands of persons.

When he came back to America he was on fire with Gandhi's spirit and went all over the country spreading warmth and inspiration. Among other places, he spoke at Fellowship House in Philadelphia, just a dozen miles from Crozer. Martin came over to hear him.

Gandhi, Dr. Johnson declared, had done five things, any one of which would have been enough to make him a great man: he had freed India of British rule; he had done it without firing a shot or uttering a violent word; he had brought untouchables within the pale of acceptability of Indian society; he had lived a personal life of poverty, simplicity and high thinking; and he had demonstrated the redemptive power of love as an instrument of nonviolent social reform.

This last point, really an orator's summary of the preceding four, struck Martin, too, as possibly the answer to his own question: Without violence or surrender how could one struggle for self-fulfillment and the common welfare? If Gandhi had resolved the paradox of the necessity of love and the necessity of force in bringing about social change, he was indeed one of the great men of all times.

Martin, too, became fired up. He began to read all the books on Gandhi that he could lay hands on. The more he read and the more he talked with others about what he read, the deeper became his faith. Now, at last, he had found a philosophy that fitted in with his natural tendency as well as with his sense of social obligation.

Fellow Students

Life at Crozer, of course, was not devoted exclusively to philosophical discussion and meditation. And Martin participated fully in the nonintellectual aspects of campus life. As usual, he made friends easily. Of the hundred or so students of the Seminary, only about a dozen were women, most of whom commuted. Thus, the Crozer student body was essentially male, like Morehouse, but differing in interracial composition.

Among the half-dozen Negro students was Martin's Morehouse classmate, Walter McCall. He had entered Crozer a semester late but caught up with his class before graduation.

Among the white students, two of Martin's friends were Dupree Jordan and Francis Steward. Both were from Georgia. Steward brought his family to the seminary with him and lived in one of the apartments furnished for married men. Martin frequented the Steward home. After graduation, Steward returned to preach in his native Georgia.

The Crozer students came from all parts of the country and from abroad. They were so friendly with one another that it was difficult to detect differences among them on the basis of color or previous residence. Normal contacts usually blossomed into free-and-easy companionships. But there was a notable exception.

One of the students, from North Carolina, found it difficult, apparently, to accept Negroes as associates. He would, for example, use the word "darkie" now and then. It was not always clear as to whether he did so unintentionally. However, his basic attitude did emerge clearly by means of a dramatic incident.

The students in their more informal moments sometimes indulged

in horseplay. One prank was to slip into a hallmate's room during
his absence and overturn his bed, chairs and other pieces of furniture. Everybody, including Martin and the North Carolinian, would
engage in these forays periodically. There were no watchful room-
mates, for the Crozer students were lodged separately.

One day the North Carolinian found his own room upset. Angry, he
came straight to Martin, told him that he knew who had done it,
and to the shock of several students, who were standing about snicker-
ing over the incident, pulled a pistol, threatening to shoot Martin.
Martin, outwardly calm, simply said that he had not been a member
of the gang that had done the upsetting, which was the simple truth.
It just happened that he was not in that particular group.

Fellow students crowded around the North Carolinian, made him
put up his gun and told him what a terrible thing he had done. Later,
they brought the matter before the student government but Martin
refused to press charges, preferring to let the matter drop. But both
student body and faculty felt that such a serious act could not be
brushed aside. After much soul-searching, the North Carolinian
publicly confessed his wrong and apologized.

By the time Martin graduated, he and the North Carolinian had
become friends. Years afterward, when the North Carolinian ran
out of funds while passing through Atlanta, he felt close enough to
Martin to look up his old schoolmate and ask for a small loan. Martin
was glad to let him have the money as a gift.

His nonvindictiveness in the room-upsetting case increased Martin's
popularity immensely. He was easily the man of the campus in the
eyes of his fellow students as well as the faculty. He was elected
president of the student government and was considered by all to
be the current seminarian who was most likely to succeed.

The round of studies and campus activities left little time for off-
campus explorations. But Martin did attend the Penn Relays during
each of his three years and took in a few parties with friends in
Philadelphia and in the smaller town of Camden, just beyond. He was
in Philadelphia rather often, for he took several special classes in
philosophy at the University of Pennsylvania to supplement his courses
at Crozer.

Martin ordinarily had no difficulty in moving in and out of public
places. But now and then he realized that his familiar friend Jim
Crow had come north, too, venturing forth from his hiding place
whenever he thought that it was safe to do so.

One evening Martin and Walter McCall were taking an automobile
drive with two girls on a New Jersey highway, a few miles out from
Camden. As they reached the little town of Maple Shade the party

decided to stop for something to eat. Entering a restaurant and taking a table, they soon realized that the waitresses were passing them up. They remained a few moments longer to be sure of this, then asked for the proprietor, who, vague at first, finally made clear that he was not going to have their table served.

The quartet knew that like most Northern states, New Jersey had a civil rights law that prohibited racial discrimination in public places. Determined to see the matter through, they continued to sit, talking things over among themselves. The proprietor became angry when they would not leave. Going outside, he took his pistol, fired into the air, and announced in a loud, clear voice: "I'll kill for less."

Calmly the quartet arose and left but returned in a few moments with a policeman. The proprietor, now frightened, was arrested. Martin and his companions asked several of the other people in the restaurant, who looked friendly, if they would testify as witnesses. Three, who were students at the University of Pennsylvania, agreed to do so.

The case was turned over to the Camden NAACP, the closest branch in the state, and a suit was entered against the restaurant proprietor. The NAACP counsel felt that there was a good chance of winning. However, the witnesses, upon second thought, decided against testifying. For lack of such objective evidence, the suit petered out. And so, Jim Crow, almost caught, once again escaped penalty.

The only invitation to "make yourself at home here, any time" that Martin could afford to accept was that offered by the Rev. J. Pius Barbour, a Morehouse man, brother to the Rev. Russell Barbour of Nashville and a friend of the King family. J. Pius had blazed the way at Crozer, being the first Morehouse graduate to study there. Martin has said that Barbour's house, which was about two miles from the Crozer campus, was like a second home to him. There he would watch TV, eat and argue at length with the learned and loquacious divine.

Practice Preaching

When it came to acquiring experience in the tasks of the ministry, Martin had an advantage over most of his classmates. As the son of a preacher, he had heard inside discussion of church affairs since childhood. In 1947, while yet a junior in college, he had been ordained and elected assistant to the pastor at Ebenezer. Each summer when he returned to Atlanta from Crozer, his father more or less took a vacation, letting his son get the feel of operating the church.

Ebenezer was well run and ably administered. It was bit odd that a church with a membership of such modest economic resources should stand up so well financially. Everybody in Atlanta knew that Ebenezer was debt free and had money in the bank. Moreover, it did not engage in raffles, lotteries or any of the other coin-producing stunts used by some of its sister churches.

Part of the credit for all this went back to the Rev. A. D. Williams, Martin's maternal grandfather. He was known as a good businessman and, whenever there was a money-raising campaign in the community, he was the logical leader of it. He seemed to have the knack of persuading people to give freely to worthy causes. No doubt his quiet humor helped. One amusing incident arose out of his misuse of a verb.

The Rev. Mr. Williams had had a course in theology at Morehouse but his grammar at times reverted to that of his pre-college days. In reporting the amounts that had been raised to one of the preliminary conferences of a fund-raising group, the Rev. Mr. Williams had said: "Mr. Jones done give $20. Mr. Smith done give $15 and I done give $25."

The next day, one of the more proper Auburn Avenue businessmen telephoned Martin's grandfather that he wanted to see him immediately and, when the clergyman came, gave him a lecture on the correct use of auxiliary verbs. "Thus you see," he concluded, "you should have said: 'Smith has given $15, instead of Smith *done* give $15."

The clergyman was a bit miffed but thanked his friend and went away. A few nights later the final reports were made; the minister, with a twinkle in his eye, told the group that his grammar had been corrected but that, when he looked over the figures for the total contributions made by all, he found that "I done give a hundred dollars but the gentleman who corrected me *has* given nothing."

The Rev. Martin Luther King, Sr., further advanced the financial soundness of Ebenezer. Under him, the church rolls expanded from six hundred to four thousand, about half of whom were active. Most of these members were skilled, semiskilled or unskilled laborers. Some were domestics. In recent years as the children of the church grew up, more and more of them were continuing in school through college. There was a sprinkling of post office employees and public school teachers but few doctors, lawyers, businessmen or college professors. J. B. Blayton, the certified public accountant, C. A. Scott, publisher, Professor Melvin Watson of Morehouse College, Dr. J. H. Cochran, pharmacist, Attorney S. S. Robinson and Dr. M. L. Jackson, physician, were exceptions.

The Rev. Mr. King, Sr., made every member conscious of his share of responsibility for supporting the church work. All persons on the books were reminded of their "church bills" by letter and by the visit of a church officer. A mimeographed statement was issued each month which listed the contributions of church members. It carried on the outside cover the following encouragement:

OUR STEWARDSHIP

The Bible refers to prayer about five hundred times, to faith less than five hundred times, and to material possessions about one thousand times. Sixteen of Jesus' thirty-eight parables were clearly concerned with stewardship of material possessions. We wonder if anyone ever said to Jesus, "Lord you emphasize money too much."

Tithing is not a way to finance the Church. It is a relationship with God. No one should plan to tithe merely in order that the Church might have money. Paying the tithe is a symbol of our recognition of God's ownership of all wealth.

Any church member unable to give was, of course, excused from doing so, but those who willfully opposed the church program in this or any other regard received a sharp reprimand from the pastor. The Rev. Mr. King, Sr., could be harsh and embarrassing. However, this was seldom necessary, for the income and expenditures of the church were clearly set forth and the books were always open for inspection. The congregation knew what happened to its money and knew that the share expected of each member was a fair apportionment.

The Rev. Mr. King saw to it that the church provided a good living for the pastor and his family but he was extremely careful in handling all collections. Ebenezer had a budget and operated within that budget. Before the new education building was built in 1955, Ebenezer had more than $100,000 in reserve funds in the bank. As of April, 1958, the current bank balance was a little more than $25,000.

Thus, if Martin wanted a model for a well-organized church, he did not need to look beyond Ebenezer. The principles of carefulness with the people's money and at the same time budgeting generous support for the pastor and his home were not wasted on the young minister.

Moreover, since Ebenezer was essentially a congregation of working-class people, Martin was thoroughly familiar with the high charge of emotion—the shouting and the beautiful but full-throated singing—and the general direct behavior of the evangelical denominations to which the majority of Negroes of America belong. This background at Ebenezer was thus a balancing weight to the intellectualism of Crozer.

Martin also moved about in the world of state and national Baptist conventions. There the atmosphere was dominated by the elections that came at the closing sessions. While engaged in "politicking," the ministers of the gospel were scarcely distinguishable from more mundane politicos. The trading of votes and influence at these conventions was brisk and sometimes sordid. Again Martin obtained another first-hand view of the realities of organized religion not included in the Crozer curriculum.

Excelsior

In 1951 Martin received his B.D. at Crozer Seminary. Besides being class valedictorian, he was also recipient of the Pearl Plafkner award for scholarship, and the Lewis Crozer Fellowship of $1,200 for two years of additional study in the graduate school of his choice. Martin had done better—much better—at Crozer than at Morehouse. Possibly it was the interracial situation, more than any other factor, that had stimulated him to do his best. He felt a compulsion to do well, for whatever he did, he felt sure, would be accredited not just to him as a person but to the Negro people as a whole. As he told William Peters for *Redbook* magazine:

I was well aware of the typical white stereotype of the Negro, that he is always late, that he's loud and always laughing, that he's dirty and messy, and for a while I was terribly conscious of trying to avoid identification with it. If I were a minute late to class, I was almost morbidly conscious of it and sure that everyone else noticed it. Rather than be thought of as always laughing, I'm afraid I was grimly serious for a time. I had a tendency to overdress, to keep my room spotless, my shoes perfectly shined and my clothes immaculately pressed. . . .

Martin thoroughly fulfilled this social obligation at Crozer. His three years there had been almost entirely without pain or strain or blemish. There had been no abiding problems of money or family or scholarship. There were no major defeats, no disasters. He was successful; he was happy. The days at Crozer had been golden.

On to Boston

Martin's intentions of continuing his education beyond Crozer evoked mixed reactions among his friends and neighbors in Atlanta. Some felt that he had been in school long enough and was already sufficiently trained—especially for the Baptist ministry. There were not many Negro Baptist churches in the nation that had a pastor with more than two earned degrees. Some spoke of the danger of becoming "overeducated"—particularly for congregations that would most likely be lower class or at best lower middle class. Anti-intellectualism could be annoying when leader and followers were culturally far apart.

These demurrers were usually silenced when Martin revealed that

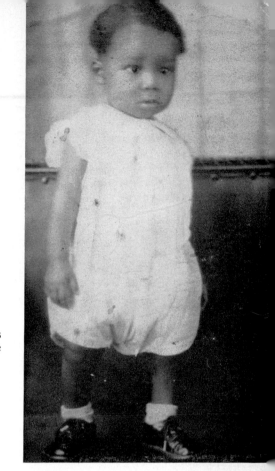

Martin at age two in his family's home in Atlanta where he spent the first nineteen years of his life.

Family portrait: (left to right) mother, father, grandmother (Mrs. A. D. Williams); (seated) brother A. D., sister Chris, and Martin.

Coretta is held by her mother in front of the Scotts' early home near Marion, Alabama. Sister Edythe stands close by.

Coretta's parents, Mr. and Mrs. Obie Scott, in their present home in Marion.

On December 5, 1956, Coretta King appeared with Harry Belafonte and Duke Ellington at the Manhattan Center, New York City, in a musical program supporting the Montgomery Improvement Association (pp. 177-78).

Coretta found Martin a serious student and attractive escort when they met in Boston in 1952.

The wedding was held in Marion, Alabama, June 18, 1953.

The new generation: Yolanda Denise ("Yoki") and Martin Luther King III.

Mass meeting: overflow crowds gathered frequently in Montgomery's churches to hear their leaders during the bus boycott.

King is booked during the wave of arrests touched off by the boycott (p. 137).

King calms an angry crowd from the front porch of his bombed home on January 30, 1956. Mayor W. A. Gayle (left) and Commissioner of Public Safety Clyde Sellers (right) also spoke (p. 135).

Three important leaders of the Montgomery Improvement Association: (left to right) Attorney Fred D. Gray, the Rev. Ralph D. Abernathy and the Rev. Robert S. Graetz.

King addresses the vast crowd gathered before the Lincoln Memorial at the climax of the "Prayer Pilgrimage for Freedom" on May 17, 1957 (pp. 195-96).

Mildred Grossman

More than thirty-three states were represented among the thousands who took part in the pilgrimage to Washington, D. C.

New York Times

M. K. Gandhi's grandson, Rajmohan Gandhi, and Roy Wilkins, Executive Secretary of the N.A.A.C.P., congratulate King following presentation of the coveted Spingarn Medal.

White House Conference, June 23, 1958: (left to right) Lester B. Granger, Martin Luther King, Jr., White House Administrative Officer E. Frederic Morrow, President Eisenhower, A. Philip Randolph, Attorney General William P. Rogers, Presidential Assistant Rocco Siciliano, and Roy Wilkins (pp. 217-25).

he Kings with Vice-President nd Mrs. Nixon at ceremonies ι Ghana marking the birth f the new nation, March 5, 957 (p. 181).

Wide World

After his arrest in Montgomery on September 3, 1958, King affirmed his innocence and charged police brutality (pp. 225 ff.).

With the letter opener protruding from his chest, King rests after near-fatal stabbing in Blumstein's Department Store in Harlem, New York City. Standing by are N.A.A.C.P. President Arthur B. Spingarn and Mrs. Robert Johnson, wife of a Congregational minister.

Vernoll

he had a $1,200 fellowship in his pocket. Everybody agreed that that made a difference. This also partly answered the objections of those who felt that, young as he was, Martin ought to take time off from studying to get some "actual experience."

And there was also the fact that Martin had been assisting the pastor at Ebenezer. His father wanted to keep Junior close to him, and as part of the attraction he was demonstrating that he could stay in the background. In 1950 Junior had been promoted to associate pastor. The thought running through the elder King's mind was that somewhere in the future he would gradually retire, letting his son take over and thus continuing the succession. He agreed that maybe, after all, it was a good move for his son to get his education completely out of the way while he was still young.

And so in the fall of 1951 Martin Luther King, Jr., packed up his green Chevrolet, his graduation present from his parents, and drove on up to Boston. He was going back to school; really he had never stopped. He had merely taken his usual summer vacation.

Martin enrolled as a candidate for the Ph.D. at Boston University in 1951. At that time Boston University and the University of Southern California were leading centers for the study of personalism, and Martin was especially interested in this rather new turn in modern philosophy which placed great emphasis upon the value of the human personality. Moreover, he had been studying textbooks written by Edgar Sheffield Brightman since his early student days at Morehouse and Crozer. Dr. Brightman was a leading light of the Boston University faculty.

From Day to Day

Martin's life in Boston was very different from his life at Crozer. Working for a Ph.D. is largely an individual, isolated journey with a great deal of research and little time for general exploration and social life. The concentration is often so intense that the student has to restrict his orbit to his classes, the library or laboratory, his project and his advisors.

For the first semester he had a room at 170 St. Botolph Street, about a seven-minute drive from the University, where several other B.U. students, mostly white, also had quarters. Martin ate out at various places. In time, he discovered Mrs. Jackson's Western Lunch Box, run by a brown-skinned woman from Kentucky, who specialized in Southern cooking. Hers became a favorite eating place for Martin and some of his friends, including Mrs. Mary Powell of Atlanta.

During his second semester in Boston, Martin and another Morehouse man, Philip Lenud, who was studying for his B.D. at Tufts

College, took a suite at 397 Massachusetts Avenue. This gave them a large living room, two bedrooms, a kitchen and bath for $60 per month. It was high rent, but they kept the apartment for two years by saving on the food bill and trying their hands at home cooking. Phil was adept at this; Martin learned some cooking from him but usually "did the dishes," according to Lenud.

Phil and Martin lived across the street from the Savoy Ballroom, where many an evening they saw students from Harvard and the Massachusetts Institute of Technology crowding in to dance to Dixieland jazz. Since this was not their style, Phil and Martin never went over, although they visited the Totem Pole and other night spots occasionally.

As an extracurricular activity, Phil and Martin organized the Philosophical Club. This started out as a weekly get-together of a dozen or so Negro graduate students who were studying at various institutions of higher learning in and about Boston. On a weekend evening they would come together, drink coffee and talk. At each meeting, somebody would read a paper on a subject of his choice and the others would try to pull it apart. At times these sessions were so exciting that they lasted past midnight.

In a short time the reputation of the club spread, and in due course it became both interracial and coed. Later, when Martin left Boston, he said that what he missed most were the evenings at the Philosophical Club.

At the university, Martin was able to study with the famous Dr. Brightman for but a semester and a half. Brightman was taken ill and soon afterward died. This short period was enough, however, for Martin to feel the force of Brightman's intellect and personality. Martin rated him as both a great scholar and a great teacher, and Brightman rated Martin A.

Next to Brightman, Martin's most impressive teacher at B.U. was L. Harold DeWolf, a disciple of Brightman, who did in theology what Brightman did in the philosophy of religion. There was one great difference, however: Brightman believed that though God is *infinite* in love, he is *finite* in power, thus explaining the strength of evil and the limitations of God in contesting against evil. DeWolf, on the other hand, believed that God is infinite in power as well as in love. Martin must have made a favorable impression upon DeWolf, too, for the teacher later said, "Of all the doctorate students I have had at Boston University—some fifty in all—I would rate Martin King among the top five."

Martin also did well in his other courses. His program called for forty-eight semester hours of classwork, examinations in four related fields of study, a dissertation and a reading knowledge of two foreign languages. Martin also managed to take several courses as a special student in philosophy at Harvard. This strengthened him theoretically and gave him a critical view of personalism. Harvard was then under the influence of the great Alfred North Whitehead, a realist.

But the decisive development that occurred during Martin's stay in Boston was not brought about by any professor or seminar. It was a girl, a coed from Alabama, who, like Martin, was in Boston on a special mission.

VII - Coretta

WHEN Martin Luther King first met Coretta Scott he liked her. He liked what he saw, and what he saw was a fine face and figure enhanced by a pleasant manner. Knowing nothing of her personal history he could hardly have guessed that had he met her some few years back she might have sorely tested his inclination to nonviolence, and might even have frightened him away.

At Antioch College in Yellow Springs, Ohio, Coretta had mystified her schoolmates and teachers. They did not understand how a Negro girl, just out of Alabama, could have such poise and naturalness in mingling with white people. It was almost unbelievable.

These qualities were no longer so baffling when one came to know Coretta and her background. The explanation lay in the particular piece of Alabama in which she was born and reared and her very definite reaction to the people and things about her.

Marion

Coretta was born April 27, 1927, in Perry County, near Marion, Alabama. Languid and conservative, Marion was a typical county seat of a typical Southern Black Belt county. In the town square stood the courthouse, with the customary columns infrequently white-washed or painted, and surrounded by a low, flat-topped wall on which the folks in from the country sat when they became tired of milling around. On a bright Saturday afternoon, the white and colored people

—looking very much alike, with the whites perhaps a little better dressed—filled the square, moving slowly in and out of the stores, talking and laughing, sitting and looking. When Coretta was a girl some families came to the city in automobiles, many more had horses and mules, one or two had oxcarts.

Perry County's power relations were suggested by its broad cotton plantations and by the statistic that of its people twenty thousand were Negro, seven thousand white. The whites, of course, owned and ran things; the Negroes were mostly sharecroppers, tenant farmers, domestics and laborers.

But not all. Sandwiched in among the big plantations were Negro freeholders, and out in the county, in the community where Coretta was born, the twenty-odd Negro families had owned their land as far back as the Civil War. One of Coretta's grandfathers had two hundred acres; the other, three hundred. Negro landowners exercised a quiet independence which a plantation hand could not afford. They worked their own farms, mostly with their own large families— Coretta's paternal grandfather had twenty-six children—marketed their crops and realized what was considered a good living.

During the depression years, these farmers naturally suffered with the rest of the region, and since then many of the young people, here as elsewhere, have left the farm and the South.

But the tradition of the self-reliant Negro was strong and manifested itself in various ways. For example, Mr. Hamp Lee, who owns his own funeral home just off court square, still remembers the time when Negroes had many businesses on Marion's main street. The best known of these was still there during Coretta's day. This was Childs'— a bakery, confectionery, grocery and general store. According to oral history, Old Man Childs got his start with $2,000 he received for using his influence to persuade Negro voters to support a certain set of local politicians. At that time Negroes were permitted to vote in large numbers, before their wholesale disfranchisement in 1901.

The Childses—the old man and his three sons—baked the first "light" bread that Marion tasted and supplied it to private homes, restaurants and boarding schools. The store was famous for its pastry and candy. It had a soda fountain at which the customers could sit and sip soft drinks. The establishment was popular with the younger set and a welcome relief for the adults, because in the white-run stores of Marion it was unthinkable that Negroes would sit at the soda counters. Even when they bought packaged ice cream "to take out," it was not handed to them over the soda counter, but around it, at the end.

The Childs store prospered for years, but the three sons, who ran

things after the death of their father, refused to supply light bread
to other grocery stores. The Childs brothers wanted to maintain
a monopoly on the local retail bread and pastry trade. Consequently,
the other merchants began to import bread from the outside, from
national bakeries. They undersold Childs'. The brothers made other
unfortunate business decisions which, in combination with the increasing competition, drove the store into debt and, finally, out of
business.

In politics the color line was rigid. All public offices in Marion
and Perry County were held by whites. Though Negroes outnumbered
whites 3 to 1, white voters outnumbered Negroes 30 to 1. And the
local White Citizens Council in 1956 said that there would be no
more colored registrants.

Yet race relations in and about Marion were quiet. Nobody could
remember a lynching or race riot, and as late as 1957, when a Negro
shot down, but did not kill, a member of a white mob threatening
the colored man's home, no charges were pressed against either the
Negro or the white man. The wounded mobster recovered, and although the Montgomery and Birmingham press carried the story, the
local paper ignored it, in the interest of peace. Both the Klan and
the WCC worked quietly but had little open support.

The color line, as a matter of course, extended to education. For
the higher training of the whites there had been for generations a sort
of religious finishing school for girls and a military junior college for
boys. These fitted into the pattern of female gentility and the male
martial spirit that is supposed to be characteristic of the old South.

Marion and Perry County traditionally have been hostile to educated
Negroes and Negro education. The state teachers college for Negroes,
founded here in 1874, a few years afterward suffered "an incendiary
fire" and moved to Montgomery, where it has since flourished. For
a long while the county made only slight provision for the public
education of Negro children. As late as 1941, when Dr. Charles S.
Johnson published his *Statistical Atlas of Southern Counties,* he reported that Perry County was spending twelve times as much for the
education of each of its white children as for each of its Negro
children. Accordingly, illiteracy was ten times greater among the
county's Negroes than among its whites.

It has been only within the past decade that school authorities
have recognized the doctrine in race matters of equal though separate.
Ironically, this came when the nation, through the United States
Supreme Court, had moved on to declare the separate-equal formula
outmoded.

After the Civil War, much of the South, prostrate and bitter, was like Marion, unable or unwilling to provide education for all of its children—especially its black ones. Accordingly, the American Missionary Association, working hand in glove with the Freedmen's Bureau of the federal government, established colleges and academies throughout the former Confederate States. It was the same impulse, working through the Baptists, that founded Morehouse.

The AMA, founded as a branch of the Congregational Church, has a notable record in the field of Negro education. It is partly responsible for the existence of Fisk and Atlanta University as well as for numerous high schools and training centers. Historically, the AMA and similar religious organizations represented the high tide of humanitarianism that began to sweep over the nation just before the Civil War. Young men and women from Yale, Oberlin, Brown— but strangely few from Harvard—came south during the Reconstruction period to help bring about a cultural democracy. These most idealistic of carpetbaggers were often from well-established families and were top students in their classes. Some of them gave up lucrative careers, even marriage, in their devotion to the belief that if it could be demonstrated that the freedmen and their children could absorb American culture they would be readily admitted to political, economic and social equality in American society.

We now know that this was a Utopian dream, but in 1865 it seemed altogether reasonable and likely. This was an hour of faith that sustained some of our brightest young minds in what was possibly this nation's most altruistic intellectual trek. Dr. DuBois has written that these teachers came south "not to keep the Negroes in their place, but to raise them out of the defilement of the places where slavery had wallowed them."

In these schools the children of the ex-slaves caught a different vision of America and of white people. They saw instructors of refinement and scholarship living and working together among their students in an atmosphere of brotherhood and devotion. If ever, this was a "band of angels."

The AMA founded the Lincoln School at Marion during the 1860's. Some of the local whites resented everything the school represented: Yankee equalitarianism, educated Negroes and the symbolism of the name of the Great Emancipator. Fred Brownlee in his book *New Day Ascending* tells of the early days at Marion and other places, when the teachers needed guns to protect themselves from violent attack. White teachers, who came from the North to work in AMA and other such schools, did not expect social intercourse with the white Southern townspeople. Despite all this, one white man of Marion, when he noticed that the Negroes themselves were raising funds for Lincoln, donated land to it.

The AMA also encouraged farm and home ownership. In this connection, Lincoln School officials bought an eighty-acre plot near the campus, subdivided it and resold the land to Negroes for building homes. These families still own this property today.

In a word, the Marion that Coretta was born into was predominantly the plantation South, but it was also a little of New England and a little more of "Negro independence."

Growing up in Perry County, Alabama, Coretta Scott saw much. She saw every type of white person from the "big house" aristocrat to the poor-white scrub farmer, to the friendly AMA scholars. She grew up knowing that all white people were not the same.

Likewise, she saw Negroes who had given up struggling against the system that made sharecroppers and day laborers of them; who bowed and bent before the white overlord; who took out their frustrations in fighting among themselves, drinking and carousing in the small-town dives. Other Negroes, she saw, struggled to make "something out of themselves." They resisted the corruption of spirit in all the ways that human beings resist. She, too, like Martin Luther King in Atlanta, could not but choose. She, too, had a family that helped her make a favorable choice.

Family

Coretta "takes after" both her father and mother. In physique she is a cross between them—brown skin, curly hair, thin lips, pug nose, square jaw, well-built shoulders, hips and legs. In temperament, she is a little of each also, but in this Coretta is mostly Coretta, rather special unto herself.

Her father, Obie, was christened Obadiah. His name, therefore, was Biblical rather than African in origin. He has a longish face, slightly slant eyes that look at you inquiringly, a strong, short, well-shaped nose, and thin lips that normally are pressed together determinedly but can break easily into a gentle smile. When he laughs, his eyes twinkle. He has a strong chin. He wears his cap at a sporting angle.

His mind works fast and everybody knows that the proprietor of Scott's store has a good head for figures. He himself will tell you that in his last year in school, in the seventh grade, he used to help the eighth-grade scholars with their arithmetic. Like Martin Luther King, he is a poor speller. He depends upon his wife for general reading and information, aside from business.

Mr. Scott has always been a hard-working man and today owns his general store, his home, three trucks for hauling wood, a chicken farm and considerable land. A generous-hearted man, he has "for-gotten about" accounts that have never been paid up by both his white and Negro customers.

Withal, he is resolute, not easily flustered. He appears to operate thoughtfully, with deliberate speed, so to speak. His quiet optimism that things will be all right in the end is apparently indestructible.

Somewhat in contrast, Coretta's mother, Bernice McMurry Scott, is tall and fair. Her hair is straight. There were both American Indian and Caucasian strains in her ancestry. She has a strong face and like Obie and Coretta has a well-shaped, somewhat short nose with an upward curve.

Though she has had little formal schooling, she likes to read Negro papers and magazines, and keeps up with radio and TV news. She does a share of her own housekeeping and runs the store while her husband is out trucking. She is strong and handy and can drive herself to town in the family car or in one of the trucks.

Tomboy

Like Martin, Coretta, was the second of the three children: her sister Edythe was two years older; her brother, Obie Leonard, three years younger.

As she grew, Coretta developed such great physical strength that her father used to brag about her as she lifted small bags of feed and boxes that Edythe could not budge. Now and then, when the children helped out in the garden and fields, Coretta always led or, at least, kept up with the leading harvester.

Coretta was one of those tomboys who outrace and outclimb any boy around. She was a fighter too—and one with a temper. Her constant companion and antagonist was her cousin, Willie McMurry, who despite a paralyzed right arm was full of mischief. He and Coretta would box, wrestle and fight. Then they would meet the Horton children at some predetermined spot and work off more energy by further scuffling.

Willie and Coretta would roam the woods, wading in their favorite creeks, imaginatively fishing with a worm on a pin, catching crawfish with their bare hands. Once they cooked a chicken all by themselves and at another time made a pie. Their most dangerous game was hitting wasps' nests, then running away.

Coretta could beat either Edythe or Obie Leonard. She was one of those battlers who believed in striking first. When she hit, it was not girl-like with the open hand; she balled up her fist and struck blows that could hurt. On more than one occasion she ran Obie Leonard down and knocked him flat. She would chase Edythe into the fields, dashing after her with a hoe or rake—anything at hand.

By the time she reached high school age, however, Coretta had tempered her belligerence. Willie was shocked the day she declined his invitation to box with him. Moreover, she was told that people would not like her if she continued to be bossy and "provoking." By this time she was beginning to pay some attention to what her schoolmates thought about her. She began wanting to be "a nice young lady." She was growing up. But this new behavior pattern did not change Coretta's basic personality. Today, she is still strong, unafraid and thoroughly capable of fighting back when necessary.

Books and Teachers

From an early age Coretta had been interested in getting an education. Perhaps she picked up the idea from her mother. Mrs. Scott wanted the children to have the schooling that she had missed. In her own day, the community itself had to provide whatever education there was, since the county was not doing so. Her school was appropriately named for its location, the crossroads where it stood. It was open for but three months of the year, and in some years was not open at all. Among other problems, it was difficult for the Negro country farmers to get—and keep—a teacher, for she was not paid in cash but in kind—mostly eggs, hams, chickens and syrup.

Coretta's first school was also the Crossroads School. It was no longer the same frame building that had served her parents, but it stood in the same place. Coretta went through the six grades as the brightest child in her class. She learned her three R's easily, sang songs and recited poems on the school programs. She was especially fond of "Paul Revere's Ride."

Coretta next attended the Lincoln High School in Marion. This was a turning point in her personal history. Not only did the institution open up a new world to her but Marion, a "big place" of some two thousand or more souls, also meant a larger and fuller life.

Coretta spent six years in the Lincoln School. For the first three years she lived in Marion, rooming with friends of the family with her sister Edythe, who was at the school the same time. The girls paid $2 a month for their room, for which they provided their own wood and coal.

At Lincoln Coretta had both white and Negro teachers, and thus not only learned to know white people as friends, but saw them mingling with Negroes as equals. This relationship was very different from the sharp race line of Marion and Perry County, where contacts between Negroes and whites were usually on the basis of master and servant, landlord and tenant, or poor white versus poor Negro.

But at Lincoln everybody was equal—at least, so it appeared to be.

Coretta got on well with all her teachers. Miss Olive J. Williams, who was colored and from Howard University, taught Coretta music, but it was Mrs. Frances Thomas, white, who after classes taught Coretta to play the trumpet. They used the same horn, after each other, wiping off the mouthpiece before passing it on. Mrs. Thomas, who was secretary to the principal and wife of the social studies–physical education teacher, liked both Edythe and Coretta—Edythe for her talent in writing and Coretta for music.

The Lincoln campus was well kept. The buildings were old fashioned and high ceilinged but comfortable and clean. The grass was neatly trimmed, the floors waxed. Here the well-trained and friendly teachers discharged their responsibilities punctually and with due regard for the other middle-class virtues.

Faculty members lived on the campus in the special dormitory for them. They ate in the common dining hall, sometimes together, sometimes with students. In such an atmosphere of free association, skin color tended to become much less important than individual personality.

Coretta did not spend all of her time on the Lincoln campus. Life in the city of Marion provided an exciting world for a rural girl: meeting friends at courthouse square, shopping at the five-and-ten-cent store, eating ice cream with boys at Childs'. Coretta herself never had a clash with white persons in town or in the country, but she remembers that white children sometimes marched along the sidewalk three and four abreast and would not yield when Negro children approached. Usually, the Negro children stepped aside into the street, but sometimes they marched on in stride, brushing up against the whites. Nothing much came of these brief encounters beyond the touching of shoulders or a push or two; never a real fist fight.

In Marion Coretta had but one job with a white employer. For about a week she helped a white public school teacher with housework. Coretta was not happy in this employment, for this teacher's attitude was far different from that of the Yankee school ma'ams of the campus. When Coretta was fired for letting the dinner burn, she felt relieved.

For her last two years at Lincoln, Coretta lived at home. The Perry County school board finally accepted its obligation to transport Negro graduates of the Crossroads School to the nearest high school, which meant Lincoln. Accordingly, the board rented one of Mr. Scott's trucks, which he converted into a home-made school bus. Mrs. Scott was given the job of bus driver.

Now back in the country, young Miss Scott was able to take charge of the choirs at her family's church—Mt. Tabo—that was just a block down the road from the Scott store and home. A church of African Methodist Episcopal Zion denomination, it had a membership of about 150. The Scott children had grown up in it. Coretta was christened there as an infant and baptized when she was twelve, just after having been "converted" by a visiting evangelist, the Rev. J. H. Cherry of Montgomery. Years afterward the Rev. Mr. Cherry was to direct the chief transfer station of the motor pool during the Montgomery bus boycott and to serve on the executive board of the Improvement Association with Martin Luther King.

Everyone seemed to be pleased with Coretta's choral directing. The Christmas and Easter musicals were well attended. Finally, when she had to leave, little gifts were showered upon her, including $8 in cash and a pair of bedroom slippers.

To keep three children in school was expensive for the Scotts. Although tuition at Lincoln was slight—only $9 per child annually— when the other expenses, including books and clothing were added, they came to an appreciable sum. Moreover, the tradition was strong in the rural areas that children should go to work early and help their parents support the household. Despite his generous nature, Mr. Scott did not see his way clear to financing a college education for his daughters and son. Mrs. Scott, on the other hand, was willing to make any sacrifice for their going on in school.

Coretta understood her father's attitude on the cost of higher education and did not hold this against him. She knew of his struggles. She was grateful to him for having done so much with so little.

Under the circumstances she could not expect the expense of a college education to fall on him. It was her own problem. She was hopeful and quietly confident that a path would open for her. This early in her life, Coretta had begun to believe in a kind of destiny: "What is for you, you will get, providing you strive for it as best you can. There is no need to fret, because if it's for you, it will come."

She had reason to be hopeful, for a few months before graduation, she received the happy news that she had been granted a scholarship to Antioch College. Now the future looked suddenly bright with promise: she was going to college, to the free North, to limitless possibilities.

Antioch
It was actually Edythe who had opened the way for Coretta at Antioch. Despite its reputation for liberalism, the college had not admitted Negro students to full matriculation until the 1940's. Antioch reached the decision to do so about the time that the Lincoln School

chorus, under the direction of Miss Williams, made its tour through the Midwest. One of the stops was at Antioch. Edythe was a member of the chorus.

The songsters made a good impression, both as singers and as people. Accordingly, Antioch's Race Relations Committee offered a scholarship to the valedictorian of the class of '43 at Lincoln. That meant Edythe, who thus became the first full-time Negro student at Antioch to live on the campus.

At first this was a great experience for Edythe. But after a while her role as a glasshouse specimen began to grow wearisome. She tired of the endless discussions of "the race problem," the "ohs!" and "ahs!" She was depressed by those who were not happy about having a Negro student on the campus. She began to yearn for anonymity, for people and places where she could simply be herself and relax. After three years she gave up and transferred to Ohio State University at Columbus, where Negro students had been attending for years and in considerable numbers.

But Edythe had stayed at Antioch long enough to clear the way for Coretta, who came there in the fall of 1945 on a similar race relations scholarship. By the time she entered there were other Negroes at Antioch, and the campus had gone through the first and perhaps necessarily painful phases of adjusting to students of color. Moreover, Coretta, less subjective and more self-sufficient, could adjust. She was psychologically well balanced, and like Martin Luther King had a natural tendency *not* to respond immediately and impulsively to stimuli. When in doubt, she usually acted or spoke after second thought.

Antioch, like Lincoln School, was a child of New England humanitarianism; and its first president, Horace Mann, was himself a part of the mid-century intellectual exodus that flowed west as well as south.

Dr. Mann died in 1859. Thereafter none of the succeeding administrators did very much about implementing the race relations principles of Antioch's first president.

The Antioch of Coretta's day was best known for its work-study program. Here was a college that geared its curriculum to provide (1) a liberal education, (2) actual work experiences for its students and (3) joint student-faculty responsibility for campus government. Half the year the student studied his books; the other half he worked at a job for regular pay—in Yellow Springs, Chicago, New York— anywhere, as long as the faculty approved. This plan enabled good students to earn their way through college, though this was but a by-product of the program. The main point was the real-life, on-the-job experience. Naturally, it would take longer to get a bachelor's degree at Antioch. It took Coretta six years, 1945-51.

The college gave Coretta a good general education: a broad grounding in the humanities and the social and natural sciences. Expecting to become a schoolteacher, she majored in elementary education, but took as much music as her requirements would allow.

As it happened, Antioch's one Negro member of the faculty, Professor Walter F. Anderson, was head of the music department.

Of the speakers who came to the campus one remembered Coretta from the time he spoke at the Lincoln School in Marion. This was Bayard Rustin, a young, articulate Negro idealist whose devotion to causes would take him as far as India—and afterward to Montgomery, Alabama.

Coretta found time somehow to take part in student extracurricular activities. She had a minor role in Gilbert and Sullivan's *Iolanthe* and sang with the college chorus. She also found time for social life. Coretta made friends easily. It was not a great leap from natural friendship with white teachers at the Lincoln School to similar associations with white teachers and students at Antioch. Among the students, she found friendships easier with girls than with boys. When Coretta first went to Antioch, eyebrows would be raised if a mixed couple went to a play or movie together. However, before she left, such pairs would pass almost unnoticed on the campus, although they were still considered odd in the town of Yellow Springs. Ohio was far more liberal than Alabama, but it was no Utopia. Despite the state's civil rights law, some restaurants would not serve Negroes, and most hotels—especially in southern Ohio—avoided housing Negro guests.

And yet friendships transcended race lines—especially among the white students at Antioch and Negro students from Central State College and Wilberforce University, both less than ten miles from Yellow Springs. Coretta also had friends in Cleveland, one of the most liberal cities in the country for race relations. One young man tried to persuade her to give up Antioch and transfer to Western Reserve University there.

Coretta thus got a broad view of the wide range of reactions from young white and Negro adults along the sometimes invisible color front. Moreover, she got glimpses of parents directly and indirectly influencing the social contacts and selections that her fellow students made. One case stuck in her memory.

A male classmate used to single out Coretta for walks and talks about life in general and music in particular. He was born in New York of a middle-class Jewish background but had grown up in Wheeling,

39805

West Virginia. His major interest was political science, but he had a talent for the piano and a feeling for nature. Coretta's early life and musical interests drew them together. When a folk festival was being presented at Wheeling, he invited a station-wagon load of his student friends to be his guests at his home. Accordingly, Coretta and four other students made the trip.

When the group got to the city limits, the young host, still full of enthusiasm, stopped the car and telephoned his parents. They would meet the group downtown, have dinner together, and make further plans. As he came back to the car, Coretta asked him if his parents realized she was a Negro girl. His face reddened. He had never thought of that. Later when the students and family met at the restaurant, the manager would serve the racially mixed group only in a private dining room. The group declined this offer.

The boy's parents, though troubled by their decision, were not quite prepared to have a Negro girl as a house guest. They solved the dilemma by putting up both Coretta and the other students in quarters provided for out-of-towners who came to Wheeling for the festival. Back at Antioch this once-promising friendship faded. It is often too much even for a young idealist to stand against home town and family.

During her second year at Antioch, the Negro magazine *Opportunity* asked Coretta to contribute an article to a special issue it was putting out on "Why go to college?" Among other things, Coretta wrote: "Antioch college is a good place. . . . I'm glad I came North to a mixed school. . . . A college education has offered me more than the chance to better my condition, to acquire prestige, to earn my living. It has opened a lot of doors in different directions."

Coretta's college generation were not the radical revolutionaries of the Depression decade. They suffered the conservative backwash of World War II. The cold war and Senator Joseph McCarthy would drive the eggheads to cover. About as far left as she got was the NAACP, the American Civil Liberties Union, and a fleeting glance toward Henry Wallace.

Back Home

Coretta made her musical debut on Tuesday night, November 9, 1948, at the Second Baptist Church in Springfield, Ohio, a few miles from the college. About a hundred persons attended—some from the college, others mostly from the Negro church congregation. Walter Rybeck, a white fellow student, accompanied Coretta. Modest as it was, it was nevertheless an exciting event as the beginning of her career.

Coretta sang regularly with the choir of the Second Baptist Church and had several other out-of-town recitals. One of these, in Harrisburg, Pennsylvania, was arranged by her former teacher, Miss Olive J. Williams.

In her *Opportunity* piece Coretta had also indicated the range of jobs she had held as part of the work phase of her education. She had served as a waitress in the college dining hall, as a counselor at Karamu Camp, a well-known interracial cultural center in Cleveland, as a teacher in the Yellow Springs nursery school and as an assistant in the Antioch music library.

Coretta's work assignments would finally take her as far away as New York City. These jobs were all helpful experiences and strengthened the independence and resourcefulness that she had manifested all along.

One summer Coretta was allowed to go back to Marion and work in her father's store as a school-approved work assignment. There she set up double-entry bookkeeping and a more systematic method of checking credit accounts. Father Scott beamed.

For Coretta it was the longest visit that she would have at home during her six years at Antioch. During her stay, Coretta and her old friend Willie, now a high school teacher, decided that it was time for Marion to have a first-class recital. The artist, of course, would be Coretta and the locale would be the Lincoln School. Even in one's home town a public program has its headaches and its surprises. The chief headache was that facilities for promoting such an event were meager. The surprise was the response of the white townspeople.

Willie, Obie Leonard and Coretta made all the arrangements. When a suitable accompanist could not be found among the colored people, a white music teacher, Mrs. T. A. Wood, agreed to serve. The Marion *Times Standard* announced the forthcoming concert on the bottom of its front page, July 27, 1950. The short notice stated that special seating arrangements had been made for white persons who would attend. Although they had not authorized this provision, the promoters let it stand. Admission was 35 cents for adults, 25 cents for children.

On the day of the concert a heavy downpour cut the size of the crowd. By custom the whites and Negroes sat on opposite sides of the middle aisle, except for Obie Leonard, who, after he drew the curtain, always sat with the whites. There was a printed program. Coretta was in excellent voice.

Afterward, both whites and Negroes crowded around her, offering congratulations. Everyone seemed to speak with pride and appreciation of the talented home-town girl. For the first time Coretta felt that the whole community accepted her as a full-fledged human being.

Despite several minor setbacks, Coretta's last year in college was a good one. Although a prejudiced supervisor kept her from doing her practice teaching in the Yellow Springs public schools as her classmates did, she moved about the campus with a sense of acceptance and security. She served successfully as dormitory counselor for a group of freshmen girls, most of whom were white. Edythe had finished her work at Ohio State but Obie Leonard had come up to Central State College, just a few miles away. Thus Coretta still had home folk near her, though she did not feel a great need for their support. On the contrary, she was a real "big sister" to her "little brother" (now taller than she) as he grappled with his personal and school problems.

In the interval her father had prospered. He helped both Edythe and Obie Leonard with most of their fees. But Coretta felt that she had committed herself to proceed on her own; she accepted only minimum help from home.

Future

Coretta was slow in deciding that she would go on to further study immediately after Antioch rather than stop, rest for a while, or take a teaching job for a year or two. Some of her classmates urged her to go on. So did Professor Anderson, Miss Oldt and Mrs. Treichler. But "Where to?" was the question. Since the Juilliard School of Music in New York City, the mecca of so many college music students, was out of the question because of the expense, the New England Conservatory of Music became the logical second choice. But it too was far from being an educational bargain.

Coretta would have to have scholarship aid if she was to sustain herself financially in any professional school. Though late in getting started, she and her faculty advisors began bombarding the philanthropic foundations with letters. Some of the appeals by Mrs. Treichler were so warmly written that Coretta still saves the carbon copies: "extraordinarily attractive," "poised," "friendly" and "one who could inspire young pupils to make up tunes and sing them" were some of the descriptions.

Coretta's last work assignment was at the Riverside Branch of the New York Public Library. She loved New York but was so busy that she did not get much chance to explore it, spending most of her free time in music lessons with Miss Ora Witte, who gave Coretta extra coaching free of charge. She, too, recommended the New England Conservatory of Music and told Coretta that if she got there to ask for Madame Marie Sundelius.

So on graduation day, Coretta faced an uncertain future. She remembers now that, as she said good-by to Antioch, she had a feeling of relief that a long journey had been completed. At the same time, she was most grateful for what Antioch had done for her. Although she had not received a scholarship grant, she was still hopeful. She went back to Alabama to visit her family for a few weeks before pushing on again. For she must go on. If music was her destiny, a way would open.

On her way from Marion to Boston, Coretta telephoned the Jessie Smith Noyes Fund, one of the foundations to which she had applied, and received the welcome news that a letter had been mailed granting her a $650 scholarship. Coretta came into Boston floating on a cloud of joy.

Cool Culture

The conservatism of Boston is legendary. Coretta found the city cool and remote rather than rebuffingly cold. The people at the conservatory were friendly enough but the atmosphere of a professional school was not that of Antioch. At the rather fashionable rooming house where Coretta lived and did household chores in exchange for her room rent, the other residents were white and not known to her. Although she had had ample experience in standing alone, those first days in Boston were lonely.

But work has a way of dispelling loneliness. Coretta was registered for the four-year course with major emphasis on voice. She passed her audition successfully. As she sang, she noticed that one of her auditors was more responsive than the others. Luckily this was Madame Sundelius, the very teacher Miss Witte of New York had recommended.

Soon Coretta was immersed in the conservatory routines. Between them and her household duties her days were full. Then, in February, 1952, she met the young man who was to change the course of her life.

Romance

When Martin King met Coretta Scott he was a confident young man. He had every reason to be; everything seemed to be in his favor. He had finished Crozer with distinction and had enjoyed a delightful summer running his father's church just about as he pleased. He had arrived in Boston with a fat scholarship, a Chevrolet and every prospect of success.

At twenty-two he no longer felt girl shy, but he was finding the Boston girls exceptionally withdrawn and reserved. When he complained about this to Mrs. Mary Powell, an old friend from Atlanta who was also studying in Boston, she offered to help. After a few days, she suggested two names. It so happened that Martin had already met one of the girls—a tall coloratura from Texas; but the description of the other girl fascinated him. He persuaded Mrs. Powell to get her telephone number and also to put in a word for him.

So on a Thursday evening in February, Martin King telephoned Coretta Scott. Brashly he asserted that he was "like Napoleon at Waterloo before your charms." When Coretta suggested that this was obviously absurd since they had never seen each other, he insisted that her reputation had preceded her. Ordinarily Coretta would have laughed and hung up but there was something appealing about the voice and personality that came over the phone. Then, too, so many intellectuals were bores; so many reverends, stuffed shirts. This one appeared to be pleasant and perhaps entertaining. She agreed to have lunch with him the next day.

Promptly at noon the next day the green Chevrolet drove up in front of the conservatory. She was waiting, protected from the inclement weather by her topcoat, scarf and umbrella. He appeared to be a little smaller, she thought, than she had expected him to be from the baritone voice.

When they got to the restaurant and she took off her rain garments, he got a better look at her. They both quietly surveyed each other from tip to toe. He took in her well-built figure but reserved his comments for her bangs and curly hair, that she was then wearing full length. He said, "You have some *great* hair," drawing out and playfully emphasizing the word *great*. She smiled. She, too, liked what she saw, including his gentlemanly manners.

At lunch the conversation sailed along smoothly enough. When Martin raised an intellectual question—something about the class relations of society—Coretta discussed it with him quite naturally. "You can talk about things other than music," he commented approvingly, "about ideas!" When he asked her for another date, she suggested that he might escort her to a party to which she had been invited the next night.

Before he left her at her stop, he had already made up his mind. "You have all of the qualities that I expect to find in the girl I'd like to have for a wife," he said suddenly. It left her almost speechless.

In the months that followed, they saw much of each other. For Coretta there were no longer any empty Sunday afternoons. For Martin the girls back home began to seem very far away indeed. Now and then, he would remind Coretta of the observation that he had made when they first met: "You have all of the qualities that I expect to find in the girl I'd like to have for a wife." Inevitably they began to talk of marriage. This was a hard question for her, not because she doubted her love for him but because there was also her career to think about. When she had thought of marriage at all, Coretta had hoped that the right man would come along about a year or so after she had completed her education and when maybe she had got started as an artist. From that point of view, Martin had appeared on the scene four or five years too soon. Moreover, she had never intended marrying a preacher. Despite Martin's modernity, would not the wife of a minister have to give up any thoughts she might have of a separate career for herself?

They talked about all this at length. Martin did not press her, but told her that he did not see why marriage and a career might not be combined: "Look at Adam Powell and Hazel Scott," he said. The Rev. Mr. Powell is the minister of one of the largest Negro Baptist Churches in the world and has represented Harlem in New York's City Council and in the United States Congress. His wife, professionally Miss Scott, has continued her public appearances as a pianist.

In the end, Coretta realized that she was so deeply in love that if need be she would give up her career. She knew that she would not be happy without him. And it might be possible to realize some, if not the whole, of her dream of being an artist.

On June 18, 1953, they were married. The wedding, which took place down in Perry County on the lawn at Coretta's home, was the biggest social event the colored people of Marion had seen in some time. The Rev. Martin Luther King, Sr., performed the ceremony. Brother A. D. was the best man. That Coretta should return home for her marriage and that it was open to everybody who could come touched the hearts of friends and neighbors. Education had not "ruined" her, they said; the young "Reverend," too, they thought was friendly and did not "put on airs."

Southward Bound

The romance and subsequent marriage did not interfere with the young couple's studies. They realized that their further education was the main business of their being in Boston and arranged their pleasures accordingly. In Boston they were lucky in getting a four-room apartment for $35 per month at 396 North Hampton Street, within a block of the conservatory. Here they remained until they left Boston for the South.

Coretta's economic problems had also eased by means of state aid from Alabama. Most Southern states were willing to help pay for the education of their Negro students, if they went out of the state for courses that were provided for white students at the state's all-white universities. Thus, Alabama would help finance a Harvard Ph.D. for a Negro whom it would not let study at the University of Alabama. This is partly the reason why many Negro scholars in the South have training superior to that of their white counterparts.

After marrying, Coretta decided that perhaps she should shift from the four-year course in voice to the three-year course in public school music. As a minister's wife, she would have a better chance for a part-time career as a music teacher than as a concert artist.

After graduating from the conservatory, Coretta spent the summer in Atlanta, at the home of her parents-in-law. Even then she knew that her next home would be 309 South Jackson Street, Montgomery, Alabama.

VIII - Decision at Montgomery

CORETTA was through at Boston, but Martin had to go back for three more months to complete his residence requirements.

He was making considerable progress on his dissertation. He had chosen as his topic of investigation the philosophies of Paul Tillich and Henry Nelson Wieman. This choice had grown out of a real-life situation. Back in 1935 a few religious leaders had come together at Fletcher's Farm, a quiet retreat at Proctorville, Vermont, for ten days of discussion. Instead of the quiet communion expected, the group became involved in a vigorous but highly intellectual debate between Tillich and Wieman.

Dr. Paul Tillich is a German-trained professor, a leader of the Christian socialists in Europe and an anti-Nazi exile who came to live in America and teach at Union Theological Seminary in New York. Dr. Henry Nelson Wieman, American-trained, was an equally prominent light of the Divinity School of the University of Chicago. Both men are recognized religious philosophers and have ardent followers. Their main difference at Fletcher's Farm was over the nature of God. This controversy continued through the years. Martin was set the task of identifying and resolving their differences, if possible. He was to do this by a full examination of their writings, subjecting them to systematic analysis and comparison. Professor DeWolf was Martin's chief advisor for this study.

By the end of the summer of 1954 Martin had completed his research. The main job remaining was to write up his findings. For this he did not need to stay in Boston; the dissertation could be submitted by mail. A faculty committee would read it critically and send it back for revision. After its acceptance the candidate would appear for an oral examination in defense of what he had written. If he passed this, he was a Doctor of Philosophy. The awarding of the degree at commencement would be a mere formality.

So in August of 1954 Martin was free to leave Boston. For several months previously he had grappled with the twin question of whether to take a position with a college or a church and whether to stay in the North or return to the South. After much meditation he made a choice that turned out to be fateful: he would go to Montgomery, Alabama, as pastor of the Dexter Avenue Baptist Church.

His father did not think well of this decision. He wanted to keep Junior near him to groom him as his successor—at least, for a while. Then, too, he had a bad impression of Montgomery as a place to live in. Back in the 1920's he and a few other Baptists had stopped in Montgomery between trains on the return trip from a church convention in Texas. They found it difficult to find a restaurant. Moreover, when they boarded a streetcar the conductor, after taking their fares at the front entrance, had told them that they would have to get off and get on again at the back door for Negro passengers. Incensed, King refused to go around to the back door and demanded his money back. The trolley operator rudely refused to return it. A clash almost ensued. Some of King's companions finally persuaded him to get off. They then walked to their destination.

Montgomery had thus left a bad taste in Martin Luther King, Sr.'s mouth. In later days when Negroes there told of their experiences on the buses he always knew very well what they meant.

As usual, Junior listened attentively to everything Daddy had to say—and then made up his own mind. He felt that he wanted to work for a while in the Deep South and that Dexter was just about the type of church that would give him a good start. So as early as May, 1954, the young clergyman was flying in once each month to preach, then flying back to his studies at Boston. But after that last summer, he and Coretta were both free to come to Montgomery to live.

The Martin Luther Kings, Jr., were able to move into the parsonage at 309 South Jackson Street a few weeks after their arrival in town early in September. They lived with Mrs. Sallie Madison at 1136 East Grove Street, while the parsonage was being repaired and painted for their occupancy.

The first year in Montgomery for the Kings was uneventful. For the young pastor, it was the usual process of getting to know his congregation, tightening up the church organization and establishing

himself in the community. In this he was successful. He preached well
and was friendly with everybody. About the only thing against him
was his youth. One elderly spinster, when she first saw him in the
pulpit, whispered to her seatmate, "I wonder if our little boy up
there doesn't miss his mother." But everyone soon realized that young
Dr. King was in full command of his church. Attendance and financial
support increased steadily. King did a good deal of parish visiting,
but found time, after hours, to work on his dissertation.

Coretta King was also very much interested in establishing herself.
Her biggest job was learning her role as the wife of the young minister.
The church members, as usual, made overtures of friendship and, at
the same time, examined her critically. They decided that she was
attractive and pleasant but slightly remote. She was careful to honor
the aged "brothers" and "sisters" who were the pillars of the church
and not to show partiality. (Southern Negroes often refer to fellow
church members as "brothers" and "sisters.") She declined to join
any Greek letter sorority but did associate herself with several of the
church clubs.

Mrs. King got on as well with the older folk as she did with the
young matrons and "socialites." She preferred to talk about books and
music and topics of the radio and TV newscasts rather than gossip.
She was still very close to Lincoln, Antioch and Boston. Montgomery
was in part a college town and the intellectuals that went to church at
all more often went to Dexter than elsewhere. Thus, she found a
congenial atmosphere.

The young minister's wife also liked staying at home, working
about the house. Her husband felt that she stayed in too much but
he realized that the home is a woman's domain.

The parsonage was a good, comfortable, rather old-fashioned
house. It was built the way most frame houses were built down South
during the twenties and thirties. It had the usual box shape that many
architects deplore, but what can one do on a narrow city lot? South
Jackson Street, where the house stood, was quite wide and afforded
space enough for a small lawn between the street and the sidewalk as
well as another green plot between the sidewalk and the front steps.
The driveway ran down the right side of the house, and there was a
large back yard. The house itself had a full front porch with the
familiar wooden columns.

Inside, it was obvious that the house had been arranged to fit the
needs of a pastor. To provide space for receptions, the inevitable
living room, which ran across the full width of the house, also flowed
into the dining room. This space could, however, be cut off into three
separate rooms by French or sliding doors. All in all, it was a good,

serviceable dwelling. The repairmen had done a good job of reconditioning not only the house but also the furnishings, which were rather plain pieces but not severe. The furniture was meant to be comfortable but not luxurious.

There was not much that Mrs. King could do to add her touch to the parsonage. But she did get in a baby grand piano, a television set, a couple of African "heads" for the walls, and several West Indian gourds and art pieces for the mantels that were above the closed-in fireplaces. The house was heated by individual gas jets. King himself added an air-conditioner to the den, which also cooled the family bedroom.

Soon, the couple became used to the parsonage and felt at home in it. Unless the weather was cold, the front door stayed open. Church members and other friends found it convenient to drop in from time to time.

Mrs. King had not given up her own career. As soon as she felt that church and home were secure, she began working in a few public appearances for herself. In November, 1954, less than three months after their arrival, she went down to Brunswick, Georgia, for a recital at the Shiloh Baptist Church. Her Montgomery debut came March 6, 1955, at the First Baptist Church. About a thousand persons were present. This was the church of the Rev. Ralph D. Abernathy, a new friend of King's. Soon afterward, she did about the same program in Camden, Alabama. But with the coming of her children, her career had, temporarily at least, to be laid aside. Her first child, Yolanda Denise King, was born on November 17, 1955.

Meanwhile the Rev. Mr. King worked hard on his dissertation. It ran to 343 pages. He made all the corrections demanded by the faculty and successfully passed the oral examination. The Ph.D. in systematic theology was awarded to him on June 5, 1955. The summary of his "contribution to knowledge" included these conclusions:

Tillich and Wieman have at the forefront of their thinking a deep theocentric concern. Both are convinced that God is the most significant Fact in the universe. This theocentric concern leads Tillich and Wieman to the further assertion that God is not man. They see a qualitative difference between God and man.

The most important words in Tillich's conception of God are "power" and "being." The most important words in Wieman's conception of God are "goodness" and "value."

Both Tillich and Wieman reject the traditional doctrine of creation. For neither of them is there a super-natural being before and above all beings as their creator.

Wieman holds to an ultimate pluralism, both quantitative and qualitative. Tillich, on the other hand, holds to an ultimate monism, both qualitative and quantitative. Both of these views have been found to be inadequate. Wieman's ultimate pluralism fails to satisfy the rational demand for unity. Tillich's ultimate monism swallows up finite individuality in the unity of being. A more adequate view is to hold a quantitative pluralism and a qualitative monism. In this way both oneness and manyness are preserved.

By late fall of 1955 it could be said that Martin Luther King, Jr., had both feet in Montgomery. He was successful and well liked; he had his Ph.D., a wife and a daughter. Atlanta, where his own family lived, was less than two hundred miles distant; and Marion, where his wife's family lived, but eighty-four miles away. Except for his unusual training, Martin, Coretta and Yoki presented a picture of a young American family that could be duplicated in almost every town in the land. They were reasonably secure and confident about the future. An active, happy and quietly successful life, apparently, lay before them.

Der Tag

Then came December 1, 1955. Mrs. Rosa Parks, a soft-spoken, attractive Negro woman, refused to "move back" on a crowded city bus so that a white passenger could have her seat. For that, the bus driver had her arrested. The reaction of the Negro community was massive.

The Montgomery bus boycott was like the bursting of a huge dam. Pent-up fears and resentments, latent hopes and aspirations came to the surface. The torrent exposed real race relations and revealed the true mood of Southern Negroes, usually hidden underneath a daily masquerade of self-effacing courtesy.

As a struggle against overwhelming odds, the boycott took on a timeless quality. The Little People, through their wit and faith, outsmarted the big, awkward and evil forces. Thus, the boycott was a triumph, perhaps the most sustained mass action of the American Negro in the twentieth century. It fascinated liberals and progressives and gave heart to submerged multitudes the world over.

The story of the boycott itself is not the subject matter of this book: that tale, with all of its curiosities and mythology, belongs to history and social analysis. It has been told in part and will be told in more copious detail elsewhere. But, it is legitimate to the province of biography to inquire into the true relations of Martin Luther King to the boycott—what did he really do?—and to note the influence of the boycott, in turn, upon him. This was his great moment in history.

How did he meet it? Did it change him? What did it do to his home
and family and his way of living?

About all this, the facts are more interesting than the fictions.

Martin Luther King did not precipitate the Montgomery bus strike;
that was done by Mrs. Rosa Parks. Neither did he think up the idea
of the boycott. Credit for that must go to an unidentified professional
man and a teacher. King did not create the Montgomery Improvement
Association but was himself chosen by the MIA. Nor did he impose
his will upon the organization; rather, most of its decisions were the
results of collective thinking.

Above all, the impulse and stamina of the boycott movement came
from the thousands of Montgomery Negroes—the cooks and maids,
the laborers, skilled and semiskilled workers, housewives and students—who were regular bus riders. They were the people who
picked up and swept along their leaders and bore them up whenever
the morale of the leadership sagged.

If there ever was an indigenous mass movement, this was it. The
notion that the big moguls of the NAACP, sitting in council at 20
West Fortieth Street, New York City, and looking over a giant map
of the South, put their finger on Montgomery and said, "There we
will put on a bus boycott," is absurd.

As a matter of record, for the first two months of the boycott, the
NAACP would not touch it because the goals of the boycotters did
not meet the minimum standards of the civil rights organization. Until
February 1, 1956, the MIA was seeking a "first come, first served"
arrangement on the buses, with Negroes seating themselves from rear
to front while white passengers, in reverse, would seat themselves
from front to rear. This plan would not have violated the Jim Crow
pattern at all and was already in practice in several Southern cities.
On the other hand, the objective of the NAACP was—and is—to
destroy segregation itself. The MIA moved up to the NAACP position
only after negotiations for "first come, first served" had failed.

The next question follows naturally: why then did the boycott occur
when it did and in Montgomery?

There may be no conclusive answer to this question. Human events
often display a capriciousness that defies man's ability to explain, let
alone predict, their course. Yet with benefit of hindsight and careful
study, it is possible to see that the Montgomery buses presented the
logical target in a general situation that was crying for corrective
action.

In the first place, the race relations pattern of the bus service was
so old fashioned that it just could not have persisted much longer
under any circumstance. It was crude and inefficient, violating the

cardinal maxim of good business that "the customer is always right." There were few places in the world of twentieth-century business where the principal customers were so rudely mistreated as were the Negro bus riders of Montgomery. They made up 70 per cent of the trade.

Moreover, no modern rapid-transit system could afford the delay of having passengers get on the front of the bus, pay their fares there, then get off to reboard the bus at a back or side door. During the most crowded rush hours this is what the bus drivers of Montgomery required of Negro passengers, in order that they would not press close to white passengers, who might be standing in the front aisle. Bus drivers have been known to leave the controls of their vehicles and take recalcitrant Negro bus riders by the arm, pulling and forcing them to the rear door of the bus. Imagine such a thing in New York! The traffic requirements of a modern urban community would make such "country" behavior ridiculous.

But in Montgomery—and in other places in the South—the whims of Jim Crow blinded the bus company and its employees, perhaps unwittingly, to the practices of efficiency and ordinary good business manners.

These same obsolete attitudes, apparently, blinded the city fathers. Had the Montgomery City Commission looked at the complaints of Negro bus riders from the cold economic point of view or had they realized that race relations on the buses did not fit the city's progress that they were so eager to promote, they would at least have taken a moderate or reasonable approach to the difficulties.

Instead, the Jim Crow bogeyman was, obviously, all that the commissioners could see. They viewed the boycott as a challenge of the whites by the blacks, in which to yield an inch would mean yielding all. And so the Negroes, who tried for two months to negotiate and compromise, were forced to raise their sights: to launch a full-scale attack upon bus segregation itself.

That the bus boycott came to Montgomery was also an indication of the weak and self-contradictory economic and social structure of the city itself. Montgomery is part agricultural, part commercial, part government-business and only slightly industrial. It is the capital city of a cotton empire that is fading away; whose acreage since 1930 has fallen 60 per cent. Its big houses and plantation sharecroppers hark back to the good, old, mythical days of the antebellum South. All of this is symbolized in the statue of Jefferson Davis that stands imposingly before the capitol and the oft-repeated catch phrase that Montgomery is "The Cradle of the Confederacy."

In those good old days (that probably never existed for more than a few Southerners), the Negroes were, according to the romantic tradition, sleek and fat, polite and submissive, given to singing and dancing generally but becoming sad and mournful when "massa" was lowered into the cold, cold ground.

But that was *then*. Today, even in agriculture, cattle have pushed cotton into the background and commerce and government business are much more important to the economic life of Montgomery than Dixie's traditional crop.

Perhaps this change is best symbolized by the "cow palace" known as the Coliseum that was built to accommodate livestock fairs and business and civic conventions. It is the most striking example of modern architecture in or near the city. It has been described as a fat turtle lying on a flat plain, just outside the city and looks for all the world like a Frank Lloyd Wright creation. Architects from everywhere acclaim it. It is functionally and structurally efficient and has no built-in provisions for Jim Crow seating, entrances, exits or rest rooms as do most of the public buildings of the South. Some of these old constructions have the words "White" and "Negro" chiseled into their brick and marble. Jim Crow is thus "permanently" embedded in the material culture. But not in the Coliseum.

This does not mean that those who designed it were racial integrationists or that the state administration that ordered and accepted the blueprint for it was interested in race mixing. Rather, it means that those responsible for the building were not so preoccupied with the race question at the time that they would ruin the functional efficiency of the conception by imposing false principles upon it. Chances are they forgot about Jim Crow while concentrating on utility and beauty.

In this sense, the Coliseum represents modern, progressive Montgomery—and the South—with its face toward the future. In the opposite way, the statue of Jefferson Davis symbolizes the past. The people in their attitudes show the same Janus-faced dichotomy: some are turned forward, others backward; some attempt to look both ways at once; still others cannot make up their minds; many are divided within themselves. It is a great and widespread frustration.

Thus, under the pressures of conflicting progressive and reactionary forces, the socio-economic structure of the city was exposed in all of its weakness, its lack of integrity and inner harmony. It was a sort of unbalance and stress that affected most businesses and public as well as private behavior.

Like the bus company, some of the local commercial houses did not know a customer when they saw one, if his skin happened to be black. They were not sure about saying to Negroes, "Thank you, *sir*," or "As you say, *Mrs.* Jones." It was difficult for a white woman clerk in a downtown store, who called her own maid at home by her first name, to know that when a Negro woman came up to her counter to make a purchase in the store she was to be addressed as "Mrs." even though, in fact, this customer might work somewhere as a maid. More than that, some of the white clerks could not or would not say "Mrs." when they knew that the Negro customer was a schoolteacher. These confused or adamant salesgirls got little help from the store management, which at times would—unbusinesslike—rather lose a dollar than yield to courtesy.

The newspapers did not help much either, for their traditional policy of never printing "Mrs.," "Miss" or "Mr." before the name of a Negro had been only recently modified to the rule of printing such a title if it appeared in an article that came in through an outside news agency such as Associated Press, United Press or International News Service but not printing titles for Negroes in stories of local origin. Thus Mrs. Rosa Parks was often referred to in the daily press as "the Parks woman."

And so, as the old cotton culture was pushed aside by the new economic order, the old paternalism had to give way before a more impersonal equalitarianism. At best it was painful. The politicians made it worse. They told the white people that it was not necessary to change the old way of life, if they would but stand firm.

The Negroes knew better. Brotherhood and democracy aside, they knew that they were customers and they knew how customers were to be treated. They would stop trading here and there after experiencing a discourtesy and would pass the word around as to which stores were most businesslike in their dealings.

But for the masses of Negroes, daily bus service was a necessity. There was no alternative to it. Some fifteen thousand of Montgomery's fifty thousand Negroes, schoolchildren, workers, shoppers, rode the buses every day and the rude treatment of them by some of the bus operators was intolerable. Such treatment was constant and the grievances accumulated. When petition after petition for relief to the bus company and the city fathers ended in the wastebasket, there was nothing else to do but stop purchasing a service that was no longer acceptable. The leadership guided this mass resentment into appropriate and peaceful channels.

Many Hands

In the great task of channeling the popular upsurge, Martin Luther King had much help. The main organizational form of this assistance was the executive board of the Montgomery Improvement Association. It was unwieldy, with some thirty-odd members and extremely loquacious, being heavily weighted with clergymen. The board wasted much time and often moved toward its goals by indirection. Of it could be said what John Adams once said of our national legislature: "The business of Congress is tedious beyond expression . . . every man in it is a great man, an orator, a critic, a statesman; and therefore, every man, upon every question, must show his oratory, his criticism, and his political abilities."

Nevertheless, the MIA board, like Congress, accomplished much good. The whole body or one of its numerous subcommittees was always in session during the boycott year (1956) and most of the board members devoted themselves to the common cause more than they did to their churches, businesses or even homes. For better or worse, the MIA board was the brains of the boycott.

There were many striking personalities on the MIA board and a review of their relations to King and the boycott is revealing.

Abernathy

Foremost was the Rev. Ralph D. Abernathy, who gave the MIA its name at the organizational meeting December 5, 1955, and throughout the boycott year was second in command. He and King were very different personalities and as a leadership team complemented each other splendidly. Abernathy was sometimes jestingly referred to as "the barefoot boy from Marengo County." This was where he was born and grew up, in the heart of Alabama's rigidly segregated Black Belt. Perhaps his reactions to this way of life made him tough.

Physically, Abernathy was short and stout, brown skinned, with blunt but well-formed features. He loved to eat and sleep. He looked like an ex-athlete who had lately neglected his exercise. He was a sergeant in World War II, when he made good use of the resonant baritone voice that he relied upon in civilian life for leading songs as well as for preaching and speaking. Abernathy had been educated at Alabama State College and Atlanta University.

As an operator, Abernathy had a boldness that King lacked. At times he would push when King would hesitate. Sometimes at committee meetings, he appeared to sleep, but whenever the talking was over and the time for deciding came, he would come to life and often take over, putting the motions and beating down the minor objections. Abernathy would clown if he thought that that would help drive home his point. But, underneath this ribald humor was a resolute will, thoroughly alive to what was happening. Abernathy adopted whatever measures he felt that practical necessity demanded. Driving toward the same ends, King would strike a deft, graceful jab, while Abernathy slugged and walloped.

Whenever somebody said that as a leader Abernathy was superior to King, they would both laugh at this—or at any other effort to pit them against each other. King has said that Abernathy was his alterego; Abernathy has returned the compliment. In discussing the new mood of the Southern Negro, King stated that "the new Negro has replaced self-pity with self-respect; self-depreciation with dignity." Abnernathy put the same thought in his colorful, homey directness: "The Negro no longer grins when he isn't tickled nor scratches where he isn't itching."

Jo Ann

Mrs. Jo Ann Robinson is correctly named. Earlier photographs show a slim, light-skinned, long-haired maiden of striking good looks and eyes that shine with a faraway glow. Time has matured some of these features (she was 39 when the boycott started) but it has not dimmed her devotion to social justice. Jo Ann, as everyone calls her, is a dedicated person. She can sew, cook and keep house but all of these feminine arts are forgotten when some child—especially a Negro child—is abused. She tried married life for a short while but soon decided to go it alone. She likes people, is an excellent teacher, and appears to be a modern woman, but cannot conceal her belief that mystical forces intervene in human affairs. Like Joan of Arc, she feels that the spirits commune with her at times and that thought waves result in mental telepathy. And yet she is a member of Dexter Avenue Baptist Church. She is from Macon, Georgia, but just as well could have come from Salt Lake City or India. She was educated at Fort Valley State College in Georgia, Atlanta University and Columbia University, New York.

Jo Ann blends her metaphysical view of life with direct social action. She is a quick thinker and extremely creative in formulating ways of getting things done. At many a conference, when the "enemy" made a calculated maneuver, it was Jo Ann who first spotted the move and countered it. Once the Mayor of Montgomery was appointing eight white persons and three Negroes to a committee on the basis of the number of organizations represented in the meeting. Jo Ann immediately saw what this meant and politely interrupted the Mayor to point out that actually there were as many Negro organizaions as white organizations represented in the meeting. The committee became eight to eight.

Pierce

Jim Pierce is so tall that when he is up on a speaker's platform he appears to be moving about on stilts. Standing beside King, Pierce looks like the old comic strip hero Mutt next to his sidekick, Jeff. And when Pierce wants to whisper, he has to bend down and over in order to reach King's ear.

Professor James E. Pierce, who is dark, bespectacled and long-winded, knows more about the history of race relations in Alabama than King and Abernathy combined. He, too, is from a Black Belt county—Lowndes—and yet has developed a twentieth-century view of the world. He attended the University of Toledo (A.B.) and Ohio State University (M.A.).

Pierce taught economics and political science. He was a folksy sort of professor, knowing anecdotes about every politician in the state. His studies of Negro registration and voting in Alabama were widely used. On the way to many a conference, Pierce and Jo Ann briefed King—relatively a newcomer—on the background of the Montgomery or Alabama situation. Pierce was conservative in his liberalism and indirect in his tactics, in marked contrast to the audacity of Abernathy and the immediacy of Jo Ann.

Gray

Everyone agreed that the bus boycott could not have been successful without its legal wing. There were some who felt that the boycott success was altogether a court victory. This, of course, was a narrow view and overlooked the essential nature of a mass movement. At any rate, the legal boobytraps that Southern law-making and law-enforcing agencies have strewn about the no-man's land of the battle for equality and integration are so great that, without excellent legal guidance, social action groups are bound to set off explosions.

And excellent legal guidance is precisely what the Montgomery boycotters were fortunate to get from Attorney Fred D. Gray. When the boycott first broke, he was but a year out of law school. He was another local boy who made good. Born in Montgomery and first educated in local elementary schools, Gray attended the Nashville (Tennessee) Christian Institute. Being something of a "boy preacher," he was ordained after graduating from this denominational training school. He returned to his native state to receive his B.S. degree from Alabama State College, then decided to take an LL.B. at Western Reserve University in Cleveland.

Like many another young barrister getting started, Gray had hardly enough money to outfit his office. Yet from within his modest quarters

of bare walls and naked floors, Gray launched a legal offensive that
threw the large and well-equipped legal staffs of the city, county and
state attorneys into confusion. Gray seemed to amaze the opposition
with the legal holes he found in Alabama and Montgomery bus segregation laws.

In court, thin and as plain in appearance as his office, he displayed
a mental acuity as apparent as his youthful idealism. While pleading
a case, his tenor voice would sometimes sing out with a note of
earnest sincerity. Meanwhile most of the opposing lawyers seemed to
bark, growl or just drawl.

Gray met with the MIA board so often that he was considered a
board member. When the Mayor and other city commissioners re-
sorted to a "get tough" policy of harassing the bus boycotters, it was
Gray who filed a suit in federal court which asked not only that all
bus segregation laws be declared unconstitutional but that an injunction be issued against the city fathers, restraining them from interfering with the civil rights of Negro motorists and pedestrians.

The rage against the Negro community was centered upon the
MIA leaders and Attorney Fred Gray. The local press broke a story
that Gray, aged twenty-five, had a draft deferment from military service. The White Citizens Council wrote to the draft board protesting
this deferment. Actually, Gray had been classified as 4D since 1948
on the grounds that he was a part-time, assistant minister at the Holt
Street Church of Christ. Immediately after the WCC protest, Gray
was reclassified as 1A.

In the meantime, another effort was made to spike the MIA's
legal guns. One of the Negro women complainants in the suit withdrew from it. Her economic position was weak—she was a housemaid
and had an invalid dependent relative. She received a telephone
threat and "advice" from one of her employers. Soon afterward, she
appeared at the Mayor's office and announced to him and the newspapermen who were conveniently present that she had not of her
own free will consented to have Gray represent her. Accordingly,
Gray was arrested and charged with barratry, or, in the grand jury's
phrase, "unlawfully appearing as an attorney for a person without
being employed by that person."

The press played this up. Through it all, Gray, quiet and pensive
looking, never betrayed fear or nervousness. After a while and on
second thought, the opposition attorneys discovered that they had
slipped up on their law. Since the case had been filed in federal
court, on federal property (the U.S. post office building), the city,
county or even state courts had no jurisdiction. They dropped the
charge against Gray. Although Negroes kept a straight face when

they were downtown, there was many a chuckle back in the Negro community.

In the white community the rage against Gray mounted. Despite it all, he did not curb his legal activities in the least. He was the chief counsel for the MIA, defending its leaders when they were charged with conspiracy and its automobile drivers when they were arrested for real or trumped-up traffic violations or when their voluntary motor pool itself was assailed in the courts.

An involuntary compliment was paid to Gray's legal argument that state bus segregation laws, because of a technicality in coding, did not apply to the buses in Montgomery. This very argument was borrowed by the state attorney's office when it attempted to extricate the Alabama Public Service Commission as a party from the suit that Negroes had filed in federal court.

Another left-handed compliment was the campaign waged to get Gray off the scene and into the armed forces. The White Citizens Council redoubled its efforts. The local draft board put Gray on schedule for his preinduction physical examination.

Gray fought back quietly. He appealed his reclassification. The main pastor of the Holt Street Church of Christ took a leave of absence; accordingly, Gray became the full-time pastor. Moreover, Gray's wife was pregnant. Many people thought that a full-time minister, who was also a husband and a prospective father, would not be rushed into the peace-time armed forces.

But the appeals board sustained the local board, and Gray was given his preinduction test. The newspaper camera men were on hand to photograph him half naked. He was ordered to report for induction on August 16, 1956. Gray appeared to be resigned to his going. The MIA sponsored a Fred Gray Night in tribute to him and collected several thousand dollars from public subscription for a farewell purse.

But there were a few of Gray's comrades who felt that at least one more try should be made. As a last resort, General Lewis B. Hershey, head of the National Selective Service, was asked to intervene. General Hershey did, and asked the local draft board to review the case. Negro newspapers (and a few others) were openly charging that Gray was being "railroaded" because of his activity in the bus boycott and for the NAACP. The local white press, denying this charge, urged that "Negro Attorney Fred Gray, like other young men, should go."

So, when August 16 came, everybody was waiting and watching.

Gray did not go. He was not inducted. Neither did his local board review his case; rather, three of the five board members resigned.

The white press in news stories, editorials and letters to the editor shrieked and fumed. The White Citizens Councils organized a committee to urge mass resignation of draft board members throughout the state. A dozen-odd members of local boards responded. Some boards refused to call up any draftees at all. With a rare show of wit, one of these boards added a new classification, 4D-G, to its series (meaning 4D-Gray) and announced that all of its eligibles were being placed in this fictitious category until Fred D. Gray was drafted.

As the excitement increased, Alabama Congressmen and Senators got into the act, questioning and attacking General Hershey or, at least, appearing to do so. The Southern rights champion Senator Richard Russell of Georgia, chairman of the powerful Senate Armed Forces Committee, was quoted as saying that he would probe the matter.

The adverse publicity and pressure upon the narrow shoulders of Fred Gray were so great that some of his friends felt that perhaps, after all, he should go on into service. On the other hand, the Negro press—notably the *Afro-American* and the Birmingham *World*—stood by Gray, and Hershey, all the way.

Hershey, quite wisely, had taken a sound position administratively. He had not overruled the local board; all he had done was to ask the board to reconsider Gray's case in the light of his changed status. A less anxious board could have gone through the formality of a review and still found the registrant eligible—and shipped him off.

While the revolt of the draft boards seemed to be petering out, despite the best efforts of the newspaper and the WCC, the anonymous letter writers and telephone callers stepped up their pace. Moreover, the police began to harass Gray by following him about, stopping his car for examination and checking his driver's license. When Gray made this known to the public, the embarrassed Commissioner of Public Safety said that the police had been following Gray about only to protect him. Why Gray was never let in on this secret was not made clear. But this kind of protection was discontinued.

It was obvious to both sides that Gray—and Hershey—meant to ride out the storm. Time was on Gray's side. On December 14, 1956, he would be twenty-six years old and thus beyond the draft age limit. When that day came, Gray was paid another unintended compliment: his birthday was front-page news in the Montgomery papers.

He had won. It was a crushing public defeat for the opposition. Gray never mentioned that. Neither did the Negro community openly

cheer. But the victory gave heart to many. At one of the mass meetings, an elderly "sister" said: "We see, God is still God; right still
wins." Gray had given everyone a demonstration of quiet courage
and self-possession.

Graetz

It is an easy joke that Bob Graetz single-handedly made the MIA
an interracial body. He was its lone white member. On public occasions he was displayed as a token of the integration ideal of the organization. There were, of course, other conscientious whites in
town and a few, like the Rev. Thomas R. Thrasher, who stood
up boldly for liberalism in race relations. But the Rev. Robert
S. Graetz was the only one who identified himself with the Negro
struggle openly and participated regularly in the deliberations of its
action groups.

Personally, Graetz was eager to do this; fortunately it also coin-
cided with his economic and professional interests. Graetz was minister of Montgomery's Negro Lutheran congregation. He was located
at the junction of a white and Negro neighborhood. With his plump,
attractive wife and ever-bounding children, he lived in the parsonage,
next door to the church. He and his family were friendly to all who
would stop to chat or visit.

Bob Graetz was German on his father's side and English on his
mother's but oddly Irish in appearance—sandy-haired, slim, vigorous,
boyish and full of fun. Like King, Abernathy and Gray, he was of
less than average height, and like them he was under thirty.

Born in Charleston, West Virginia, Graetz graduated from the
seminary of Capital University (Lutheran) at Columbus, Ohio. While
there he manifested a moderate interest in Negroes and Indians. He
served his internship at a predominantly Negro church in Los
Angeles. Like Martin Luther King, he was a newcomer to Montgomery,
having arrived in June, 1955.

Graetz heard about Mrs. Rosa Parks' incident soon after it occurred and pushed his way into the very first mass meeting that
the MIA put on. This was the great overflow meeting at the Holt
Street Baptist Church on December 5, 1955.

The Rev. Mr. Graetz was useful to the MIA beyond his services as a public symbol. He was a member of the local white ministerial organization and worked hard at the task of interpreting the
true views of the Negro community to the white community, and vice
versa. He wrote round-robin letters to white ministers and helped
arrange a few secret, interracial meetings. But his appeals were not

very successful, for the white ministers were generally immobilized by
personal misgivings and threats of reprisals from hostile boards of
directors or congregations.

Violent elements of the white community sought to punish Graetz
for his disloyalty to the tribal call of color. They labeled him a
"nigger lover." They threatened to silence him and, if he did not heed
the warnings, even to kill him. The newspapers highlighted his
activity and anonymous telephone callers and letter writers went to
work on him. He was arrested by the sheriff for helping out in the
voluntary motor pool. One night his automobile tires were slashed,
and sugar was poured into his gasoline tank.

But Graetz—and his family—persisted, still smiling, unembittered,
but inwardly saddened by the realization of the hold that primitive
hate still has on man. During the trials of the MIA leaders, Graetz
suggested the symbol that MIA members for a while wore on the
lapels of their coats or blouse fronts. Underneath a little paper cross
were the words: "Father Forgive Them."

In the summer of 1958 when Graetz left Montgomery for a new
charge, an interracial church in Columbus, Ohio, he was given a
special send-off with gifts, including several hundred dollars in cash.

Nixon

There is much about E. D. Nixon that fits the romantic image
of a heroic labor leader. For one thing, he looks the part; for another,
his struggles for personal achievement and social responsibility remind us of the American dream of log cabin to President. Nixon is
a Pullman porter and owes a great deal of his inspiration for civic
action to A. Philip Randolph, the grand old man who built the Brother-·
hood of Sleeping Car Porters.

Nixon is a big man with big shoulders, big hands and feet, and an
open, plain, dark, clean-shaven face. He is a man of force and when
the newly formed MIA was fumbling over the question of whether
it should come out publicly with its speeches and programs, it was
Nixon's voice that rasped out, "If we're gonna be mens, now's the
time to be mens." This stiffened the backs of some of the preachers,
who at this early date were apprehensive.

Nixon is another local boy who has made good—the hard way.
He had all the difficulties of poverty, a large family that required his
labor as a child, and very little opportunity for education. Despite
his vigor and self-confidence, he is sensitive to his own short-comings.

Nixon was quite proud of his son, a talented folksinger who was
known professionally as "Nick LaTour," and of his own material
success. Besides his home and his automobile he owned several parcels

of property and had money in the bank. He would hint broadly that this was better than some of the M.A.'s, D.D.'s and Ph.D.'s had done. Moreover, Nixon had been fighting for civil rights for years and when Montgomery Negroes appeared to be largely indifferent to such a struggle. For a long while he was head of the state NAACP, with Mrs. Rosa Parks as his secretary. He admired her gentleness and quiet efficiency; she, his raw courage and aggressiveness.

Nixon could have been president of the MIA. He himself withdrew his name from consideration because as a Pullman porter he would be out of town a great deal and because he felt that someone better educated should speak for the organization. Nixon, however, agreed to be treasurer. In that position he worked hard and rallied labor and other support for the organization.

As the mass movement became world famous, Nixon could not put away the vision of what might have been if on that fateful afternoon of December 5, when the MIA was being organized, he had agreed to have his name placed in nomination for the presidency. Accordingly, on occasion he so strongly projected his part in the creation and development of the MIA that many a passing reporter came away with the impression that Nixon really was *the* man. For example, Bob Hamilton in *Peace News* for April 20, 1956, wrote a feature article under the caption "The Man Behind the Man." In the course of this interpretive essay Hamilton said: "Listening to him (King) speak confirmed in my mind the belief that oft-times the sole determinant as to whether or not a man will be great is the amount of formal education he has. This by no means discredits Rev. M. L. King, but I say that if Nixon had had King's education, Montgomery would have stirred much earlier than December 1955."

In the *Militant,* William Bundy did a special article entitled "E. D. Nixon—Trade Unionist, Negro Leader." Among other words of praise, Bundy wrote that he was told by a white man in Birmingham, Alabama, that "an old time Negro trade unionist in Montgomery . . . was, as much as any other single person, 'at the bottom of the whole movement there.' " Bundy also quoted the French author, Daniel Guérin, who spent some time in the South during his tour of the United States in 1948. Guérin met Nixon and described him as "a vigorous colored union militant who was the leading spirit in his city." (This was doubtless true at that time, 1948.) Guérin went on to say that "Nixon has both feet on the ground. He is linked to the masses. He speaks their language. He has organized the work of race defense with the precision and method of a trade unionist. Men like E. D. Nixon (to name only him) incarnate the alliance which has at last been consummated between the race and labor."

In a full-page article in the Chicago *Defender* for May 26, 1956, on "The South at the Crossroads" one of the sub-captions announced that "Boycott Was Idea of Pullman Porter."

And as late as September, 1957, after honors had been passed out to many, Nixon's fraternal lodge brothers gave a testimonial to him. The resultant news article that was inspired by this occasion in the Atlanta *Daily World,* contained the following:

The Montgomery Improvement Association, The Rev. Martin Luther King, Jr., President, is a culmination of the dream of E. D. Nixon, civic-minded leader and militant citizen of this city. . . . This dream became a reality on December 5, 1955, when MIA was organized and he was offered the position as president. Casting aside this possible bid for fame, Nixon told the Association's members: "Dr. Martin Luther King is your man. He is better prepared and the people will follow him." With this terse reply Nixon gave a leader, not only to Montgomery, but to the world.

In *Liberation* for December, 1956, Nixon himself took pen in hand. He began his article, "How It All Started," with this paragraph:

On the night of December 1st, 1955, I sat for a long while on the edge of my bed. After a time I turned to my wife and said, "You know, I think every Negro in town should stay off the buses for one day in protest for Mrs. Parks' arrest." My wife looked at me as if I was crazy. Then I asked her, "What do you think?" "I think you ought to stop day dreaming, turn out that light and get some sleep."

Seven paragraphs later, Nixon added:

Then all of a sudden, as I sat there on the edge of my bed, some ideas came to me: why not ask the Negroes in Montgomery to stand up and be counted? Why not start a protest for Mrs. Parks? Why not stay out of the buses? Why not start a Montgomery Improvement Association? I decided that it was time for mass action. Despite my wife's reaction, I felt that the Negroes in Montgomery were at last anxious to move, prepared to sacrifice and ready to endure whatever came.

Many of Nixon's colleagues, who knew better, smiled at these wistful, wishful versions of what actually happened. Charitably they would say that the newspapermen may have misunderstood or misquoted Nixon. One man, less charitable, with a copy of *Liberation* in his hand, said, "Yes, everybody misquotes Nixon—even Nixon himself."

Others

There were, of course, many other striking personalities on the MIA Board. Mrs. Rosa Parks was the calm and beautiful symbol of the patient bus rider, who, though slow to anger, once aroused became implacable. Mrs. Euretta Adair, wife of a wealthy physician, was a perfectionist, seeking always to shape the MIA into the intellectual ideal of the books she had read. The Rev. B. J. Simms ran the voluntary motor pool more efficiently than the city buses were run. Rufus Lewis patiently devoted himself for a while to the boycotters' transportation problems, then went back to his first love, registration and voting. The Rev. J. H. Cherry, who years ago had "converted" Coretta to Christianity on one of his visits to Marion as an evangelist, directed the transfer center of the voluntary motor pool. The Rev. B. D. Lambert was an orator whose hypnotic effect was as great upon himself as upon his audiences.

The Rev. H. H. Hubbard, big, stout, light-skinned, was like a fatherly patriarch while little, dark, Rev. G. Franklin Lewis was like a remote intellectual who shrank from any clash of personalities. Together with Nixon, Miss Ida Caldwell, a shirt factory worker, represented organized labor. Mrs. Irene West, erect, gray-haired, bespectacled, despite her sixty-two years, drove every day in the voluntary motor pool. Like Mrs. Parks, she was an adornment of the movement.

In the closing months of the boycott, the Rev. S. S. Seay, whose sharp accent made him sound like a British West Indian, moved closer to the MIA summit, standing next to Abernathy in power and influence. From the beginning the Rev. A. W. Wilson bravely offered his church, the Holt Street Baptist Church, for the big mass rallies. He ran his church like an efficient business. But the most beautiful church that Montgomery Negroes owned, "Old Ship," was seldom used for mass meetings since, as its pastor, the Rev. W. J. Powell, explained, the church was located in what in recent years had become a poor white neighborhood. The Rev. H. H. Johnson openly challenged all who covertly threatened him.

P. M. Blair, a businessman, was best known as "the bronze mayor of Montgomery." Another businessman, C. W. Lee, made good use of his technical skill in accounting. Dr. Moses Jones, an independent thinker, represented the medical profession. There was also the Rev. U. J. Fields, a shining comet that later somehow fell out of its orbit.

This was the galaxy in which King moved. There were many stars. Together and separately, they helped him lighten up the Montgomery heavens and remove the darkness from the path of the walking feet.

Secretaries Help, Too

King was also greatly helped by his office staff. All during the boycott but especially at the beginning, there were numerous volunteer workers in and out of the office, at times too few, at other times

so many that they got into each other's way. Most of these youthful
volunteers were high school and college girls. But some volunteers
came in to do office chores after a full day on a job. One or two, like
Mrs. Annie Bell Smith, even had children at home; a few were out-
of-town visitors, who, like Delores Williams, had come to town to
see relatives and friends but ended up working for the MIA.

These were all Negro youth. Where was the idealism of white
youth—the young intellectuals, the members of the Sunday schools,
the pro-labor liberals? Was the tribal call so fiercely inhibiting?

During the whole boycott year, only one white youth—a girl—
offered to work for the MIA cause. She was from the North, had a
daytime job, and was willing to help in the office at night. But her
presence would have been too risky. The night problems included
the ever-watchful police.

The regular office staff, employed part time or full time, included
the Rev. R. J. Glasco, King's administrative assistant, who handled
the ordinary daily details; Mrs. Erna Dungee, attractive and with
a subtle sense of mimicry, who kept the records of income straight;
down-to-earth Mrs. Hazel Gregory, who worked closely with Glasco
and during the year of the boycott turned out oceans of mimeographed
sheets.

King was especially fortunate in his two secretaries. The first was
Mrs. Elmer Henningburg Reynolds. She was a well-dressed, dashing
young matron, who, with her secretarial skill, assisted Martin and
Coretta in putting together the first draft of his dissertation and filled
in as his church secretary, when the young lady who had this job
had to leave the position before her successor could take over. Mrs.
Reynolds helped King much more in learning the ins and outs of his
new environment, for she knew well the personalities of the Dexter
congregation, of which she was a prominent member. Mrs. Reynolds
was interested in civic and cultural movements quite sincerely but
mostly in a social sense. She believed in her civil rights and human
relations organizations and won many new members to them, including a few liberal whites whom she persuaded to join or make
contributions. It was difficult for anyone to refuse a cause so well
represented.

In December, 1954, Mrs. Reynolds lost her husband, a victim
of heart failure. She was recovering from this bereavement when
the boycott burst upon Montgomery. Although she kept busy professionally as a secretary, she agreed to help King out after hours with
the letters that were flooding in on him. Often they would work till
midnight; at times, to 1 or 2 A.M.

But after about two months, when the psychological pressures were added to the long hours of toil, the pace became unendurable to her. The daily stories of the harassment of the boycotters by the police, the filthy, anonymous telephone calls, the bombing of King's and Nixon's homes were building up tension in everyone. Then came the mass indictments of the grand jury and the announcement that on February 22 the Negroes who were involved in the Montgomery Improvement Association were to be rounded up. On the eve of the mass arrests, Mrs. Reynolds was tense all that day. That night she woke herself up screaming. It was too much; she had to give up the job. King understood. Everybody understood.

King's other secretary was Mrs. Maude L. Ballou, who remained with the MIA throughout the boycott and afterward. It was possible to organize the office after Mrs. Ballou came on as a full-time employee. She was a tall, light-brown young woman, with an intellectual-looking forehead and expressive eyes. She was both an idealist and an efficient worker. King had no reservations about having her handle his most distinguished visitors or the urbane newsmen, for she was at once intelligent and sincere. However, she bruised easily when she saw the machinations of the "men of God." She was appalled when she heard about Abernathy's remark to Mrs. Dungee: "You girls see us not only when we're dressed up in our spiritual robes; you see us as we really are, in our spiritual B.V.D's."

Mrs. Ballou was very protective of King. Next to Mrs. King, she realized probably more than anyone else the impact of the boycott ordeal upon him personally. She felt sorry for him. She could see or sense his weariness and distress. She tried to ward off the hosts of callers who swarmed in to see him. She tried to explain what King meant and what he intended to do whenever what he actually did or did not do was misunderstood. She answered all criticisms of him. Perhaps this shield was in part an extension of her mothering urge. She had a husband and children of her own.

Some of Mrs. Ballou's close friends would tease her, from time to time, about her boss. The dialogue would go like this:

"How are you today, Maude?"

"I am fine, thank you."

"And how is Leonard [her husband]?"

"Oh, he's fine, too."

"And how are the children?"

"Oh, they are fine, too. Everybody's fine."

"Well, then how is L. L. J.?"

Mrs. Ballou would smile or blush, for she knew that the initials

L. L. J. stood for Little Lord Jesus. That was the private name that some of her friends had for King because they knew that Mrs. Ballou thought so well of him.

Outpost

Help came, too, from an outpost of the campaign. Dr. Richard Harris partially converted his pharmacy into a transfer station for the motor pool. He installed extra chairs for the comfort of the tired waiting travelers. He kept on hand a petty-cash fund for emergency needs of the MIA. Often he himself could be seen, round-faced and round-headed, wearing earphones and mouthpiece while mixing drugs. In that way he could fill prescriptions and relay directions and S.O.S. calls for the transportation service at the same time. Dr. Harris was perhaps the best example of the businessmen who committed themselves to the cause. It was not easy for the "enemy" to put pressure upon him, for his relatives owned the building that housed his store and 90 per cent of his soda fountain and drugstore customers were Negroes.

A number of individuals voluntarily came forward with personal assistance and succor. Some of the men of the Dexter Baptist Church served as a voluntary patrol, guarding King's home at night. Some ex-servicemen did likewise. But the man above all others who gave of his time in this way was Bob Williams, a friend of King's at Morehouse. Willams had preceded King to Montgomery by three years and was teaching voice at Alabama State College. A first-rate tenor himself, he developed spendid choruses and soloists.

Williams was as fastidious as King about his clothes and almost as winsome. Dark, lean, pleasant, he was very much the college-bred man. He was also impatient with pretense or red tape. Devoted to King, Williams served as his trusted chauffeur, driving him to the trains, airport, Birmingham, Atlanta and other nearby places. When King was out of town, Williams would often stay at the house, protecting Coretta and Yoki. He made himself available at all times. "Anything for Mike and the cause," he would say. Williams was not a complete convert to nonviolence. His friends twitted him by saying that had he been on hand when the bomb throwers appeared, nonviolence would have faded in a flash—a flash from Bob's gun.

Something Special

Thus Martin Luther King did not operate in a leadership vacuum. He was aided and abetted on all sides; surrounded and supported and reinforced. Collective action resulted from collective thought.

What, then, did King himself add to the situation?

In brief, Martin Luther King was the spokesman, the philosopher and the symbol of the Montgomery bus boycott. In these roles he was without a peer and gave the additional dimension to the movement that helped make the struggle epic.

There were many good speakers, ranging from the moan-and-groan preachers to the old-line orators, and the quiet, scholarly lecturers. But King was by far the best of the lot. He established close rapport with the people. No matter who gave a pep talk, the mass-meeting audiences were never completely satisfied unless they heard from King. They believed in him. One "sister" said that when King spoke she felt that God himself was near; another testified that when she heard King's voice she could also hear the rustle of angels that she could see dimly, hovering over him.

To many a mother, here was her symbolic son: neat, clean, well-spoken, smart, good-looking, manly. To many a childless woman here too was her son. At the same time, King was to the predominantly female audience the father symbol: strong, wise, protective. When it was suggested that King represented the father-son complex, one woman who may not have understood the term said, "Oh yes, Father, Son—*and* Holy Ghost."

The men, too, liked him. He was easy to get along with, the kind of person one would choose for a brother. At the mass meetings the identification of speaker and audience was apparent. The flow of sentiment between leader and followers was immediate. Even to an outside visitor King was, at the least, a young, brave, modest, intelligent, handsome, articulate man. To the newsmen King was highly quotable. Even to those whites who came in direct contact with him, he may have exemplified the personal qualities, aside from color, that they really wanted for their own sons—or even for themselves, although they would not have admitted it. Objectively, King was a personification of much of the Western world's middle-class ideal of the educated man.

The revolution in race relations in the South would turn up many leaders. Almost all of them would be, in some degree, wise and strong spokesmen, expressing a mass urge. But seldom would these leaders add a fresh concept to social thinking as King did with the philosophy of nonviolent resistance. When he struck that chord, he drew a response from men everywhere who were followers of Jesus Christ or Gandhi; also from all others who were weary of war and conflict. This, too, gave him a universal appeal.

IX - Hero at Montgomery

AS president of MIA, Martin Luther King was not an immediate and unqualified success. As a negotiator—and this was part of his job—for the first two months, he was actually a failure. The MIA leaders met twice with the city fathers and bus company representatives and several times with a citizens committee that had been appointed by the Mayor to work out a settlement. No settlement was reached; negotiations broke down.

This surprised King. Apparently, he had expected these negotiations to approximate the old bull sessions at Morehouse and Boston, in which there was the give-and-take of honest opinions, ending with all present agreeing upon the points established, shaking hands and parting in good humor.

King had to learn that the Montgomery negotiators were not interested in intellectual shadowboxing. Their concern was the struggle for power—that is, profits for the bus company, votes for the politicians and maintenance of the *status quo* in race relations. That a proposition was logical was of less importance than its probable effect upon the economic or political situation, including white supremacy. That "first come, first served" seating on the buses was fair and that other Southern cities practiced it was beside the point. King was not prepared for the tactics he encountered. Accordingly, he was outraged and twice lost his temper.

It may not have been his fault, but the fact was that after two months of negotiation King and his MIA colleagues had nothing to show. King even offered to resign.

During this early period, King's philosophy of nonviolent resistance was only gradually taking form. When he made his debut as president of MIA at the initial mass meeting, December 5, he did not mention Gandhi or anything directly relating to the Mahatma's theory or practice of social change. His speech was just one more appeal to principles of Christianity and democracy, to fair play and compassion for those in the opposition camp.

But during December and January, King and others had time and need to think about strategy. Miss Juliette Morgan, a white librarian, wrote a long letter to the editor of the local morning paper, December 12, in which she compared the bus strike to Gandhi's famous salt march to the sea. This was perhaps the first clear statement of nonviolent mass resistance as a possible technique for the boycotters. Other liberals, pacifists and Christian socialists who wrote in or who drifted into town added their push to the doctrines of Gandhi and Thoreau.

Practical events were proceeding along the same line. King, at the suggestion of some of his friends, applied for a permit to carry a pistol. The sheriff turned him down although King had received numerous threats.

Nonviolence, therefore, was not a ready-made concept that was imposed upon Montgomery; rather it was an evolution which arose in part from the personal and intellectual inclinations of Martin Luther King and the practical situation that confronted Montgomery Negroes. They found it difficult to secure arms and knew that the opposition had the preponderance of physical power. In case of a conflict, Negroes knew that the Alabama National Guard, the state patrol, county and city "peace" officers would not be on their side.

King himself, during the boycott's first two months, was almost unknown as a public personality. He was just beginning his career and was still known chiefly among his circle of family friends, schoolmates and church members. Although he had preached from many pulpits, he was most often referred to as the son of the Rev. Martin Luther King, Sr. He was, of course, relatively new to Montgomery though he was rapidly making his mark as a progressive religious and civic leader. In the first weeks of the boycott, both city officials and newsmen turned to Attorney Fred Gray, a local product, for information about the MIA. Gray passed the ball to King.

It was not surprising then that during December and January, when King was quoted in the papers, his words were only an item in the story and his name was scarcely in the heading. As late as

January 19, 1956, a local reporter could write, "There seems to be uncertainty in the minds of the white community over the identity of the director of the bus boycott." He then went on to "reveal" that King was "the boycott boss."

If, in the early days of the struggle, King did not emerge as a public figure or philosopher and had to learn the facts of life as a negotiator, he was successful in two of his many roles: first, as a presiding chairman of the MIA Board; secondly, as a spokesman at the mass meetings.

Everybody testified that King knew how to get along with all types and classes of people. He also persuaded them to get along with each other. By example, he was democratic, patient and optimistic. C. H. Parrish, a Negro and a sociologist from the University of Louisville, sat in on a MIA committee that met one evening for four or five hours. Dr. Parrish recalled that, during all that time, he never heard King give a direct command or contradict anyone. This was typical. King's way was to ask for volunteers for this or that task, and for the views of everyone on a topic before suggesting that somebody make a motion for action to be taken. At the mass meetings, King and the crowds were as one. From the very first, he was a hit with them.

Thus, Martin Luther King, though unknown and unloved beyond his immediate environment, had the staunch support of his MIA colleagues and the masses of the Negro community. This proved to be a firm base, essential and certain, from which could be launched whatever else the future might require.

Bombs and Suit

For King and the movement, the turning point came when the boycott was about two months old. On January 30, 1956, King's home was bombed and two days later Montgomery Negroes filed suit in federal court against the bus company and the city fathers.

The bombing of a home, under any circumstances, is sensational news. In this instance it also posed the question: how does a man act when word gets to him that dynamite has been exploded outside his front door while his wife and baby are behind the door? It is enough to release volcanic emotions in anyone.

On this particular Monday evening, King was speaking at one of the frequent mass meetings. When the news came to him, he hastened home at once, but walked calmly through the milling crowd of Negroes and policemen which he found clustered about his lawn. Inside he found the Mayor and the Commissioner of Public Safety as well as his wife and baby and a lady friend of the family. These public officials had received word of the bombing before King and had rushed to the scene to investigate.

The crowd of Negroes was in an angry mood, both because the house of their leader had been attacked and because the police were now trying to push them back from the house, so that the crime detectives, photographers and reporters could do their work, and street traffic could be cleared.

After a while, the police tried to make the crowd disperse and go home. An attractive, well-dressed woman on the sidewalk, Mrs. Beautine DeCosta, said to one of the policemen, "Go get Rev. King. We will not leave until *he* says that his family are not hurt and that everything is all right." The policeman obligingly went inside, and King came out, calm and resolute, flanked by the Mayor and the Commissioner of Public Safety. Clearly and strongly, King spoke to the people: "He who lives by the sword will perish by the sword. . . . We are not advocating violence. We want to love our enemies. Love them and let them know you love them. Do not get your weapons. Put them away. I did not start this boycott. I was asked by you to serve as your spokesman. If I am stopped, our work will not stop, for what we are doing is just, and God is with us." The crowd, now quieted, exclaimed, "Amen."

The Commissioner of Public Safety then spoke briefly and haltingly of law and order, and the Mayor said, if not very forcefully, that white people did not condone violence.

A photographer snapped a picture of the three while King was speaking. It made the front page of the next morning's paper. It showed King with his right hand raised in a gesture that blotted out the face of the Mayor. This was symbolic of things to come.

King was now page one news not only in Montgomery but through-out the nation. The news services, radio and TV spread his name from coast to coast. The local press still referred to King's wife as "Coretta King," without the "Mrs.," and to Mrs. Mary Lucy Williams, a friend who was in the house when the bomb exploded, as "the Williams woman."

Other headlines were forthcoming. Two days after the bombing, the bus boycotters filed suit in federal court calling for the end of bus segregation and asking that the Mayor and other city officials be restrained from violating the civil rights of Negroes. This suit indicated that Montgomery Negroes were abandoning their "first come, first served" proposal, which had been rejected, and that they were dis-gusted with the city commissioners for faking a settlement of the boycott with unauthorized persons. Also, the suit was a counter-thrust to the Mayor's get-tough policy with Negro motorists, who were giving boycotters free rides, and Negro pedestrians, who clustered on street corners for these pickups.

In effect, the suit meant that the MIA had finally moved up to the ideological position of the NAACP and was now attacking not only "unfair" Jim Crow, but the whole Jim Crow principle.

The bus fight began to make sense in terms of the rulings of the United States Supreme Court against racial segregation and the national outlook on the issue of desegregation.

The suit was a jolt to the city fathers. The special harassments of motorists and pedestrians stopped overnight.

Counterattack

It was now the turn of the opposition to make a move. It came with massive force and was meant to break the back of the boycott and teach a lasting lesson.

On February 21, after a press buildup of an eight-day investigation, the Montgomery County grand jury returned indictments for 115 leaders and key participants in the boycott. The specific charge was conspiracy to destroy a legitimate business. The grand jury also made its general position clear. Without a word about federal law or the United States Supreme Court, the jury report contained these words: "In this state we are committed to segregation by custom and by law; we intend to maintain it." The sheriff's office announced that on the following day it would begin the roundup of those who had been indicted.

The Negro community was stunned. But a few hours after the first impact of the news had worn off and the names of the indicted persons became known, the Negro community relaxed. It realized that a fair proportion of Montgomery's top Negro religious, civic and educational leaders were on that grand jury list. As groups and individuals here and there discussed what was just about the only current topic of conversation, it became ludicrous that the moral and ethical symbols of the community should be branded as criminal. And so, on street corners and in the cafés, in churches, and in homes, on the campus and in automobiles, smiles blossomed into laughs.

Accordingly, when the deputy sheriff came for the Rev. Mr. Abernathy, the picture that the photographer got was one of a smiling Reverend. When the Rev. Mr. Hubbard went down to give himself up to the law, he joked with his arresting officer, saying that as a taxpayer providing the salary of the officer, he should have made the officer come for him. Others called up the sheriff's office to ask if their names were on "that list" and, if they were, volunteered to go down. Nobody attempted to run and hide. A huge but orderly crowd assembled in front of the county jail to see what went on. The mood of good-natured hilarity was so prevalent that the sheriff told the crowd: "This is no vaudeville show." What the sheriff may not have realized was that many of his deputies were also laughing and joshing with the "criminals" they had been told to round up. In the excitement, even the editor of the morning paper apparently forgot that it was George Washington's birthday; his editorial on the father of our country did not appear until the next day.

Enter King

Martin Luther King was not in town when the mass arrests began. He was at Fisk University in Nashville, delivering a series of lectures that he had promised before the boycott started. He kept in touch with things, but he was off the scene—and "out of camera." So, it was Mrs. Parks whose picture appeared on the front page of the New York *Times* and who was mentioned in its editorial. Abernathy was much photographed. The picture of him and a stout lady member of his congregation joyously hugging as he came out of the county jail was one of the candid shots of the year. The morning paper ran a full page of scenes from the roundup. Good humor pervaded the photographs and spilled over into the accompanying stories. Nobody seemed to be mad at anybody. It was more of a spectacle than anything else. Those arrested were treated courteously and released immediately on bond.

King hurriedly concluded his lectures and left Nashville for Montgomery by the way of Atlanta. There his father and a group of Negro leaders tried to persuade him not to return to the dangers of Montgomery. King told them that he *had* to go back. He was right—the people were expecting him. Mrs. King declared that she was going back too, and she did.

So, when word reached the newsmen that the MIA leader was arriving, they tried to intercept him at the city limits. Some were waiting for him at home. King rushed away, picked up his chief lieutenant, Abernathy, who had been running things in his absence, and went on down to the county jail. There the newsmen were gathered in full force.

He was photographed as he was being booked. Outwardly he was calm but he betrayed an inner nervousness by his habit of pulling his lips in slightly between his teeth. The photograph went out over the nation. The afternoon headline read, "Rev. King and 88 Others Booked on Boycott Writs." King was thus again "in camera" and was to remain so for quite a while.

That night at the mass meeting it was clear that leaders and followers were committed to fight to the end. Several of the twenty-four ministers in the indicted group took the floor to affirm their faith and determination to go on "all the way."

This irrevocable commitment involved King personally. From the very beginning he had been conscientious about his responsibility as leader. But now that he felt fully the spirit of the people, he moved to a deeper realization of his identification with them. That they would not desert the common cause he was sure. They had slammed the door on compromise. Nobody seemed to be afraid any longer. Policemen and jails had come to mean little. All doubt, apparently, had been swept away.

At some point in the lives of most men there come moments when they lose all self-consciousness; when they forget the minor details of existence and ignore personal comfort and convenience. They merge their individual spirits with something larger and more powerful than self, surrendering completely to a principle or a cause or a person. There is a free flow of sentiment and emotion, unrestrained and uninhibited, direct contact with universal life forces. It is a feeling of sacrifice and elation. It is a moment of reality.

Such moments are rare for most men, but for Martin Luther King and his MIA followers these moments would be frequent during the boycott year. After February 23, King and the "Montgomery protest," as they euphemistically called it, were one. Actually, he was willing to lay down his life for the cause, and so were his followers. At some of the mass meetings, a feeling of crisis seemed to descend upon the crowd. Word would come of some unexpected move by the enemy, some diabolical maneuver, some setback, some crushing disappointment. The audience would moan for a while as though in physical pain—and then there would be the counter-affirmation, a resurgence of faith and resolve, ending up on a high note of exhilaration.

Or, in contrast, some act of extreme sacrifice or devotion would come to light. The audience would hear about some brother or sister who had "gone the last mile" or resisted a great temptation to turn back or go over to the enemy. The good news would sweep through the crowd and Martin Luther King, giving voice to it, would float with the audience on a wave of joy. Nothing else in the world seemed to matter. These were moments of reality.

King could easily have ordered his followers into battle. They would have marched against the enemy, not caring that such a one might have thousands of guns. That, instead, he told them to love their enemy and express their opposition to injustice by self-discipline and organized, peaceful resistance was the most creative approach to race relations twentieth-century America had seen.

The day of arraignment for those indicted and arrested was February 25. Accordingly, the MIA set that date for a prayer pilgrimage, during which everybody was to walk wherever he went, shunning the use of private automobiles, taxis or any other form of motor transportation. Thus nonviolence was now projected positively as a weapon in the campaign. The newspapers played up this aspect and the local morning daily ran a special article on Henry David Thoreau, the American father of passive resistance or civil disobedience.

The Press Comes to Town

The reaction of the nation to the mass arrests ranged from surprise to outrage. The Washington *Evening Star* said that such an act was "beyond belief," while its neighbor, the Washington *Post* called it "monumental folly." Many papers elsewhere agreed in substance with the *Afro-American* when it said: "If Montgomery city officials wanted to solidify and strengthen the determination of colored people to continue the boycott, they couldn't have done any better than to arrest 24 pastors."

This was true. Instead of destroying the boycott, the mass arrests had cemented it and drew national attention and support to it. The boomerang completed its circuit, striking those who first flung it at the Negro community. The New York *Journal-American* remarked that "the brains in this crisis are mostly on the Negro side. The perspective and the sense of destiny are entirely on the Negro side."

All manner of organizations offered sympathy and support. Pro-MIA editorials filled the press of the North and West. The Southern press was generally silent or against the boycott. Civil rights, religious and interracial groups issued statements, passed resolutions and sent money, clothes and shoes, and a carton of foot salve. Congressman Adam Clayton Powell demanded that the President of the United States guarantee the safety of the indicted Negroes. Roy Wilkins, NAACP head, compared the mass arrests to the terror of totalitarian governments. Dr. Ralph Bunche of the United Nations, a Nobel Peace Prize Winner, saluted Montgomery Negroes as "a fellow American and as a fellow Negro." This was strong support from this paragon of calm discernment.

Following the start of the boycott some of the metropolitan papers and the big radio and TV chains had sent in reporters and cameramen for special spot stories. By the time of the arraignment all the large news-gathering agencies realized that big stories would be coming from Montgomery and north Alabama, where Miss Autherine Lucy was attempting to get into the all-white state university. Some papers

assigned what were humorously called "war" correspondents to
the "Southern Front." Some thirty-odd outside newsmen were in town
for the arraignment and by the time of the trials the number had
doubled. Among them were M. K. Kamath of the Press Trust of
India; Keith Kyle, London *Economist;* Daniel Morgaine, *France-Soir*
of Paris; Wayne Phillips, New York *Times;* Peter M. Lizagor,
Chicago *Daily News;* Charles Whipple, Boston *Globe;* Bob Denley,
International News Service; Dan Berman, New Brunswick, New Jersey,
Daily News; Farrell Dobbs, *Militant,* New York; Abner W. Berry,
Daily Worker, New York.

The Negro press also sent some of its star reporters to Montgomery:
Charles Loeb, Negro Newspaper Publishers Association; James
Booker, *Amsterdam News,* New York; Ethel Payne, Chicago *De-
fender;* William Fowlkes, *Ebony* and *Jet,* Chicago; L. O. Swingler,
Tri-State Call-Times, Memphis, Tennessee; James Huger, Louisville,
Kentucky, *Defender;* Al Sweeney, *Afro-American,* Baltimore; Evelyn
Cunningham, Pittsburgh *Courier* and Emory O. Jackson of the Scott
News Syndicate. Nick Chris of the United Press and Rex Thomas of
the Associated Press ran the Montgomery offices for their news ser-
vices. The New York *Post* sent down two artists, Burt Silverman and
Harvey Dinnastin, who did drawings of courtroom scenes, where no
photographers were allowed.

Montgomery had not been the center of so much attention since
the inauguration of Jefferson Davis as President of the Confederacy
in 1861. Between the arraignment and trial dates, the reporters and
cameramen overran the town in search of background and pictures.

They followed King about wherever he went. They were waiting for
him at his home when he got up in the morning. They rode with him
to his office or to his church or mass meeting and came home with
him late at night. They swarmed over the campuses, interviewing
teachers and students. They talked with bus drivers, bus riders and
ex-bus riders. They stopped at service stations, waylaid city officials
and camped in the offices of the local papers.

It was a cosmopolitan lot: friendly, forward, warm, generous,
incessantly smoking and talking. It gave the slow-moving town a
fillip. The sympathies of the working newsmen were definitely with
the boycotters. Their personal views were much stronger than they
could afford to show in their news stories and radio-TV comments.

The Negro community enjoyed these visiting journalists and "mike
men" immensely; some of the whites did, too, though a majority of
them seemed to squirm from time to time. The WCC often ducked
the reporters.

Negroes would race to their radios and TV sets, spinning the dials from station to station, trying not to miss anything about Montgomery. Many persons saw themselves on TV for the first time; others began reading and carrying about with them the daily New York *Times*.

Though most of the publicity was about the mass movement as a whole, the image of Martin Luther King increasingly came into focus. Credit must go to the Hartford (Connecticut) *Courant* for perceiving this. Its editorial of March 10, 1956, was possibly the first one on the MIA leader as such. Entitled "Martin Luther King, Negro Leader," it said:

Emerging from the racial conflict in Montgomery, Alabama, is the growing leadership of a Negro clergyman, Martin Luther King. By virtue of his intelligence and piety Mr. King has gradually become the spokesman for passive resistance. It is well to remember his name. For if this movement is successful, as it appears likely, the Reverend Dr. King will become not only a national hero among his race, but the continuing spearhead in the fight against segregation.

On the same date, the Pittsburgh *Courier* ran two articles on Gandhi and the Montgomery movement; the Chicago *Defender* mentioned King and Abernathy as examples of courageous ministers of the South; and William Worthy, special correspondent of the *Afro-American,* wrote that the struggle in Montgomery reminded him "of some of the underdeveloped and newly freed countries I have visited in Asia: Indonesia, Burma, India and South Vietnam . . . a few able leaders at the top being relentlessly pushed from below toward a goal of a more abundant life but at the same time severely handicapped by an absence of trained personnel in the technical, educational and administrative spheres."

The Trial

The trial began on March 19 and lasted for four days. By common consent of prosecution and defense, the King case came first, for the evidence and testimony would be generally the ⁄ same for the whole group under indictment. The atmosphere was electric. The situation was filled with all manner of suggestion for the historian of social change.

The courthouse was old, high-ceilinged and inadequate for the crowds—mostly Negroes—that squeezed in each day. The segregation line was, at times, hardly visible. For example, although counsel for the defense and counsel for the prosecution sat on opposite sides of the same table, they came together at the end of the table. These lawyers were frequently conferring and passing things back and forth among themselves and during the four days of the trial appeared to fraternize quite often.

King and the others had been indicted under a 1921 state antilabor law which held that a conspiracy to boycott, without a just cause, that did injury to a business was criminal. The prosecution, therefore, set out to prove that the MIA was such a conspiracy, that its cause was not just, and that it intended to, and in fact did, injure the business of the bus company.

The defense, of course, denied these allegations and held that what the MIA did was no more than exercise traditional rights of free speech and assembly and that its intent was not to injure the business of the bus company but to bring about fair treatment of bus customers.

The prosecution established quite easily that the MIA financed the operation of the motor pool, which was an alternative transportation facility, for the ex-bus riders. The MIA was shown to provide gasoline and repairs for those who used their cars and to supply some drivers to supplement those who also drove in the free-ride pickup system. The defense contended that there was nothing illegal in this procedure.

The prosecution was less successful in proving that the MIA had used force to prevent Negroes from riding the buses. Of the three witnesses on this point, the defense revealed that one was employed as the janitor who cleaned up the very courtroom in which the trial was being held and could not, therefore, be looked upon as a free agent; that another could not identify the man who was supposed to have threatened to "whup" the witness if he rode the bus again; and the third turned out to be a maid employed by the Mayor's mother-in-law.

The Mayor himself was put on the stand. At one point he was asked by the defense counsel: "Does Beatrice Jackson work for you?" The Mayor answered disdainfully: "I have told you fellows twice she don't work for me." At this, defense attorney Billingsley jumped to his feet, pointedly objecting to that kind of answer. The Mayor retreated.

When the next question was put to him: "Does she work for you as a maid?" The Mayor responded: "No, sir, she don't."

Negroes in the courtroom gave each other a look and a sly wink—a Negro attorney had made the Mayor say *"sir."*

Another high point was the parade of witnesses by the defense. Some of them told the story of efforts that had been made by Negroes to get bus officials and city fathers to improve the bus service, prior to the boycott. On this testimony the court heard Mrs. Thelma Glass, well-spoken, self-possessed teacher, and Mrs. Sadie Brooks, dignified president of the federated colored women's clubs. These were types that the white community seldom saw and did not know. These Negro women struck the worldly-wise newsmen as standard American types.

Especially impressive were the stories of the regular bus riders, who reported alleged abuses by bus operators. The natural wit of the testifiers and the unintended humor of some of these situations were matched only by the senselessness and crudity of the treatment they described.

The prosecution denied that the bus operators were discourteous and contended that in the early days of the boycott buses had been hit by bricks and bullets while passing through Negro neighborhoods. The defense asked for proof that those indicted had committed any of these acts.

None of the Negro witnesses would say a word that would involve the Rev. Dr. King in any way. The Rev. U. J. Fields, then recording secretary of the MIA, skirted the edge of contempt by his indirect, evasive and at times impish answers to questions that the prosecution put to him. Actually, he appeared to toy with the solicitor. Accordingly, he was the hero of the moment in the Negro community. After court hours, wherever Negroes met, they would laughingly ask, "Man, did you see Fields playing with them today!"

At one point a local white newsman single-handedly appeared to have broken the state's case. He had been put on the stand by the prosecution but he testified that in his numerous visits to mass meetings he had never heard King advocate the use of force in any manner but had heard him say on several different occasions that those who disagree with the "protest" should be loved.

It may have been that the prosecution actually knew so little of the inner workings of the MIA that it did not know where to probe and punch. Apparently, the state, with all of its reputation for spies and stool pigeons, had failed to penetrate the councils of the MIA. Yet it is strange that the mass meetings, some of which had outside loud-speakers to accommodate the overflow crowds, were not tape-recorded. Such evidence would have greatly strengthened the prosecution's argument.

In a move of doubtful strategy, the defense put King himself on the stand. This was an unnecessary gamble. On the other hand, it was the big chance of the prosecution to break him down or at least discredit him with his followers. The prosecution fumbled this opportunity, failing to break through at weak points or to force King to incriminate himself or plead the Fifth Amendment. It was one thing for King's followers on the witness stand to duck and dodge for him but it would be a different matter entirely for the leader himself to avoid the truth. Gandhi's satyagraha, translated loosely as "passive resistance," means literally "adherence to truth." Martin Luther King would decidedly have lost stature had he failed to meet this test—and the world was looking.

As it turned out, King, on the witness stand, was self-possessed and easily disposed of the questions put to him. When he had finished and stepped down from the stand, it took the judge's gavel to hold back the applause of the courtroom crowd.

When the evidence was all in and the closing arguments were being made, an informal poll was taken among the visiting newsmen. They voted three to one that the defense had outargued the prosecution but voted five to one that despite this the verdict would go to the prosecution.

The courtroom Negroes had expressed privately the general view of Southern Negroes that they had little confidence in the justice of Southern courts. But there was the hope against hope that perhaps this would be the exception, because the world was looking and because the defense had deported itself so well.

The crowd was proud of the Negro lawyers. Attorney Arthur Shores was already famous as the attorney for Miss Autherine Lucy. Fred D. Gray, of course, was the home-town favorite. His colleague, Charles D. Langford, was there with the supporting evidence of his legal research. Peter Hall, suave and urbane, was an accomplished cross-examiner, while Orzell Billingsley, if he had done nothing more than make the Mayor back up, had stamped himself as a fearless defender. The NAACP had its Robert Carter on hand, but the judge would not let him participate in the arguing. National Negro religious bodies were also represented by counsel who, like Carter, were restricted to whispering advice from time to time.

When the final pleas were concluded, everybody expected the judge to take the case under advisement for a few days and then come forth with his decision. It was, therefore, shocking when the judge delivered his decision almost before the attorneys had resumed their seats. He found King guilty.

For a moment the courtroom was almost silent. Nobody had been prepared for such quick action. However, after a few moments, the defense attorneys recovered their composure and indicated that they would appeal the verdict. King was released. Court was adjourned.

King and his wife were with his attorneys now. As they put their papers into their brief cases and gathered up their hats and coats, friends came up to shake hands and say encouraging words. Some women had tears in their eyes.

After a while, King and the group around him began to move out of the courtroom. The crowd moved with them, down the stairs to the first floor, then onto the stone steps of the courthouse. There the TV cameras and microphones were set up, waiting. Newsmen swarmed about, asking King what he would do now—call off the boycott? What was the next move?

His answer was unmistakable. With his hat pulled down firmly, his left hand in his pocket, his right fist clenched but not raised, and his wife standing next to him, he said, "The judge's verdict will not increase or decrease in any way my interest in the protest. The protest goes on!" Somebody asked, "Will there be a mass meeting tonight?" Somebody in the crowd answered, "Yes, and everybody will be there!"

The spirit of the people was rebounding. They cheered and waved to the cameras. King and his wife smiled and waved, too. "Hail King!" somebody said. "Hail *the* King!" somebody answered. "King is King!" shouted yet another. And this was the headline that the *Afro* used on its front page. Many other papers carried similar leads.

The news of the verdict went out to the world. With it went the picture of the determined but nonvindictive leader and the undaunted people who stood beside him.

That night there was a series of mass meetings—for no one church could have held the crowds. Each of the gatherings was jammed. C. W. Lee, a Negro businessman, usually quiet and reserved, presented King to the audience with the words: "Here is the man who today was nailed to the cross for you and me." Singing and shouting, weeping and laughing, everybody let himself go. This was indeed a moment of reality. For a neutral observer, it was hard to see how life could deny the little that these people yearned for so passionately.

Even while urging his followers to continue the "protest" King could still speak with compassion of the man who had sentenced him:

We must not totally condemn Judge Carter. He was in a tragic dilemma. Maybe he did the best he could under the expedient method.

We are not bitter. We are still preaching non-violence. We are still using the weapon of love. We are still using the method of passive resistance. I feel confident that as this case moves up through the higher courts, somewhere along the way the decision will be reversed.

And let us not lose faith in democracy. For with all of its weaknesses, there is a ground and a basis of hope in our democratic creed.

All the world now knew of Martin Luther King. He was part martyr and part hero. Under the most favorable conditions imaginable his star had been shot into the heavens. Circumstance and history, opposition and support had combined, it seemed, to make him known around the world. He was up there now, a veritable satellite, for all to see. There was nothing that his enemies could do about that. Their guns were powerless to shoot him down. He was completely out of their range.

X - The Good Press—and the Bad

THE miracle of Montgomery, of course, was the way the Negro community launched and sustained its economic boycott and the way it was organized and piloted nonviolently through a sea of provocation to a successful conclusion.

But it was equally significant that the story of this struggle and victory got through to the world. Without a doubt, it was the best reported real-life serial of the American Negro that the world had seen in many years. And Martin Luther King, symbolic of the movement, became more widely known and in a shorter space of time than any Negro leader since Marcus Garvey and the "Back to Africa" crusade of the post-World War I days.

The influence of the press and other media of communication in focusing upon King as the chief individual item of the Montgomery story was decisive in shaping the image that took form in the public mind. Also remarkable was the breadth of interest in the Montgomery story, covering the whole range of political and ideological views as well as geographical location and type of publication.

The *Nation* of March 3, 1956, in its lead article by editor Carey McWilliams, quoted King and observed that his name had "a fine echo," but it was the New York *Times* that did the first detailed biographical sketch of the boycott leader. This appeared on March 21 and was unsigned.

The *Times* described King as a "rather soft-spoken man with a learning and maturity beyond his twenty-seven years. His clothes are in conservative good taste and he has a small trim mustache." Then followed short paragraphs on King's philosophy, his family background and education—"Southern born, Northern trained." Abernathy and Gray were mentioned also, the writer remarking that the boycott leaders were mostly between twenty-five and thirty-seven years of age. Accompanying the sketch was a good, single-column picture of King, serious looking, with his hat on.

King's speech in Brooklyn on March 25 was well reported in the New York press. Nonviolence and the example of Gandhi were his theme. M. K. Kamath, newsman from India, characterized King as brilliant and compared him with Gandhi.

About this same time, Dr. DuBois, who had known and evaluated every national Negro leader since Frederick Douglass, wrote: "Can Passive Resistance Win Over Race Hate? I doubt it. But if it does, then Mohandas Gandhi and the Black Folk of Montgomery have shown the world how to conquer war." Later, DuBois would give his estimate of King: "Honest, straight-forward, well-trained, and knowing the limits."

Time for April 2 had the courthouse steps photograph and reported the King trial as the first for the indicted MIA officials.

The April issue of *Liberation,* publication of pacifists and Christian socialists, ran an article by King in which he asserted that the Montgomery movement up to that time had established eight propositions:

1. We can stick together.
2. Our leaders do not have to sell out.
3. Threats and violence do not necessarily intimidate those who are sufficiently aroused and non-violent.
4. Our church is becoming militant.
5. We believe in ourselves.
6. Economics is part of our struggle.
7. We have discovered a new and powerful weapon—non-violent resistance.
8. We now know that the Southern Negro has come of age, politically and morally.

The King article was later reprinted separately by CORE (Congress of Racial Equality) with an introduction that said, in part:

The technique of non-violence, spotlighted to the entire world by the effective Montgomery protest against bus segregation, is not unprecedented in the struggle against racial discrimination in the United States.

In the early 1940's the enthusiastic response to A. Philip Randolph's plan for a Gandhian March on Washington was a principal factor in the enactment of wartime FEPC (fair employment) legislation.

Even in the deep south, passive resistance has been practiced before. A similar bus boycott was conducted in the summer of 1953 by Negroes in Baton Rouge but it received little publicity.

The pioneer of non-violent direct action techniques in United States race relations is the Congress of Racial Equality (CORE), a national federation of local interracial groups, founded in 1943. These groups have abolished discrimination at restaurants, theaters, skating rinks, dance halls, amusement parks, swimming pools and other public places in borderline states as well as in the North, middle west and far west. They have also worked to eliminate racial barriers in employment.

Liberation also carried an article, "Montgomery Diary," by Bayard Rustin, who had known Coretta at the Lincoln School and later at Antioch. He was on the editorial board of *Liberation,* had visited India and was well versed in Gandhianism. He brought suggestions and support from the organized pacifist movement to the MIA.

The *New Leader* of April 2 used on its front page cover a close-up of the courthouse-steps picture of King and his wife. The London *Economist* of April 7 also reported the King trial.

Abner W. Berry, in his column "On the Way," for the Sunday *Worker,* April 8, wrote: "While Marxists have had no direct contact or influence on the Montgomery bus protest movement, it conforms to predictions made by Marxists." This was a remarkably modest claim, considering its source. Credit was also given to Gandhi for predicting that American Negroes would most likely be the first Americans to adopt his philosophy.

Jet for April 12 had a picture of King and his wife on its front cover and inside a five-page feature article on "Alabama's Modern Moses." One of the seven photographs used was, apparently, from the Montgomery police files, showing King with his jailhouse number, 7089, hung about his neck. The article, written by *Jet* editor Bob Johnson, one of King's schoolmates at Morehouse, gave a thumbnail sketch of King's family, education and other personal history.

The Norfolk, Virginia, *Journal and Guide* of April 14 had a front-page streamer: "Dixie Black Moses Says Boycott Fight to Finish." The article was the first of a series. Editor P. B. Young, Jr., himself had visited Montgomery for this first-hand account of the situation there. The piece began on page one and all of page thirteen was given over to pictures of boycott leaders and scenes. Of the twenty-three photographs, King was in twelve. A second article, the following week, went more deeply into King's background, reciting the story of his education and early doubts about entering the ministry.

The April 21 issue of the Pittsburgh *Courier* concluded the "Life Story of Rev. M. L. King, Jr." by Evelyn Cunningham. This personal sketch was made against the background of the first of the mass trials.

Beginning of the End

Events continued to move; accordingly, on April 23, a headline in the Montgomery papers (and elsewhere over the nation) read: "Intrastate Bus Segregation Is Banned by the Supreme Court." The court had so held in the case of Mrs. Sarah Mae Flemming, who had sued the bus company in Columbia, South Carolina, when a bus driver forced her to move to "the Negro section" of the bus on which she was riding. NAACP attorneys represented Mrs. Flemming. Her case had been in court since 1953.

The National City Lines, which operated the buses in Montgomery, immediately dropped its policy of segregation. But the Montgomery civil authorities, among others, held that the Flemming decision for Columbia, South Carolina, was not binding on Montgomery, Alabama, and demanded that the bus company continue segregating, and secured an injunction from a local court to sustain this position.

Amid the confusion there was some question as to what Montgomery Negroes would do. King was turned to for the answer. The Montgomery *Advertiser* of April 25 quoted him as saying: "No change"—the boycott would continue until the situation was clarified.

Meanwhile several other Southern cities dropped bus segregation —but not Montgomery.

Requests for speaking engagements were flooding the MIA headquarters. When Governor Coleman of Mississippi learned that an invitation had come to King from an organization in that state, he "advised" King not to come. On April 24 King replied that he had been unable to accept the invitation. "However, if I had accepted the invitation, I would feel it my moral responsibility to come to Mississippi in spite of your cautious warning. . . . I think the state of Mississippi could well profit from a gospel of love."

La Paix, published in Fort-de-France, Martinique, West Indies, on April 25 quoted King in a front-page report, under the double-column lead: *"Où en est le conflict racial en Alabama."*

The Baltimore *Afro-American* for April 28 announced that "the passive resistance demonstration movement against racial segregation on buses [had] reached Capetown [South Africa]." The issue there

was the restriction of native African passengers to the upper story of
the double-decker buses.

The *Afro* of May 12 used as the heading over one of its stories,
"Rev. King is 'King' in Montg'ry." The story then added: "To the
underprivileged citizens of Montgomery, who have for long years
suffered the injustices and pains of segregation, the Rev. Martin L.
King is just that—a king."

On the other hand, reporter Art Carter continued, "to the white
citizens, at least the vast majority of them, the 27-year-old minister
is 'an outsider,' 'a stirrer-upper,' 'an agitator' . . . 'a meddlesome
northerner.' " Then followed a half-page résumé of King's work and
philosophy.

Under date of May 14, A. J. Muste, who had spoken impressively
at Crozer while King was a student there, issued his "letter from
the U.S.A." in which the prominent pacifist declared that the main
force that was drawing Southern leaders together in a common struggle
"was the deep conviction—recently acquired by some of them—that
Gandhian nonviolence [was] so beautifully exemplified in the Montgomery struggle. . . ."

In May, Miss Eve Merriam released her book of verse, *Montgomery,
Alabama, Money, Mississippi, and Other Places.* Perhaps as Mrs.
Eleanor Roosevelt wrote in her endorsement of the thin volume, it
was more "a social pamphlet than . . . poetry." Yet its focus was
positive and sympathetic. One of the poems was entitled, "Martin
Luther and Other People"—the other people were Rev. Mr.
Abernathy and the Rev. Mr. Gaetz [Graetz]: "We'll hold with the
Lord, we shall not ride." Another of Miss Merriam's pieces was
about the "plain-talking splendor from Mrs. Rosa Parks."

On May 17, anniversary of the Supreme Court's school desegregation decree, King spoke in New York at the Cathedral of St. John
the Divine. He has listed this as one of his most important speaking
appearances. The title of his sermon for the occasion was most
suggestive: "The Death of Evil Upon the Seashore." In developing
this theme, he first recounted the trials of the Israelites, then went
on to say hopefully, "In our struggle for freedom and justice in this
country we have gradually seen the death of evil." A picture of King,
with the Right Rev. Horace W. B. Donegan, Bishop of New York
and the Very Rev. James A. Pike, Dean of the Cathedral, appeared
on the front page of the Chicago *Defender* of May 26.

In the middle of May, Mrs. Almena Lomax, a journalist who injects
her own personality into whatever she writes for her newspaper, the
Los Angeles *Tribune,* began a series on Montgomery, which she

called "the happiest city in the U.S.A." By this she meant the élan
of the Negro boycotters. She dubbed King a "20th Century Moses"
and went on to say that he had "great virtuosity, both as an orator
and a philosopher. . . . Undoubtedly King is the 'king,' this movement's
leader . . . its crucified symbol, its blood and body-of-Christ, its
inspiration, its aim and aspiration, also its central, guiding mind."

Mrs. Lomax's focus and enthusiasm were not restricted to King,
however. The "heart" of the movement, she asserted, "is Abernathy,
'talking in tongues' so to speak, with the packed church of the old
women of Alabama . . . the old women are sweet, and the young
women of Alabama are lovely. . . . But the men are, for me, gallant
and full of inner grace and outer gentleness. . . . It is a land of lovers.
. . . And Abernathy and King, 29 and 27, are lovers no less."

For a rally at New York's Madison Square Garden, scheduled for
May 24, King was billed with Miss Autherine Lucy, Gus Courts, who
had defied the White Citizens Council and voted in Mississippi, and
Dr. T. R. M. Howard, who was then spearheading the Mississippi
civil rights fight. These personalities were advertised as "Heroes of
the South." However, King could not keep this engagement and Montgomery was represented instead by Mrs. Rosa Parks and E. D. Nixon.

This turned out to be a huge and successful venture. Among the
speakers were Mrs. Eleanor Roosevelt, Roy Wilkins of the NAACP,
A. Philip Randolph of the Brotherhood of Sleeping Car Porters,
Congressman Adam Clayton Powell, Charles S. Zimmerman of the
International Ladies Garment Workers Union, Dr. Israel Gold-
stein, President of the American Jewish Congress; also there was
an array of entertainers, including Tallulah Bankhead and Sammy
Davis, Jr. The daily and weekly press gave the meeting wide coverage.
Several thousand dollars were raised and divided among the NAACP,
the MIA and various other organizations working for civil rights in
the South.

This New York rally was but one in the series held throughout
the nation on or near May 28—the date designated as "A Day of
Prayer." At one time Congressman Adam Powell had also suggested
that Negroes and their friends should stop work for an hour on this
day, thus dramatizing their solidarity with the "front-line soldiers
in the battle of the South." Many mass meetings were held in the
South and North but the work-stoppage idea was dropped.

Hue, a pocket companion magazine to *Jet,* ran a feature in its
June edition entitled "How the Bible Beat Jim Crow in Montgom-
ery." It was a six-page spread with two-thirds of the space in pictures.
King was in half of the ten photographs.

Surprisingly, King received an unfavorable notice in the British Manchester *Guardian*. Alistair Cooke, American correspondent for the paper, traveled through several of the southeastern states for a series that he called, "The Ordeal of the South." The fourth chapter in the serial was on Montgomery, "City of the Boycott." Cooke's sympathies here were primarily with the bus company and municipal officials. He remarked that

Montgomery is to feel like a culprit city, for, again, the northern reporter's instinct is to ignore the bus company . . . and to be welcomed as a brother-in-arms by the Rev. Martin Luther King, jun., the young Negro organizer of the boycott who flies in and out of the airport a couple of times a week buying station wagons from "neutral" outlanders as the Arabs go scouting for Soviet planes. . . . He is a young, bland man with solemn good looks. . . . He is also, they [the whites] say, a very smooth article and as willing to be the cat's-paw of the NAACP. . . .

The local Montgomery press reprinted the Cooke piece. Negroes and their friends, who knew Cooke mainly as a master of ceremonies of the first-class Sunday TV show *Omnibus,* were shocked. They had been sure that he was a liberal.

The *Guardian* declined to print a rebuttal to the Cooke piece on Montgomery though it did publish a letter of Henry Lee Moon of the NAACP that was critical of the whole series.

The End—Almost

On June 4 the federal district court ruled that bus segregation laws of Alabama and Montgomery were unconstitutional. The three-judge panel voted two to one in favor of the petition that had been lodged by Montgomery Negroes on February 1.

News of this decision crowded the headlines and drowned out almost all other news for Montgomery. What would the Negroes do now? everybody was asking. Was the boycott over? Again, reporters, local and national, were on King's trail. When they caught up with him, his answer was: "We shall *not* go back to the buses until the situation is clarified."

There was a great deal of confusion because it was not clear whether local officials would be "good sports" and concede that their game was up. The officials, however, determined to resist to the last, although they must have known that there was not the remotest chance that the lower court's order to desegregate would be reversed by the Supreme Court of the United States—the very agency that had in the first place handed down the basic desegregation decrees for the nation.

Toward the end of June, the NAACP held its national convention in San Francisco. King was one of the chief speakers. One photograph shows him swamped by the admiring delegates. He told them the "Montgomery story," relating it to the history of the Negro in America and the current world struggle of subject peoples. This same speech was later used as King's side of a debate on the Montgomery situation with the editor of a local daily, as printed in *U.S. News and World Report* for August 3.

Easily King was the star of the convention. Many thought that he, rather than Jackie Robinson, the baseball star, should have received the NAACP's Spingarn Medal for outstanding achievement. As if with prescience, the awards committee seemed to realize that Robinson was having his last year as a ball player; King could afford to wait.

At this same NAACP gathering, reporters put a question to King that brought forth strong reaction, at least in Montgomery. He was asked if the boycott technique had a broad application to other civil rights issues. He answered that it "might become the pattern in many areas of the South" and that it might be "extended to segregated schools." He qualified his statement by adding that he had not "thought through the idea fully." Thurgood Marshall, chief counsel of the NAACP and strategist of the legal campaign against Jim Crow, was quoted as responding to King's comment rather sharply, saying, "I don't approve of using children to do men's work." The Montgomery Press made much of this difference (such as it was) between the Negro leaders.

Redbook for August was the first magazine of national circulation to run a sketch of King. "Our Weapon Is Love," by William Peters, was a five-page piece with pictures. It described King as a "new and striking kind of Negro leader," who had "injected a new element into the Negro's struggle for equality—passive resistance." It was a quiet and thoughtful piece.

On August 11, King was in Chicago, appearing before the platform and resolutions committee of the National Democratic Convention. He urged "strong federal action" on civil rights, "one of the supreme moral issues of our time."

The next month, King was back in California, this time in Los Angeles, as guest speaker for the fifty-seventh annual convention of the Improved Benevolent and Protective Order of Elks of the World, where he also received their Lovejoy award. The Pittsburgh *Courier* of September 9 ran a photograph of King and Elk officials in an open automobile during the parade.

Horace R. Clayton, co-author with St. Clair Drake of *Black Metropolis,* writing in the Pittsburgh *Courier* of September 22, said that "Montgomery has become a symbol, a *cause célèbre;* a defiant act on the part of Negroes as a community which gained such worldwide publicity that it does and will stand as a landmark in the fight of Negroes (and some decent whites) for the principle of human decency."

On November 4, King preached a sermon in which he envisioned the Apostle Paul, famous for his letters to various missionary Christian groups, writing to American Christians, calling upon them to renounce segregation, praising the Supreme Court, criticizing organized religion and recommending love as the greatest virtue.

Victory with Humility

On November 14, 1956, newspaper headlines screamed, "Supreme Court Outlaws Bus Segregation." As was virtually inevitable the court had rejected the appeal of Montgomery city and Alabama state officials from the lower federal court order to desegregate the buses. The decision came while a local court was moving to break up the voluntary motor pool of the Negro community. Negroes and their friends in Montgomery and elsewhere were jubilant at the news from Washington. King described it as "a glorious daybreak to end a long night of enforced segregation."

The MIA board went into emergency session. It recommended that the boycott come to a close as soon as the court's mandate reached the city and the specific orders of injunction were delivered to the city and bus officials who were named in the original suit of February 1.

With a sense of history, the MIA convened the mass meeting to end the boycott at the Holt Street Baptist Church, where the first mass meeting at the beginning of the boycott was held December 5, 1955. The overflow crowd went to the Hutchinson Street Baptist Church, where the program was repeated.

Amid tumultuous rejoicing, the crowded churches voted approval of the MIA recommendation. The boycott was over. But at this very moment King came forward and warned his followers: "We must not take this as a victory over the white man. . . . Don't push people around. . . . If somebody pushes you, don't push back." His words on this occasion were quoted all over the nation. This was indeed the essence of moderation, asking his people not to shout "victory" even when they had earned it so well.

There were, of course, some delays and a few more maneuvers.

It was actually December 20, 1956, before the court orders were delivered and at that time technically went into force. Accordingly, King issued a formal statement, which said in part:

> Now our faith seems to be vindicated. This morning the long awaited mandate from the United States Supreme Court concerning bus segregation came to Montgomery. This mandate expresses in terms that are crystal clear that segregation in public transportation is both legally and sociologically invalid. In the light of this mandate and the unanimous vote rendered by the Montgomery Improvement Association about a month ago, the year-old protest against city buses is officially called off, and the Negro citizens of Montgomery are urged to return to the buses tomorrow morning on a non-segregated basis.
>
> I cannot close without giving just a word of caution. Our experience and growth during this past year of united non-violent protest has been of such that we cannot be satisfied with a court "victory" over our white brothers. We must respond to the decision with an understanding of those who have oppressed us and with an appreciation of the new adjustments that the court order poses for them. We must be able to face up honestly to our own shortcomings. We must act in such a way as to make possible a coming together of white people and colored people on the basis of a real harmony of interests and understanding. We seek an integration based on mutual respect.

On December 21, 1956, integrated buses rolled down the streets of Montgomery for the first time. King and other MIA leaders rode the buses, sitting up front. They were joined by a few whites, some of whom were visitors, like the Rev. Glenn E. Smiley, Fellowship of Reconciliation leader.

Civil rights had won. Integration was a fact. Every paper would quote King; every network would interview him. He was the man of the hour. He and the boycott had entered into history.

Fait Accompli

King was by this time a public figure. He had become a part of the general cultural environment. He was now known in the way that congressmen, cabinet members, governors and mayors, big-time athletes, movie actors and other entertainers are known. His picture was familiar. His opinions were sought.

The columnists began to run items on him. Thomas L. Stokes, Georgia-born but New Dealish columnist with a wide national following, made a graceful bow for the Christmas season. He wrote of the "Chivalry of Meekness" and among those he cited were "the Negroes of Montgomery, Alabama and their leaders, including the

Rev. Martin Luther King." Ecstatically, the urbane *Afro* described
King's visit to the nation's capital as "the Rev. Mr. King comes to
Washington [and] the people embraced him . . . and got a fresh
glimpse of the true ideal embodied in the American Dream."

The Montgomery bus boycott was ranked as one of the top stories
of the year—and everybody knew who the boycott leader was.

Time for January 7, 1957, printed (with photographs) its list
of "Stars in Their Own Orbits": Poland's Cardinal Wyszynski for
resisting political domination; Elvis Presley, "rock and roll artist";
Françoise Sagan, French novelist; and "Martin Luther King [who],
in year of integration progress in the South, led non-violent 381-day
boycott that ended segregation on buses in Montgomery, Alabama."

In December, 1956, Dr. George Gallup had his Institute of
Public Opinion make its yearly survey to determine "the most
admired men in the world today." President Eisenhower came out
as the number one choice. King did not place in the first ten but
did lead the list of "also rans" in the field of religion. In this category,
however, he ranked above such well-known personalities as Josef
Cardinal Mindszenty and Dr. Norman Vincent Peale. A year later,
King held still the same rank in the annual Gallup poll. Apparently, he
was firmly established.

Sinking In

There were several developments after the curtain rang down on
the boycott and during 1957 that served to drive the image of Martin
Luther King deeper into the consciousness of the American people.
These were penetrations that went beyond the spot news reporting of
whatever King was doing and saying. For example, less than two
weeks after the boycott was over, the MIA held what it called an
Institute on Non-violence and Social Change. It was a week-long
round of mass meetings, dinners and seminars and was planned
long before the date of the desegregation of the buses was anticipated.
It was meant to mark the anniversary of the arrest and jailing of
Mrs. Parks and the launching of the Montgomery movement.

All the sessions of the institute were interesting and well attended,
but it was the seminars and luncheons that gave an intellectual quality
to the conference. The necessary concentration on day-to-day action
during the boycott year had left little time for meditation and evaluation. Now it was possible to take a calm backward glance. This was
the feature that attracted the *Nation* magazine and other so-called
"egghead" publications.

At the luncheons an effort was made to place the boycott in its historical relation to the transition taking place in the South from a segregated to a racially integrated society. The rich lore of the boycott —especially the conversational exchanges between Negro domestic servants and their white "mistresses"—was given sociological interpretation by Dr. Preston Valien of Fisk University. The Rev. Glenn E. Smiley ran the seminars, giving through them a brief history of nonviolent resistance, a statement of its philosophy and a rather frank debate on its limitations.

Lillian Smith, author and a truly liberal white Southerner, though ill, sent along a thoughtful message. Dr. Homer Jack, another American exponent of Gandhianism, came and re-emphasized what had been argued at the seminars. The symposium of leaders from Baton Rouge, Tallahassee and Birmingham—places where there had been boycotts or where such struggles were then going on—was disappointing from the intellectual point of view. Rather than presenting reports on the experiences of these communities and an exchange of views, this session turned out to be an oratorical contest in which the panelists all preached emotion-packed sermons.

King himself prepared a twenty-page speech for the opening mass meeting. This was much too long and perhaps too ambitious. But it did suggest the serious effort that was being made in general to come to grips with some of the major problems of the philosophy and strategy that Montgomery had made famous.

The conference was well reported, locally and nationally. From it "the Montgomery way" emerged as an influence that was here to stay.

King was the subject of the cover story in *Time,* February 18, 1957. Lee Griggs from the magazine's Atlanta office was sent in to do the write-up. Soon after he arrived he received the inevitable anonymous telephone threat, the caller warning that "We know why you're in town and what you're planning to do, and you'd better not do it." Griggs answered back that he, too, knew why he was in Montgomery—"to attend to my own business" and hung up.

Perhaps that would-be bogeyman gave Griggs just the stimulus he needed, for he turned out a superb piece of interpretative journalism. "The Attack on Conscience" was the apt caption given the four pages of text and pictures. The cover photograph-portrait by Boris Chaliapin showed King more austere than usual—lips pressed, eyes right, head back, straight up and formidable as a rock.

Everybody liked the *Time* story, with a few exceptions. E. D. Nixon did not because his home had been left off the map which showed the Montgomery bombings. Mrs. Jo Ann Robinson felt that

the information on MIA finances was a violation of confidence on
somebody's part. The editor of the local morning paper called the
piece "incompetent, faithless reporting" but he let Griggs off scot-
free, putting the blame on "the *Time* rewrite men in New York." At
any rate, millions of readers got their chance to judge for themselves.

On April 8, 1957, Ted Poston began a biographical series on
King in the New York *Post*. Previously he had done a series on the
people of Montgomery. Now he was doing their leader, playing down
his early nonviolent tendencies, calling him "Fighting Pastor." His
was the most detailed sketch of King to date. It was done in quick,
brash strokes calculated to keep the tabloid readers awake on their
afternoon subway rides from the office. Through Poston, New Yorkers
came to feel that they really knew King. The *Afro* reprinted the whole
six instalments, thus reaching a nation-wide Negro audience.

Additional touches were added to the *Time* and *Post* portraitures
by a Japanese editor and an American who had spent some time in
Southeast Asia.

Editor A. Nakamura of the *Asahi Shinbun,* one of Japan's largest
dailies, was asked by his government to do a series on life in America.
One of the picture stories was Montgomery. It was a two-thirds-page
spread, mostly of photographs. Of particular interest was the shot
of King speaking. It was most alive, catching the animation of his
face and the expressiveness of his hands. Also there were views of
Negro high school students at graduation, the state capitol, downtown
Montgomery, an empty boycotted bus, and a segregated bus shelter
at Court Square with Negro bus customers bunched together on the
left, white customers on the right. Finally, there was an inside shot,
taken from the living room of the Ballou family, the home of King's
secretary. In the foreground, the children, dressed in their nighties,
were at play, while in the background, sitting on the divan, Mr. and
Mrs. Ballou beamed.

When Harvard-trained Ernest L. Zaugg reached Montgomery he
seemed not to be in any hurry—as were most of the other journalists.
He loafed about Montgomery for about two weeks and then did
two remarkably perceptive pieces for the Boston *Globe*. He concluded: "I have seen many mass movements, but nothing like this.
It is one of laughter and song."

George Barrett also had a point to make. He had come down to
Montgomery for the Sunday New York *Times* Magazine during the
boycott. He came back after it was over and did an "end-of-war"
piece for March 3, 1957. A year later Abel Plenn would come back
and once more resurvey the old battleground. These evaluations were

all favorable, indicating that even after the excitement of battle had passed away there was a permanent advance. Montgomery would never be the same. The new-born spirit would march on like "John Brown's body." In Barrett's article King's name was mentioned twenty-six times.

Martin Luther King and the Montgomery story were also getting into the books. Carl T. Rowan in his *Go South to Sorrow,* published in 1957, devoted one of his eleven chapters to King and the MIA, "The Cradle (of the Confederacy) Rocks." Langston Hughes and Milton Meltzer in their *Pictorial History of the Negro in America,* 1956, had a full-length picture of King and Abernathy and a short description of what happened in Montgomery.

Charles "Spinkey" Alston, prize-winning Negro artist of New York City, did "Walking" in oil. Though it was inspired by Montgomery it appeared to be closer to the Mexican motif, stylistically speaking. Much more related and also highly suggestive was "Bus Stop" by Ulrich McMillan, a Negro painter and soldier who saw and felt what went on while he was stationed at Maxwell Air Base, just outside Montgomery. Also impressive was the color print "Walking with God" by Mrs. Lila Ulrich Kopperman. There was much verse and a batch of songs, two or three of which were first-rate. But these were about the movement rather than King. But he did get into the comic books. The Fellowship of Reconciliation put out *Martin Luther King and the Montgomery Story,* sixteen pages for ten cents. Elsewhere several student groups dramatized his life.

During April and May, 1957, Alfred Duckett ran a series of second-thought articles on King in the weekly Chicago *Defender.* He raised the question: Is the Rev. Mr. King a marked man? Duckett's answer was "The most ardent segregationists realize that martyrdom of a man of King's stature would create such a crisis that Federal justice and Federal troops would have to be brought in. . . . [However] sometimes hate-filled, trigger-tense shadow men sulk along the lunatic fringes. It was thus that Lincoln was killed by John Wilkes Booth."

In Recognition of . .

During 1956 and 1957, while newspaper presses were grinding away, Martin Luther King was the recipient of what appeared to be an unending stream of awards. They came in so fast, piling up in the MIA office and the den at home, that Mrs. King decided to collect and arrange them artistically on the walls of the parsonage hall. It was a capital idea, for these walls had been bare and there was ample space to give the plaques and scrolls an interesting design.

Some of the honors were apparently little more than a bid of a local organization for a paragraph in the daily paper; others, however, were substantial and indicated further the impact of King upon the public mind.

As of the end of 1957 some forty-five different items had found a space for themselves on Mrs. King's wall of fame for her husband. Typical were the certificates, framed or unframed, and the familiar heart-shaped brassy metal plaque mounted on wood. More noteworthy were the gold Spingarn Medal awarded by the NAACP, the blue and white Cross of Malta presented by the Philadelphia Cotillion Society, and the elaborately embellished trophy from the Dorie Miller Foundation with its inscription: "Awarded to Dr. Martin Luther King, Jr. A Stout Heart and Dedicated Life to the Abolishment of Poverty, Ignorance and Intolerance and Establishment Among Us of the True Principles of Human Brotherhood. Chicago—1956."

The awards came from an astonishingly wide variety of donors. Montgomery and King touched a great many different types of people and institutions—Greek letter and mass fraternal orders, churches and religious organizations, institutions of higher education, beauty culturists and policemen.

The citations, too, were often revealing:

In recognition of distinguished Christian leadership . . . for giving the world a living demonstration of aggressive Christian social action characterized by spiritual discipline.—National Fraternal Council of Churches.

The momentous struggle of the people of Montgomery, Alabama, will record him as an uncompromising champion of enduring principles certain to be vindicated in the future order of mankind.—Unitarian Fellowship for Social Justice.

. . . expanding the area of freedom, enriching the community life and stimulating a new sense of individual dignity.—Emancipation Association of Birmingham, Alabama.

. . . courageous fighter for equal civil rights, contender for justice for all people . . . eloquent pulpit orator, scholar, student, builder, gentleman, distinguished American citizen.—National Beauty Culturists League.

. . . distinguished minister, leader and humanitarian . . . pioneering courage and unselfish devotion . . . a source of inspiration to those who believe in equal rights for all men.—Guardians Association of the Police Department, New York City.

His great gifts of heart and mind. . . . He has colored the thinking of our epoch.—Utility Club, New York City.

. . . fearless foe of injustice and inhumanity . . . foremost in fighting for the rights of Negroes. . . . Without violence and without virulence . . . awakening the conscience of the nation to the true meaning of human rights expressed in our Constitution.—Charles Evans Hughes High School, New York City.

. . . brilliance and patience of the prophets of yesterday, shepherd of a flock which cries out for leadership . . . dedicated to the principles of equality for all men.—Brandeis University Alumni Association, Boston.

. . . for distinguished services to the principles of American Democracy.— Founders and Friends of Roosevelt University, Chicago.

. . . you united the non-violent passive resistance of Gandhism with the spiritual power of Christianity . . . you have embodied the spirit of the new Negro.—Alumni, Fisk University.

Some of the above awards were sent to King but for most of them he appeared personally and made a speech. In a few cases a cash purse accompanied the plaque or scroll.

In Coretta King's display, honorary degrees also occupy prominent positions. At the 1957 commencement season King received three honorary degrees from American institutions of higher learning. In June both Morehouse College and Howard University awarded him the degree of Doctor of Laws, and Chicago Theological Seminary made him a Doctor of Divinity.

The citation of the Chicago institution, member of the Federation of Theological Schools at the University of Chicago, speaks of King as an "unembittered prophet in a major American campaign in the non-violent Christian war for equality and justice and fair play."

At Howard, the President, Mordecai W. Johnson, who had inspired King's interest in Gandhi, said in part:

You have led your people on a victorious pathway seldom traveled in human life. You have shown them how to mobilize the fullest powers of their souls for effective resistance to evil, and how to overcome humiliation and abuse without violence and without hatred in deed or in words. . . . You are a blessing to the Negro people and to your nation. . . . The example of your leadership has given hope to those who suffer from oppression all over the former slave states and those who suffer from humiliation all over the world.

The Morehouse occasion was packed with emotion. Not only was it the return of a "son" to his alma mater but the whole King clan

was represented—father and mother, wife, brother and sister—and a
host of life-long friends and teachers. President Mays could not
avoid giving a personal touch to the ceremony, and he spoke with
great feeling:

You are mature beyond your years, wiser at twenty-eight than most
men at sixty; more courageous in a righteous struggle than most men can
ever be; living a faith that most men preach about and never experience.
Significant, indeed, is the fact that you did not seek the leadership in the
Montgomery controversy. It was thrust upon you by the people. You did
not betray that trust of leadership. You led the people with quiet dignity,
Christian grace, and determined purpose. While you were away, your
colleagues in the battle for freedom were being hounded and arrested like
criminals. When it was suggested by legal counsel that you might stay
away and escape arrest, I heard you say with my own ears: "I would
rather spend ten years in jail than desert the people in this crisis." At
that moment, my heart, my mind, and my soul stood up erect and saluted
you. I knew then that you were called to leadership for just such a time
as this. . . . On this our 90th anniversary, your alma mater is happy to
be the first college or university to honor you this way.

A Man Called Hall

But this acclaim was not shared by everyone. From the very beginning King had received some unfavorable criticism. There were,
naturally, the skeptics and the reasonable dissenters. The attacks,
however, unlike the broadly-based praise, usually came from one
specific source: the active opposition. The legitimate Montgomery
dailies led the assault for the pro-segregation forces. But the "ille-
gitimate" fly-by-night-pamphlet and unsigned-handbill crowd crudely
followed the leads of their journalistic betters.

Actually, the Montgomery papers were valuable sources of information on the MIA, King and the boycott, and more day-to-day
detail could be found in these local publications than elsewhere. If
a reader could pick his way through the "angles" and "slants" of the
news stories, he could pretty well keep abreast of developments. So
much for news.

In opinion, the two local dailies, though jointly owned, were as
different as night and day. The editorial page of the afternoon *Alabama Journal* was typical of the average Southern paper that opposed
racial integration. Every twenty-four hours it would grind out a sort
of rock-and-roll refrain that "race mixing" threatened "the Southern
way of life" and must be stopped at all costs. Any reader who looked
at the editorials and local columnists for a week or so could afterward
predict what would be said on the race question without reading

beyond the first sentence of any new editorial or column. During the entire boycott year the paper published not even one letter that favored desegregation.

The morning paper—the *Advertiser*—was different. It favored segregation, of course, but did so interestingly. Its letters to the editor, printed under the caption "Tell It to Grandma," showed some variety of viewpoint; its columnists—except for the local judge who did a Monday-morning comment—were not absolutely predictable; and its editorials were well written, often oblique and almost never crude. Even the old judge was amusing in his unintended humor. He was a rare survivor of that almost extinct species of the 100 per cent tribal patriot. "I stand for the white race," he wrote and seemed altogether happy about it.

Intellectually, the editorial page of the *Advertiser* thus was worth reading. And since both papers—morning and afternoon—were the property of the same publisher, the main difference between them seems to have been the *Advertiser*'s editor, Grover Cleveland Hall, Jr.

Grover Hall was dapper, handsome and articulate when he wanted to be. He was a bit below average height, had brownish hair, a rather boyish face, large ears and nose and a well-shaped head on a good pair of shoulders. His build suggested tennis or swimming rather than the more muscular sports. His clothes revealed an almost exquisite sense of colors and fabrics. He liked mynah birds, camellias and a handkerchief in his upper coat pocket or a flower for his lapel. When preoccupied, Hall could walk through his entire office without a word to anyone. And yet he was, socially, a popular bachelor.

A local boy, he literally grew up in the *Advertiser* office. His father had been editor before him. Young Hall went as far as high school but never bothered about college. He had served in World War II but otherwise stuck close to his ink and newsprint. Even his war record was made at the typewriter. He produced the unit chronicle: *1000 Destroyed: Life and Times of the 4th Fighter Group.*

Grover Hall was widely read and a great admirer of H. L. Mencken. His prose style was deft and flexible and, when in the mood for it, he could give to any subject the light but deadly touch of a Bengal Lancer.

It was unlikely that the rising star of Martin Luther King would pass unnoticed by the *Advertiser*'s editorial page. King had become the best-known man in Montgomery and at the rate of his acceleration would soon put even Jefferson Davis into eclipse.

Until King and the boycott came along, Grover Hall had been looked upon as a liberal of sorts; at least, as an enlightened man with-

out an obvious reactionary tendency. Yet, if there was an issue between black and white and everybody was choosing sides, Grover
Hall, too, could not but choose.

At first this was not necessarily a drastic choice. Many persons felt
that had the *Advertiser* come out clearly for a settlement during the
days when the boycotters were talking about "first come, first served"
seating, a settlement would have been reached.

This cue was missed, perhaps mainly because of the assumption—
almost universal—that the Negro movement would collapse of its
own weight in a short time or that a show of force by the white
opposition would restore "sanity" to the colored folk. Grover Hall
himself had written that the whites were destined to run things and
control things "as far as the eye could see."

But as the boycott continued and the pressure became greater, Hall
saw himself pushed into the position of supporting the backward-
looking side, of destroying his own reputation as a civilized man of the
world. Now he was bracketed with the crass racists whom he dis-
dained.

Hall would defend segregation reasonably but his co-defenders—
mobs, klansmen and rough politicians—would not follow his lead.
They had no time for elegance. They tried to kill Miss Autherine
Lucy on the campus of the University of Alabama; they assaulted
Nat "King" Cole, even as he sang to an all-white audience. Later they
would mutilate the sex organs of a stray Negro pedestrian. Hall would
rail at these direct actionists as "jug-heads," "lunatics" and "criminal
idiots" but they, too, felt that they were defenders of the Southern
way of life.

Despite his best-worded editorials, Hall found himself boxed in
with the white patriots. He could not afford to favor the boycotters
after February 1 when they had become integrationists. In *U. S. News
and World Report* for August 3, 1956, Hall confessed that he was
no longer a liberal. As evidence of his Southern patriotism, he developed the tactic of making rear-guard forays editorially and hit upon
a brilliant counterthrust: the Askelon series. Taking the Biblical
line, "Tell it not in Gath, publish it not in the streets of Askelon,"
Hall collected and printed the most sensational stories he could lay
hands on of race discrimination in the North. He sent clippings of
these articles and his accompanying comments to the Northern papers.

To some extent he gave the Northern press pause. He twitted the
Yankees on their hypocrisy and their looking for Southern motes
while forgetting their own beams. But almost every time Hall felt
that he had scored a victory, along came some wild act by some
Southerner or band of Southerners that outraged everyone. The con-

clusion was unavoidable that, though the North was far from perfect, the big clean-up job on race relations had to be done in the South. This realization was disconcerting. After the effort to abduct Nat "King" Cole had shocked the nation, Hall did an editorial entitled, "It Makes Us Flinch." In it he said:

Affiliation with any section, group or organization generally involves contact with undesirable bedfellows. But offhand we can think of none so utterly odious, so abjectly stupid, so hell-bent on bringing disrepute upon the "cause" they are allegedly championing, as a certain type of Southern patriot.

It is no wonder that respectable Southerners, fighting for the legitimate rights of the South, should sometimes almost feel like chucking it all and letting the Yankees and the NAACP work their will.

Hall was similarly dismayed when churches and homes were bombed a few weeks after the Montgomery buses had been integrated. In his anger he perhaps overlooked a point made from time to time by his editorial contemporary, Ralph McGill of the Atlanta *Constitution,* who pointed out:

But let us not overlook the fact these bombings are the fruit of the tree of defiance of law and of orderly process. In all cities [where bombings had occurred] there had been leaders in the press, and in public life who had attacked the Supreme Court, the President of the United States, and the U.S. Attorney General in the most reckless and abusive terms. That this inspired the criminal fringe to action cannot be denied.

"Saint Martin"

Meanwhile Martin Luther King was leading his cohorts to victory after victory, and the world seemed to be joining in support and adoration of him. Hall, in commenting upon the boycott, had taken several thrusts at King from time to time, but on February 10, 1957, he fell upon him personally. The editorial was entitled, "Dr. King Enters Hagiology of Methodist Church." It began, "A Baptist, the Rev. Dr. Martin Luther King, has attained sainthood in a Methodist publication." Hall identified the publication, *Adult Student,* then added:

The hagiographer (one who writes of the lives of saints) who calls Dr. King "saint" is a professor of Christian doctrine at Candler School of Theology, Emory University—Claude Thompson.

In a Sunday School lesson guide, Professor Thompson writes:

". . . The Kingdom was set into history with a cross. It will not be extended without pain. . . . This is not reserved for exceptional saints like . . . Martin Luther King. . . . It must come home to every Sunday school student and teacher."

The editorial then went on for another half column with sallies against the "Eliza-on-the-ice newspapers of the North," "northern zealots" and Negro leadership.

The assault upon King was built upon two items.

1. The *Advertiser* did not usually report the Sunday-morning sermons of the Rev. Dr. King, but on Monday, January 28, 1957, it carried such a report of the previous day's services. The first few paragraphs of the account read as follows:

The Rev. Martin Luther King, Jr. told his congregation yesterday that he had a vision early one morning a year ago telling him to lead the Montgomery Negro Movement against segregation without fear.

After describing the vision to his almost-filled church a few hours after a dynamite bundle failed to explode on his porch when his family was not at home, King said in prayer:

"I realize that there were moments when I wanted to give up (leadership of the pro-integration movement) and I was afraid, but you gave me a vision in the kitchen of my house and I am thankful for it."

Early on a sleepless morning in January, 1956, King said, "rationality left me. Then, almost out of nowhere I heard a voice that morning saying to me:

" 'Preach the Gospel, stand up for the truth, stand up for righteousness.' "

King went on, "Since that morning I can stand up without fear. So I'm not afraid of anybody this morning."

This was the "vision in the kitchen" that Hall and others would refer to frequently. Actually, the Rev. Dr. King had explained his apparition not as a mystical experience of supernatural sights and sounds, but rather as a psychological release of the subconscious or unconscious mind. But who could resist the play on words of such a phrase as "vision in the kitchen"?

Three days after this item appeared, an *Advertiser* reader wrote in to say that "The voice Reverend King heard in his kitchen could have been the voice of the devil" and then went on to attack King, contrasting him with Booker T. Washington and George W. Carver, who were "too busy" to want integration.

This view was promptly challenged by another reader who favored integration and was sure that it was not the devil but the God-head that had spoken to King. "Were it not true, violence would have taken place months ago."

2. The editorial also gave the impression that Professor Thomp-

son in his article had devoted special attention to King. But examination of the publication itself reveals quite the opposite. The *Adult Student* is a little monthly magazine designed to help Sunday-school teachers and others with their weekly lessons. Professor Thompson was a regular writer for it, making suggestions on understanding and applying the Scriptures. At the beginning of one of his articles entitled "Facing the Question," he wrote: "Our question today is: What is meant by the kingdom of heaven? What does it require of me in personal living and social action?" At the conclusion of the three-page piece, Thompson had these two paragraphs:

But it is not victory without sacrifice. The Kingdom was set into history with a cross. It will not be extended without pain. The struggle being what it is, no suffering is too great for those who devotedly accept the way of Christ.

This is not reserved for exceptional saints like Toyohiko Kagawa, Olin Stockwell, Martin Luther King, Bishop Wang, or Martin Niemoller. It must come home to every Sunday-school student and teacher. *The way of peace and pardon is the way of pain.* The Kingdom comes with great tribulation.

This was the only reference whatsoever to Martin Luther King. His name was brought up this once and then in the context of four other well-known personalities. Grover Hall's tremendous reaction, therefore, was completely out of proportion to the original record.

Soon after Hall's editorial, the letters began coming in to "Tell It to Grandma." A clergyman who had been quite active in defense of segregation wrote, "Your very thoughtful editorial . . . that a Methodist publication . . . printed a recent article setting forth the incredible idea that the leader of the Montgomery bus boycott, the Rev. Martin Luther King is an 'exceptional saint,' will provoke wide concern in Methodist circles."

Then two paragraphs further on, he added: "It is difficult to associate the grotesque and irresponsible statement by the author of the *Adult Student* article, Dr. Claude Thompson, with the institution in which he holds a professorship."

The clergyman who wrote these words must have known better. He was the pastor of a large Methodist church and as such received the *Adult Student* regularly. He had only to take a look at Thompson's article to see what it really said.

Another Methodist minister, from a small town, though himself a segregationist, thought that Hall's editorial was misleading. He felt that "many people mistook this statement to mean that the Methodist Church had canonized Dr. King and thus made him a saint.

This, of course, is not true. The truth of the matter is that the Methodist Church does not make anyone saints."

Other letters came in attacking Thompson, church literature, Methodist discipline, King, the boycott and integration in general.

And then a tiny church in Selma, Alabama, made front-page news. It passed a resolution that it would withhold funds from Emory University because of the "characterization of sainthood to the Rev. Martin Luther King." Emory's dean of theology was called upon to make certain that "there will be no repetition" of articles like that of Dr. Thompson's. The news story concluded with a revealing sentence: "The Selma Church, which allocates a small portion of its budget to Emory, did not announce the amount that is being withheld."

Of course Emory University, with an endowment of millions and the backing of Coca-Cola and other big foundations, would not be so small as to make a public reply to this little church whose leaders, no doubt, were sincerely trying to do their bit to defend "the Southern way of life."

Professor Thompson withheld his fire during more than a month of distortion and abuse. He wrote privately to a friend:

> You will note that this reference to Dr. King is almost incidental to what I was saying. It was never intended to be a controversial item. However I am willing to defend the statement, particularly since it seemed necessary to do so now, for I am quite convinced that the conduct of Dr. King is far more saintly than that of his critics. This leads me to the conclusion that the people who objected to this incidental reference are looking for trouble rather than for the truth.

Then on March 26 Thompson's public reply appeared in the "Grandma" column. He wrote:

EDITOR, THE ADVERTISER—A recent editorial has taken me to task for my reference to Dr. Martin Luther King as "an exceptional saint." The editor supports his criticisms by reference to Webster's definition of sainthood.

But the church looks at sainthood a little differently than does the famous lexicographer. The Roman Catholic Church, for example, requires two things in a saint: (1) that he have been dead for an appropriate number of years, and (2) that he shall have performed some attestable miracle.

As for Dr. King, he is not dead; though doubtless some of his enemies wish he were. So on this score he cannot qualify.

But as for the other test, he has performed one of the most notable miracles in America. In the midst of a dangerously explosive situation, at grave danger to himself and his family, he guided the Negroes of Montgomery in the achievement of their legal rights as citizens of a democracy.

And he did it without violence on the part of the Negroes. Furthermore, and even more remarkable, he has refused to hate or fight back at people who have threatened him, ridiculed him, sought to bribe him, and even have set off bombs at his house.

I submit: this is a miracle of the first order.

Any other candidates care to compete with the Rev. Martin Luther King for the saintly crown in Montgomery? In my way of thinking this is amazingly similar to the way in which Jesus of Nazareth faced the enemies of His day. This is sainthood in man's church.

CLAUDE H. THOMPSON

This salvo, of course, did not end the battle. One reader characterized Thompson's reply as "pious egotism"; another labeled it "asinine" and nominated Thompson "as a candidate for the No. 1 jackass of the United States."

Neither drew from Grover Hall any explanation or apology. He held to his point. It was taken up by others and repeated far and wide, perhaps in some circles that offended Hall's sensibilities. For example, the *Alabama Labor News*—a segregationist sheet that fought national labor leaders who favored a racially integrated labor movement—in its issue of July 30, 1957, printed a cartoon of a dancing chimpanzee, waving his long hairy arms above his head. On his breast were the words: "St. King" and above the picture: "I used the church to make a Revolution and they made me a 'Saint.' "

Grover Hall himself once said in a public speech that "a newspaper has a great potential for both mischief and beneficence"; and can be "a bully, a knave, or a clod."

Lower Depths

The *Alabama Labor News* was not the only publication of its type to attack King and the other boycott leaders. The *Monthly Bulletin* of the Montgomery County Citizens Council for May 28, 1956, slammed into the advertising of King, along with Autherine Lucy, Dr. Howard and Gus Courts, as heroes of the South. The *States' Rights Advocate* of the Montgomery County Citizens Council for July 28, 1956, ran as its first-page headline: "Supreme Court Creates Racial Hate Over U.S." On page two, in a short article, "Brain-Washed with Trouble," Mrs. Rosa Parks was quoted as saying: "Support the NAACP, live up to the ideals of Mary McLeod Bethune, stick close to Christianity, don't give up faith, and one day we will have the democracy we are all hoping for." Then the editor asked: "Will we still have a free republic?"

In a front-page story for December 25, the *Advocate* gave its interpretation of bus desegregation:

Whatever the end result will be no one knows. We do know that Rev. King is one of the tools of the NAACP efforts behind the change and that only a minority of the negroes [sic] in Montgomery have followed his lead. The rest have either stayed off buses because of fear, or because they did not want to be a part of any trouble which may have been caused by their riding buses.

But bus desegregation is not the answer to NAACP's wishes. It is only the first step. King himself has said that their next actions would be white restaurants and theaters.

On February 7, 1957, the *Advocate* turned its fire more directly on King. In a single-column lead on page one it asked: "M. L. King, Leader or Destroyer of His People?" The first paragraph gave the answer:

The sudden affluence of Martin Luther King and the national publicity he has received through his efforts in the MIA and the NAACP has caused him to spread his wings and fly to other sections of the South to stir up racial unrest and agitate white people.

It was a long article which said further along:

King has advanced so far in the ranks of the communistic front organizations that he is now, or rather considers himself an authority on how to instruct negroes [sic] to break the laws of their states and escape scott free through the backing of the NAACP or that organization's splinter groups. . . .

It concluded with a quip:

When the time comes for King to settle down to a routine life as a preacher of the gospel . . . and when and if his flocks demand that he stick to preaching the gospel according to the Bible he hides behind, he will surely find it a monotonous chore . . . for how're you going to keep 'em down on the farm after they've seen Broadway?

Even so, the publications of the WCC never reached the bluntness of the regular, "legitimate" afternoon daily. The *Alabama Journal* for April 26, 1957, in an editorial, "A Visitor from Helsinki," indicated that a Finnish caller asked the editor how he might get in touch with the Rev. Dr. King. In reply "he was assured that he was in the wrong place to keep up with the movements of any fakir, mountebank and self-exploiter."

In connection with this statement some of the more sensitive and "decent" white people expressed embarrassment by what they labeled as "crude."

Even more extreme were the four unsigned handbills that were circulated against the boycott leaders.

Batches of the first one were scattered about late Tuesday night,

December 18, 1956, and early before daylight the next morning. The throwaway was 5¼ × 8¼ inches in size:

Are You Tired of Walking?

SURE YOU ARE . . . BUT WE WALK WHILE OUR LEADERS RIDE . . . IN BIG CARS TOO!

W H Y ?

Because They're Playing Us For Suckers While They Get Rich On Our Money!

NO WONDER THEY WANT TO KEEP THE BOYCOTT GOING . . . NO WONDER THEY DON'T TELL US THERE ISN'T A CHANCE IN THE WORLD OF BREAKING SEGREGATION IN MONTGOMERY

W A K E   U P — G E T   S M A R T

We'll Be Walking To Work Till Judgement Day If They Have Their Way · · · We'll Be Losing What Friendship We Have Left And Making Our Situation Worse Instead Of Better If They Have Their Way . . . We'll Be The Joke Of The Whole Country . . . Walking While Our Leaders Ride In Big Cars . . . Walking While Our Leaders Get Rich On Our Money!

DON'T SWALLOW THEIR MESS ANYMORE!

Don't Be A Fool — It's Our Money & Our Feet!

The second handbill came out about a week later, was the same size, had a shorter message but in larger type:

We been doing O.K. in Montgomery before outside preachers were born!

Ask rev. King's pappa & mamma if they like his doings -- ask him if they going to help in Atlanta.

Better quit him before it is too late!

A third appeared Thursday night January 3, 1957, with a similar message:

LOOK OUT!

Liver Lip Luther

Getting Us In More Trouble
Every Day

FUNNY BULLETS

ON

FUNNY TERMS

FROM

FUNNY PLACES

We Get Shot At While
He Hides

Wake Up! Mess Is His Business
Run Him Out Of Town!

The fourth leaflet, 4¾ × 8, was on Attorney Fred D. Gray. It appeared the night of February 7.

DRAFT DODGER
NAACP TROUBLEMAKER

This is the disgrace to our people. Such a person in the white race is an outcast, as you well know. Many complaints are now being heard, we are losing jobs, relief is limited.

The White man celebrates July 4th as Independence Day. Some Negroes have been discharged for minor offenses and Whites hired. By July 4th we are told there will be no jobs left for Negroes.

Many believe it's a Communist inspired plot being led by King, Abernathy, Graetz, Nixon and Gray. They ride high, eat good, stay warm and pilfer the funds. We walk and suffer in many ways.

Let's run these five out of the state before we all have to leave.

These handbills all purported to be speaking for Negroes. Nobody could be found in the Negro community who believed that. If the purpose of the distribution of such "literature" was to divide Negroes, the failure was complete. Actually, it stimulated a reaffirmation of faith and fired the mass meetings once again to rise up to new moments of reality.

Thus, Martin Luther King was a fact, vivid and arresting, even to many who had never seen him in the flesh. In this sense, he was a creature of mass communication. In every sense, he was a living force, a tantalizing, "upsetting" personality that stirred the emotions as a harbinger of good or evil. He had entered deeply into the consciousness of men—those who loved him and those who, as one man put it, "hated his guts."

XI - *Pilgrimage*

AND while the image of Martin Luther King was whirling about the earth—wondrously or monstrously, according to the view of the observers—he still had a life to live that was somewhat apart from the headlines. He was, after all, a human being, an individual, a person, a father, a son, with all of the needs and desires of a man seeking to fulfill his obligations to his family and to himself.

The long, hard campaign had had its effects on the home folks in Atlanta and Marion. King's father had been involved from the very first. He was all heart and motion. Anything that concerned his son concerned him. He could not be still. He wanted to do something. He would have gladly faced all danger himself, taking over the battle, protecting Junior. Again it was "O my son Absalom, my son, my son Absalom! would God I had died for thee. . . ."

What could this father do for this son? Martin Luther King, Sr., did not believe in nonviolence. He would listen patiently to what Junior had to say on this subject but his strongest inclination was to meet the enemy on the firing line and have it out with him. Moreover, on the basis of his wider experience, he often advised his son. He was in Montgomery frequently, once bringing over a bag of money to bail his son out of jail during the mass arrests. And since the city authorities seemed unwilling or unable to protect Junior from violence, his father saw the Governor.

When in town, he would sit on the platform at the mass meetings with the other "distinguished guests and visitors." He never declined the courteous invitation "to say a few words."

Martin's mother was less active and vocal than her husband. But she suffered all that any mother would suffer under the shadow of violence that hung over her child. Sister Chris, who was preparing to teach at Spelman, and brother A. D. were with Martin all the way and in every way.

Incidentally, the family had come back together as a whole. Perhaps the larger crisis that embraced Martin had helped A. D. and his father to reconcile their differences. The break had never been complete. A. D. for a long while had been living with his ever-increasing brood in the old family house on Auburn Avenue. Moreover, he had gone back to finish at Morehouse, giving up his job with the Atlanta Life Insurance Company. Unlike Martin, A. D. had always wanted to preach. Instead of taking over a small church of his own, he accepted the assistant pastorate of Ebenezer, for he felt that his father needed him. Everybody was happy for that.

Over in Marion, Coretta's mother and father also felt repercussions of the MIA campaign. When Mr. Scott got the news that a bomb had exploded at the front door of the King home, he drove to Montgomery at midnight intending to bring his daughter and her baby back with him; but Coretta would not leave Martin.

Coretta's mother kept up with what went on by every means possible. She would button-hole anybody from Marion who made a trip over to Montgomery. Occasionally she made visits there herself. She listened to all of the newscasts, read the daily white papers and the weekly Negro papers. Perhaps she was the best-informed person in her area on the boycott.

The Scott neighbors—Negro and white—knew what was going on, too. Colored friends would stop in at the store to talk and offer their assistance. Some of the white customers stopped coming. The Marion chapter of the White Citizens Council identified Obie Scott as the father-in-law of "that agitator, Martin Luther King." The head of the WCC was a son of a man who had a fatal automobile collision with Scott's truck, back in the depression days. These pressures eased off only when the boycott was over.

Coretta herself had stood up well. She admitted that when the threats first began to come over the telephone and in the mail—and then that first bomb—she was frightened and upset. But like a soldier after his first brush with the enemy, she adjusted and came to accept the fact that her home was part of the battlefield. She was sorry that she could not participate more actively in the campaign but realized that she had to take care of a baby less than a month old when the boycott started and, as everyone told her, caring for her husband, keeping him "in shape," was a contribution of the highest order to the cause.

"Frankly, I worry about him," she told a reporter. "He never has a minute to himself. When he isn't in court, he is attending meetings of the Montgomery Improvement Association. When he's home, he's always on the phone. People call him from all over the country. I try to protect him as much as possible so that he can rest, but there is little that I can do."

So much was going on in the King home that it was often difficult to get the baby asleep. Bob Williams was often around as a guard and protector. After the bombing, lights were attached to the outside of the home and were kept on all night. Whenever tensions mounted, veterans and members of the Dexter Avenue Baptist Church unobtrusively kept a nightly vigil near the King home.

Mrs. King saw her husband when he was weary and perplexed by hard decisions. She helped him in every way that she could. One way was not to complain, not to give him a guilt feeling about having so little time for his wife and child.

How did she feel when his voice and face came before her on the TV screen or when she saw the newsmen following him about as though he were the President of the United States? "I would feel proud some, but there was the greater feeling of apprehension, the danger."

The honor, she knew, was great and her own background had emphasized social responsibility, the obligation, as it was often put, "to help others and to make the world a better place in which to live." It was her husband's duty to do what he was doing but, she would add, it was a tremendous responsibility. A mistake could prove fatal to the welfare of the people. And as for the applause, it could go away as quickly as it came. King's mother felt much the same way.

Despite the boycott and the baby, Mrs. King never gave up completely her wish for a part-time singing career, an aspiration in which her husband encouraged her. In their own church, Dexter, a capacity crowd of about five hundred heard her in a recital September 30, 1956. She was described as in "good voice, though a little tight." Less than a month later, she did virtually the same program for the Olivet Baptist Church in Chicago, of which Dr. J. H. Jackson was pastor. About a thousand persons were present and the tightness was now all gone. On November 11, she was in Mobile at the Warren Street Methodist Church.

Her big engagement came in New York on December 5 at the Manhattan Center. This was the anniversary of the beginning of the boycott. "In Friendship," a Northern-based organization to aid "the partisans and victims of the Southern battle for democracy," was sponsoring the musical for the financial benefit of the MIA. Stanley Levittson, Bayard Rustin and Miss Ella J. Baker did much of the promotion. Coretta was advertised as "Mrs. Martin Luther King, Jr." She shared the stage with Harry Belafonte and Duke Ellington.

In all respects—musically, educationally and financially—the concert was a success. Mrs. King sang and then made a little speech she had written on "Why We Walk in Montgomery."

After the Manhattan appearance most of Coretta's programs included a short statement before her last group of songs. Audiences everywhere were hungry for some direct word on developments in the South.

Invitations began to pour in from all parts of the country. Although by that time, Mrs. King was expecting her second child, she was able to make a few other appearances. She sang in Philadelphia, Washington, Gary, Indiana, and Augusta, Georgia. All along she realized that singing for churches and social organizations was not quite the type of career she had envisioned at Antioch and Boston. Nevertheless, she was not fretting; actually, she was happy that she had been able to realize that much of her dream.

Recession

As we have seen, King himself responded to the pressures of the boycott positively. He had learned much. After his initial adjustments, he had risen to the occasion in almost every particular and had stood the wear and tear of the campaign remarkably well. But he was noticeably tiring. When some of his friends suggested that he take a month off, disappear and rest—"get lost," they said—his reply was: "Will the people keep on, if their leader is away?" King had come to accept his position, naturally and unquestioningly. On this his further education would not be altogether painless.

After the boycott was over and the big war was won, the recession of enthusiasm was inevitable. This psychological shift caught King unawares. During the crisis everybody seemed willing to do almost anything. There had been unity, altruism, a fusion of personalities and spirits in the common cause. Everybody was pushing King forward, finding in him every good quality that any emergency required.

But now his colleagues, relaxed and somewhat indifferent, began to look at him more normally. They began to question his judgment, to mention his shortcomings. Criticisms on matters that formerly would have gone through unanimously became sharp and prolonged.

It was almost unbelievable to King that the very people who, a few months ago, had been shouting his praises were now asking him for justification for every proposal he put forward. He felt deserted and alone. He told some of his close friends that perhaps he had outlived his usefulness in Montgomery and should leave.

This was an overreaction to the actual situation. It is true that the people had turned, not *against* King, but to some extent *away* from him. They had merely turned toward the other side of a situation that had always been there but which had been obscured by the needs of the crisis.

The psycho-moral requirements of the year-long operation were over. King's knowledge of philosophy should have reminded him of the oscillations of life. Many people had devoted themselves so thoroughly to the boycott for so long that there was much catching-up to be done in their own personal lives.

Nor did it help the general morale that King, individually, was so greatly sought after. From his hundreds of invitations to speak, he had accepted so many out-of-town engagements that he was pressed for time to think through the post-boycott program for the MIA. Even his MIA colleagues felt that he was bent on making a fortune.

It was not generally known that King never charged social betterment organizations in the South anything beyond his bare expenses. *Jet* magazine, which dubbed him "Man on the Go," listing 780,000 miles by plane and 208 speeches during 1958, might have added that for more than half of these appearances King received less than his travel and keep. Moreover, his name was so controversial that no public school or college in the South would employ his wife. Finally, it was expensive to entertain the distinguished visitors who descended upon the King household from week to week. This other side of the picture was obscured in the rush of events and comments. Writers who came to town to write about the Montgomery movement ended up by writing about King. It was easier that way. Thus, as we have seen, in Barrett's article for the New York *Times* Magazine, supposedly on the general situation, King's name came up twenty-six times.

In short, King's colleagues felt that he was taking too many bows and enjoying them; he was forgetting that victory at Montgomery had been the result of collective thought and collective action. It now seemed that everything was "King, King, King!" "This never was a one-man show," Abernathy had said long ago. Many remembered that.

Offers of attractive positions flooded in on King. He was like a
child in a candy store: which flavor was the best? Which should he
choose? Should he remain in Montgomery or go to New York,
Chicago or California? Would he like to be a college president or
the pastor of a big church or an executive of a national church
organization? Should he go into politics? Before December 5, 1955,
life had been simple: then, if any one of a dozen of the 1957 offers
had come to him, he would have answered yes by return mail.

And so the great letdown had come, and the hero was fatigued
and frustrated. There was nothing else to do but take a rest, get
himself together and decide on what course to follow. In Friendship,
the organization that gave financial and moral support to the fight
against Jim Crow, urged him to go to India and Africa. Invitations
from both Nehru and Nkrumah were lying on King's desk. Dexter
Avenue Baptist Church voted him $2,500 for a trip abroad; the MIA
added another thousand. Even the opposition forces got into the act.
The WCC publication gleefully reported that King was going overseas.
But it was *The Truth,* a fly-by-night segregation sheet, which apparently lived for but one issue, March, 1957, that ran the big front-page
headline: "King Goes to Africa." The double column subhead read:
"Purpose of Trip Not Clear; Vision of 'Gold' Coast Suspected." This
was a play upon King's previous "vision in the kitchen" and the
word "gold." "Probably the best news to come from the Capitol [sic]
City in many months," ran the opening sentence, "was the recent
announcement that Rev. Martin Luther King is making a trip to
Africa." The article went on:

Members of his congregation have been assessed $25.00 each to defray
his expenses. Some have balked outright and refused to give anything.
Others have readily agreed to donate the $25.00 to be rid of him at least
for a while. There is speculation among many in his congregation that
once he is in Africa a fund will be raised to keep him there. Others are
hoping that he will have another "vision" telling him that he should de-
vote the rest of his life as a missionary in Africa. And speaking of visions
the authorities at Mt. Vernon [asylum for the mentally ill] tell us that
there are several inmates down there who have "visions" regularly.

To Ghana

The Kings left Montgomery in the usual last-minute rush with
Coretta doing most of the packing. He went ahead to Richmond for
a speaking engagement. She picked him up there. When they changed
planes at New York, their traveling companions would include Congressman Adam Clayton Powell, A. Philip Randolph, Mrs. Louis
Armstrong, the Honorable Richard Jones, Minister to Liberia, Dr.

Ralph Bunche of the United Nations, and the Honorable Norman Manley, leader in the then forthcoming federated commonwealth of the British West Indies. The newsmen were at the New York airport, too, and it was not Powell or Randolph or Bunche or Manley that they crowded about, but King.

There was a hop to Boston, then to Santa Maria, then Lisbon. On this third leg, one of the stewards kept looking at King, then finally made the connection, "You are Rev. King of the bus fight in Alabama." He had seen the *Times* cover story. He arranged to have King sit at the controls of the plane for a few moments. King liked this so well that he announced to his fellow travelers that after a few more lessons he was sure he could pilot a plane with ease.

Powell took the party around in Lisbon. At the Monrovia, Liberia, stop, King was met at the airfield by one of his Morehouse mates, Romeo Horton, bank president. This was Africa but the real thrill came as the plane glided to earth at Accra, the capital of what in a few days would be the new nation of Ghana.

The Kings were lodged with a friendly but formal British family of Achimota College and were surprised to find everything—the school for Africans and the city as a whole—so modern.

The big event, of course, was the birth of the new nation. What had been a colony and protectorate of the British Empire would become a self-governing member of the British Commonwealth of Nations. Representatives of some sixty-odd countries were on hand for the historic occasion. Both the United States and the Soviet Union were there, hopeful of winning friends among the African peoples. Vice-President Richard Nixon was the ranking American on hand, bringing greetings and gifts from his country. It was significant that Martin Luther King had been invited along with the diplomats and public figures. This was a deliberate gesture. It was part of the policy of the native West African "brothers." King was thus given international recognition as the leader of the Montgomery movement. Also recognized were Negro Congressmen from the United States, Adam Powell and Charles Diggs and well-established leaders such as A. Philip Randolph in labor and Lester B. Granger in social welfare.

At 11 P.M. March 5, 1957, the old assembly of the Gold Coast colony was adjourned—forever. Symbolically, the curtain was rung down on the past. At 12 midnight, the new nation was born. The ceremonies were held out of doors in the polo grounds in the capital city, Accra. Under the floodlights, the crowd of some fifty thousand could see that Nkrumah and his close comrades of state were upon the speaker's stand and had on their native African robes

and their little prison caps, in commemoration of the days when the
colonial authorities had them in jail for sedition.

One minute after the stroke of midnight, Nkrumah spoke, in a
voice laden with emotion: "The battle is ended. Ghana, our beloved
country, is free forever." There was a moment of silent prayer; then
a tremendous shout went up from the people, "Free-dom, free-dom!
Ghana is free! Ghana is free!" The Union Jack came down and the
flag of Ghana—green, gold and red stripes with a single star in the
center of it—went up.

Joy was unrestrained. Nkrumah wept. King and many others wept,
too. It was a moment of reality.

The celebration continued for several days with the sessions of
state relieved by socials. The Duchess of Kent, representing the
Queen of England, conveyed the formal transfer of power and subsequently at a ball danced with the new Prime Minister. A photograph
of this graphic incident was reproduced all over the world. In fact,
"the peaceful assumption of independence" was front-page news
almost everywhere. The "talking drums" as well as the radio and
TV spread the word all over Africa.

King was enjoying himself. Nixon remembered him from the *Time*
cover picture. He invited King to come to see him in Washington
and teased Mrs. King about not having wanted to marry a preacher.

The Kings had lunch with Nkrumah privately. This was unique
for nondiplomatic visitors and was another deliberate gesture on
the part of the Prime Minister. Nkrumah, too, had used nonviolent
resistance, though not exclusively, in his campaign of "Positive
Action." It was heartening for King to talk to him and to hear him
say that the spirit of the people of Montgomery had likewise given
him great hope. King would think about this brief meeting many
times and muse that Gandhi, Nehru and Nkrumah had also been
jailed. When Nkrumah visited the United States during the summer
of 1958, he declared that King was one of his favorite Americans.

Before the Kings left Ghana both became ill; Coretta but slightly;
Martin, more seriously. He had not realized how tired he really was
but had kept going mainly on the wave of excitement. There was so
much happening that he could not afford to miss. But finally the
weakness of the flesh was manifest. An intense fever so completely
"flattened him out" that he was sure that he would die. Three doctors
were called in before a turn for the better was noticeable.

While recuperating, King was visited by a notable friend of the
Africans. Dr. Homer Jack reported the visit in the *Christian Century*
for April 10, 1957, under the caption, "Conversation in Ghana."
He began:

Of all the clergymen in Africa, one has symbolized in the past decade the best of the church working for justice and against colonialism: Michael Scott. Of all the clergymen in America, one has symbolized in the past year the best of the church working for justice and against segregation: Martin Luther King, Jr. Ironically, Scott of Africa is a white man while King of America is a black man. Appropriately, both were personal guests of Prime Minister Kwame Nkrumah to witness the independence celebrations of Ghana.

Then, Jack described Scott and King in terms of the struggle for equality in America and Africa. Both men were hopeful of the example that Ghana would set as a Negro nation. Both believed that there was "no basic difference between colonialism and racial segregation"; that nonviolence would triumph in America as well as in Africa—even in South Africa; that the church "must take the lead to find techniques to deal with both colonialism and racism"; and that "the forces of both history and Providence were on the side of freedom."

In a few days, Martin was back on his feet. Coretta felt better, too. They visited Nigeria briefly before flying on to Rome, Geneva, Paris and London. They were back in Montgomery by March 28, having been away twenty-five days.

King had always wanted to go to Africa, "land of my father's fathers." Going back had renewed his strength and faith. He was tremendously inspired and more determined than ever to push forward the frontiers of freedom in his own native Southland. He was sure that the time had come for a broad, bold advance.

To Washington

Long before King's African trip, the Montgomery leaders had been conferring with others throughout the South. The helpfulness had been mutual. Financial and moral support had flowed into Montgomery; also numerous pointers had come from Baton Rouge, where a similar bus boycott had occurred in 1953.

On the other hand, when Negro bus strikes broke out or were threatening in Tallahassee, Miami, Atlanta and Birmingham, these places all looked to Montgomery for advice and suggestion. "The Montgomery way" connoted success and nonviolence. There had been much talk of systematizing these more or less sporadic contacts. Accordingly, King, the Rev. F. L. Shuttlesworth of Birmingham and the Rev. C. K. Steele of Tallahassee issued a joint call for a Southwide conference, at Atlanta, Georgia.

The response was favorable. Almost all who were asked to come did so. Only a few pleaded "previous commitments." Thus, some sixty persons from twenty-nine communities in ten Southern states met for two days, January 10-11, 1957.

Indirectly, the conference had an ominous salute, for it was on January 10—before daybreak—that a series of bombings tore holes into homes and churches in the Negro community of Montgomery. This was the delayed reaction of the violent elements to bus desegregation, which was then almost two months old. White business and religious organizations bitterly condemned these "wild," "dastardly" and "irresponsible" acts. But nobody recognized—at least, not publicly—that there was any connection, as Ralph McGill would say, between abusive words and abusive deeds.

Abernathy's church and home had been struck, but not King's this time. Both rushed back to Montgomery, Coretta presiding at the Atlanta Conference until her husband returned the following day. Abernathy remained in Montgomery, missing the conference completely. When King got back to Atlanta he found a more felicitous salute by way of telegrams from public personalities who were endorsing and supporting the conference idea. These messages were many and varied from the North, but small in number from the South.

From the two-day session emerged a preliminary organization called the Southern Leadership Conference on Transportation and Non-Violent Integration. Officers would be elected later. Most of the sixty conferees were clergymen, with a sprinkling of state and local NAACP officials, three businessmen, two labor leaders, two college professors and one farmer. A well-worded address was issued containing special passages that were pointed respectively toward the nation, white Southerners and Negroes. America was reminded that "our democratic vitality is sapped by the civil rights issue." Southern whites were urged "to join the struggle for justice" and Negroes "to refuse further cooperation with the evil elements" and "no matter how great the obstacles and suffering . . . reject segregation." All were reminded that "non-violence is not a symbol of weakness or cowardice" but transforms "weakness into strength and breeds courage in face of danger."

As for the next tactical steps to be taken, President Eisenhower was requested to "come south immediately, to make a major speech in a major southern city urging all southerners to accept and to abide by the Supreme Court's decisions as the law of the Land . . . and use the weight of your great office to help solve the violent racial disorder arising over civil rights."

Vice-President Nixon was urged to "make a tour of the south similar to the one made in behalf of Hungarian refugees," reporting on "economic boycotts, reprisals, bombing violence directed against persons . . . who assert their rights under the Constitution."

A meeting of Southern Negro leaders with the United States Department of Justice was asked of Attorney General Herbert Brownell, to discuss the question of federal responsibilities in maintaining order in "areas where Negroes and whites who stand up for justice fear for their lives."

The conference then adjourned, subject to recall at an early date.

In a few days, replies came to King from the White House and Department of Justice. Sherman Adams, aide to Mr. Eisenhower, in a long telegram, made the point that "it is not now possible for the President to schedule such a speaking engagement as you ask. . . ." In another lengthy wire, the Department of Justice finally said that "a conference at this time would not be helpful or appropriate" though the department was daily "receiving information upon this matter" of civil rights. No answer whatsoever came from the Vice-President. The Southern white press played up these rejections at Washington.

After waiting for about a month, the conference leaders came together for a one-day session in New Orleans on February 14. Again the response was excellent. This time ninety-seven persons from thirty-five communities in ten Southern states attended. King was elected president, Abernathy treasurer. The name of the organization was changed to Southern Negro Leaders Conference and then again to Southern Negro Leadership Conference.

This was mainly a telegram-sending session. The air was literally filled with missives directed to Washington officials. A page-and-a-half telegram was sent to President Eisenhower. The main point of this message was contained in its fourth paragraph:

> While we are sensitive to the burdens of your responsible office, we believe that human life and the orderly, decent conduct of our communities are at stake. These imperative considerations leave us quite reluctant to accept as final that a speech by you in the South cannot be scheduled. It is our sincere belief that action on your part now can avert tragic situations by cooling passions and encouraging reasonableness. In saying this we are not unmindful of the immense responsibility of your office in the conduct of our national and international affairs. However, morality like charity, begins at home. Here at home, as we write, we are confronted with a breakdown of law, order, and morality. This is a sinister challenge and threat to our government of laws, drastically calling for attention and remedial action.

There was also the recommendation that the President "call a White House conference" on civil rights that would be similar to

the meetings that had been held on education and juvenile delin-
quency. And finally,

If some effective remedial steps are not taken, we will be compelled to
initiate a mighty Prayer Pilgrimage to Washington . . . we will ask our
friends, Negro and white, in the North, East, and West, to join us in this
moral crusade for human dignity and freedom.

The wire to Nixon was shorter and more pointed:

We are sorry that you have not seen fit to answer our telegram. Meantime, we note that you have been chosen to represent the United States
Government at the Gold Coast Independence Celebration March 6th,
when that first Negro country in Africa receives its freedom from colonial
domination. We are convinced that you will be better able to represent
America's defense of justice and freedom at the celebration, if prior to
your leaving for Africa . . . you arrange for the fact-finding trip we have
proposed into the South.

The conference renewed its request for a meeting with the Department of Justice and added one more thought on this matter,
asking the Attorney General "to invite all Southern District attorneys
to join in this meeting." In a statement to the press, the conference
emphasized the point that had been made in the telegram to President Eisenhower: the likelihood of a pilgrimage to Washington.

After helping fire these well-aimed missiles, King then hurried
back to Montgomery to pack his bags for his month's "vacation" in
Ghana. It was here that he got his answer from Nixon and reached
the resolution that, if Washington would not come South, Southern
Negroes certainly ought to go to Washington.

When after a month no positive word had come from the nation's
capital, the Pittsburgh *Courier* reminded its readers that the Southern
Negro Leadership Conference was "still waiting on Eisenhower."
Accordingly, as soon as King came back from Africa he consulted
with his fellow officers and found them unanimous in the feeling that
the time had come to act.

"Marching on Washington" struck a responsive chord with the
Negro people. It was action—and action rather than more talk was
what the masses seemed to want. The idea appealed to several other
Negro leaders. A. Philip Randolph had been talking about a mass
march for over a year. Roy Wilkins, not as sanguine as Randolph,
nevertheless, looked with favor on some "dignified," co-operative
celebration of the anniversary of the United States Supreme Court's
school desegregation decree.

In New York on March 25 King saw both Wilkins and Randolph.
The general conception of a pilgrimage to Washington was agreed to

and a date set for the busy executives to assemble their colleagues and advisors and get together for "finalizing" the specifics.

Accordingly, on April 5 the three leaders with some seventy-odd associates and aides met at the Metropolitan Baptist Church, Washington, D.C. This event was significant, for when A. Philip Randolph, Roy Wilkins and Martin Luther King sat down together, it meant that three fairly distinct lines of Negro leadership were joined—at least temporarily. These men were strikingly different as individuals and equally distinguishable in the strategies and tactics that they pursued in their common crusade.

Big Three

A. Philip Randolph was the grand old man of the trio. At sixty-eight he was tall, broad shouldered and philosophical. His face and manner were attractive and commanding. He was from Florida and the evening school of New York City College but he spoke with a rich natural Harvard baritone. Randolph's real education had come by way of the labor movement and the writings of radical philosophers.

When some men called Randolph a dreamer they were praising him for his cosmic views; others were damning him for not getting down to organizational particulars. Professor Abram L. Harris, formerly of Howard, later of the University of Chicago, once wrote that Randolph could initiate but could not sustain mass movements.

Randolph's most concrete and perhaps enduring achievement was the organization of the Brotherhood of Sleeping Car Porters—the labor union of the railroad passenger attendants. These men came to Randolph in 1925. He made their cause his. For a long while the going was rough. He withstood all threats and bribes; was apparently fearless and incorruptible. Today most Pullman porters need only one guess to name the man they feel should be President of the United States.

During the Second World War, Randolph led the fight against Jim Crow in employment. He threatened to march masses of Negroes and their friends to the nation's capital in a dramatic protest. President Roosevelt realized that America could ill afford such a demonstration in the midst of a world struggle for the Four Freedoms and against the "Nazi tyranny." Accordingly, the President issued Executive Order 8802, which prohibited job discrimination in war industry against any American on the basis of color, creed or national origin. This was not just a "Negro victory" but a boon for the whole nation in that it sped the maximum utilization of manpower. Furthermore, it was a step forward in the evolution of federal public policy. More than ever, Randolph was a hero.

Men on the street corners of Harlem and Auburn Avenue enjoyed repeating the true story that once at a group conference, when President Roosevelt raised his voice at something Randolph said, Randolph raised his voice back at the President. Then both men sensed what had happened, turned on their great natural charm and smiled.

When Randolph attempted to transform the emergency March-on-Washington movement into a permanent organization, he failed. But it was significant that the orientation of this effort was toward a program of "non-violent, good-will, direct action" or in other words, nonviolent resistance.

Again, in the post-World War II period, when Negroes and their friends were fighting the racial quota feature of the military draft, Randolph again was the leader. His strategy was quite similar to that which had produced Executive Order 8802 and the wartime Fair Employment Practices Commission. Speaking for the Committee Against Jim Crow Military Service and Training (later named the League for Non-Violent Civil Disobedience Against Military Segregation), he declared that unless the President issued an executive order banning discrimination and segregation in the United States armed forces, Randolph would call upon young Negro and white men to disobey their draft calls. He set a date on which this open appeal would be made.

Straightway the Senate Armed Services Committee "invited" Randolph to appear before it. He came and stated his case calmly and unequivocally, saying that unless military Jim Crow was abolished he would urge "mass civil disobedience" of what he termed unjust laws. Here indeed were shades of Thoreau.

When warned that such a move might stir violent elements as well as bring on prosecution for treason by the government, Randolph answered: "We would be willing to absorb the violence, absorb the terrorism, face the music and take whatever comes."

Fortunately, just before time ran out, President Truman issued Executive Order 9981, which affirmed a policy of "equality of treatment and opportunity" in the armed forces. Actually, this was not a clear prohibition of military Jim Crow, but Randolph considered it to be such a long stride in that direction that he called off the scheduled mass draft defiance. Again he was a hero.

That was Randolph's way. Normally he moved about the country, quietly looking after the affairs of the Brotherhood of Sleeping Car Porters and serving alongside other leaders of the labor movement. (He was one of the vice presidents of the AFL-CIO national council.) But, at critical moments, he would re-emerge as a champion of Negro rights.

Over the years he had been the father symbol more than any other national Negro leader. He looked upon Martin Luther King as a son, believing in him and offering suggestions and support but no commands.

Randolph had known about nonviolence and civil disobedience before King was born. He had come to them by a route that was completely outside of King's own life journey: the radical labor movement. King must have recalled that Bayard Rustin, who had clear views on nonviolence and who had often brought advice and support to the MIA was, in a sense, a disciple of Randolph's and had worked closely with him in the campaigns against job and military Jim Crow.

Roy Wilkins was a very different type. Unlike Randolph and King he was no orator. But he was a better writer than either. He spoke thoughtfully and without flourishes. As a journalist he knew about the subtleties of public relations and was much the best administrator of the three.

Wilkins was a Northerner. Though born in St. Louis, he was taken to Minnesota at the age of four by his mother upon his father's death. Later he attended the state university. He always had white as well as Negro schoolmates and friends. With his dual interest in general affairs and Negro affairs, he helped edit both the college daily paper and the local Negro weekly of the twin cities, St. Paul-Minneapolis.

Wilkins at fifty-five was slim, of medium height and weight, brown skinned, with a well-shaped head, a small mustache and a quiet smile. He was well dressed and urbane, without bombast or crudity. He could see the other fellow's point, reasonably. He never complained about anything personally though for years he waged a heroic fight against an intestinal illness that would have exhausted and disheartened a lesser man.

Wilkins had behind him the most substantial civil rights organization in America, the NAACP. He had come to its New York headquarters in 1931 from the Kansas City *Call*. For eighteen years he served as assistant to Walter White, the dashing executive secretary. During this period Wilkins managed the home office, while his chief was speaking, lobbying and conferring around the country. After DuBois left the NAACP for Atlanta University, Wilkins added editing the *Crisis,* the NAACP official monthly, to his duties.

Wilkins lacked White's flair and White lacked Wilkins' administrative talents. In the summer of 1949, White, with a bad heart and new wife, left New York for a leisurely trip around the world. Few expected him to return to active duty though his resignation was not accepted.

During White's absence, Wilkins, as acting executive secretary, staged the National Emergency Civil Rights Mobilization Conference in January, 1950, one of the most deftly organized and effective demonstrations that the NAACP ever attempted.

But the following spring, Walter White reappeared, rested and restless. An organizational crisis was avoided by splitting the office down the middle, making Wilkins secretary of internal affairs, and White secretary of external affairs. Things went on like this until March, 1955, when White died and Wilkins took over completely.

Wilkins himself has admitted that the NAACP has not had a broad base. Its quarter million to half million dues-paying members somehow expect the organization to work for them but do not feel that they personally have to participate often in mass action. NAACP leaders do not regard popular pressure as a strategy but only as an occasional tactic. Their chief reliance has been upon court action, lobbying, conferences and educational propaganda. The goal of the NAACP has been to have American practice conform to American (that is, federal) law. The NAACP has never sought to go beyond the Constitution or overthrow the republican form of government. In this sense, it has been a conservative, strictly legal organization. Both its method and objective were realized in its greatest victory: the United States Supreme Court desegregation decree of May 17, 1954.

King, Wilkins and Randolph, sitting around the table, were intellectuals, each in his own way; but the organizations they represented were distinguishable as religious, intellectual and labor.

Prologue

The three men, by common consent of those meeting with them at the Metropolitan Baptist Church, were named as co-chairmen of what everybody agreed should be called "Prayer Pilgrimage for Freedom." The group then went to work on other particulars. A "call" to the nation in general and the Negro people in particular was hammered out, embracing five objectives: (1) a demonstration of Negro unity, (2) provision for Northern aid to Southern "freedom fighters," (3) defense against "the crippling of the NAACP" in some Southern states, (4) mobilizing support for pending civil rights legislation, (5) protest against violence. The meeting was to be religious in character and the emphasis was to be placed upon nonviolence. It was scheduled for noon, May 17, 1957, in front of the Lincoln Memorial. This was the actual anniversary date of the Supreme Court decision.

Both King and Randolph made suggestions for putting together the program, but this task was left mostly in the hands of Wilkins. It was estimated that it would take between $10,000 and $15,000 to promote and stage the meeting. The NAACP would underwrite most of the expenses with King and Randolph contributing part of the cost from their organizations. The Rev. Thomas Kilgore, Jr., was named national director of the project, with Ralph Abernathy, his associate, in charge of the South. A half-dozen honorary chairmen were chosen along with a national sponsoring committee of fifty prominent persons. Bayard Rustin and Miss Ella Baker were borrowed from In Friendship as "special organizers."

The press was on hand for statements and pictures. Perhaps the most interesting photograph was the one used by the Pittsburgh *Courier*. It was a group shot of the three leaders in which Randolph appeared to be gazing into the far-distant future, Wilkins was looking straight ahead though not so distantly; but King, in a sidewise glance, appeared to have his eyes on his two colleagues.

When the public realized that the Negro leaders were serious about marching on Washington, there were visions and alarms, the nightmare of thousands of Negroes, dropping hoe and rake in the fields of the Southland and taking to mules or jalopies in a sort of medieval crusade northward to the nation's capital. There they would be met by a similar tidal wave, sweeping down from the slums of New York's Harlem, Detroit's Paradise Valley, Chicago's South Side and the black ghettos of St. Louis and points far west. Abernathy himself, in a moment of enthusiasm, declared that a hundred thousand Negroes and their friends would stop whatever they were doing and start toward Washington in time to be there on May 17. Most other estimates varied from 50,000 to 75,000.

On the other hand, there was apprehension that a mass pilgrimage would be fraught with danger to the Negro's cause, with hooded klansmen falling upon the flanks of the dark-skinned pilgrims, waylaying stragglers, setting up road blocks and nailing up signs, prohibiting the marchers from passing through certain cities and towns, and a pitched battle between these molesters and the harassed travelers, who by now would have run out of nonviolent good will. Then there were those who felt that in a "y'all come" mass march there would be nothing to prevent drunks and rowdies from joining up and disgracing the parade en route or at the nation's capital, "before the eyes of the world." And finally, there was the specter of the "hammer and sickle." The United Press circulated what proved to be an unsubstantiated story that "The Communist Party is making an all out effort to infiltrate the big Negro pilgrimage." The Berkeley-Albany (California) Council of Churches sincerely feared that "such a venture, no matter how thoughtfully conceived and dedicated, could all too readily be 'taken over' by dissident elements and turned, boomerang fashion, into a devastating weapon to destroy much of the confidence and respect which have been developed. . . ."

Much less imaginary was the real problem of promoting the vast undertaking within the space of five weeks. For example, the Rev. Mr. Abernathy was hopping about the South, speaking almost everywhere, but what was lacking were the technicians and organizers. The preachers could get the "rousements," but even a crusade needed a good transportation service and arrangements for food, way stations and lodgings. A corps of volunteers from Madison Avenue, the universities and the labor unions doubtless would have made a difference.

In New York most of the forward-looking unions voiced approval of the pilgrimage but were busy with their own affairs. One exception was District 65, the Retail, Wholesale and Department Store Union. Some twelve hundred members sacrificed a day's pay and then took care of their own expenses to Washington. Real support also came from the garment, transport, automobile, steel, hat and bartender locals.

Active opposition cropped up in a few places. In both New Orleans and Tampa, a lone Negro preacher denounced the pilgrimage for the daily papers. In Little Rock, Arkansas, a score of Negro ministers, passing a resolution that the march to Washington would interfere with the President, thanked Mr. Eisenhower "for all he has done to alleviate the suffering of Negroes."

As was to be expected, the White Citizens Councils opposed the pilgrimage. The Alabama group ran full-page ads in the daily papers, decrying "the conspiracy" of Martin Luther King and the NAACP "to destroy our Southern way of Life."

On the positive side, the mayors of both New York City and Los Angeles and the governors of California, Maryland, Iowa and Missouri proclaimed May 17 as a pilgrimage day. Manhattan's Borough President, Hulan Jack, campaigned for the march to Washington though he did not subsequently go himself. There were several thousand posters, handbills and a few half-page and full-page ads in the newspapers.

On May 16 the early arrivals began to appear, and on the following morning Washington knew that something big had come to town.

Most of the pilgrims had come by train, bus and automobile. Some of the notables had flown in by plane from Los Angeles, Montgomery and New York. Very few had walked. The Rev. Milton Perry, who had come over 180 miles on foot from Jersey City, was so exceptional that he became good copy for journalists in search of human-interest stories. The largest delegation—about eleven thousand—had come from New York.

The visitors had good luck with the weather: the day was clear and warm. Robert C. McLaughlin, president of the Board of Commissioners, presented the co-chairman of the meeting with the keys to the city. The crusaders were delighted to find Pennsylvania Avenue lined with flags. It was not till afterward that they learned that the decorations were there for Armed Forces Day on May 18.

When, shortly before noon, the crowd collected in the area between the Lincoln Memorial and the lake, it became evident that although the showing was impressive, it was a smaller gathering than the leaders had hoped for. Estimates of its actual size varied considerably. The leaders estimated it at 37,000, the Washington *Post* at 25,000, the District police at 15,000. Even the optimum was appreciably short of the 50,000 that had been expected and very far below the 100,000 that Abernathy's enthusiasm had conjured up. Perhaps a Saturday or a Sunday would have been a better choice. Perhaps the red scare had also done its work, especially in holding down the attendance by residents of Washington and nearby Baltimore. Or perhaps the promotion for the crusade had been too little, too late and too oratorical.

And yet it was a representative crowd. People came from some thirty-three states, and as a whole looked well dressed and reasonably prosperous. Well-known personalities from the entertainment world were spotted here and there: Jackie Robinson, Harry Belafonte, Sammy Davis, Jr., Sidney Poitier, the actress Ruby Dee and the novelist John O. Killens.

Politically, there were all points of view from left to right, but by and large it was a liberal-conservative crowd of churchgoing Negro Americans. Only about 10 per cent were white. In many ways it was a great big Montgomery mass meeting.

Some New Yorkers had smiled when they talked about going down to Washington to the "prayer meeting." They did so respectfully and patiently for they wanted to have a good look at this "King thing," as they put it. Some of them realized that the Montgomery Improvement Association and the Southern Negro Leadership Conference had evolved in a sort of pre-political climate where those struggling did not have the ballot and the guarantee of elemental civil rights. Accordingly, the tactics and techniques that were developed for such a situation might be altogether unnecessary in places where everybody voted and the states had civil rights codes and commissions to investigate discriminations on the basis of color, creed or national origin. The methods of struggle in the North were understandably more direct and forceful.

The speaker's platform was on the steps of the Lincoln Memorial. Stretching out in front of it were folding chairs for only two thousand of the audience; the others had to stand or sat on the grass. Before the day ended some fifty would faint and over a hundred would require first aid.

The Act

At the stroke of high noon, the program started. After the national anthem, Bishop Sherman L. Greene delivered the invocation, which was followed by Professor Warner Lawson's huge university chorus, singing "The Battle Hymn of the Republic." A. Philip Randolph presided, his rich baritone ringing out. His opening remarks were well worded but he seemed hurried. Perhaps he sensed that the program would be long. Nevertheless, he did make his point:

We have come to demonstrate the unity of the Negroes and their allies —labor, liberals and the church—behind the civil rights bills now before Congress, in order that they might not be strangled to death by committee maneuverings and the filibuster.

We have gathered together to proclaim our uncompromising support of the fight of the National Association for the Advancement of Colored People for civil rights and democracy under the able, resourceful and constructive leadership of Roy Wilkins, Executive Secretary.

We have come to call upon President Eisenhower, our great national and world leader, who is undoubtedly possessed of a high sense of humanity, to speak out against the lawlessness, terror and fears that hang like a pall over the hearts of citizens of color in the South. . . .

Theresa and James Gordon, youngsters from Clay, Kentucky, laid a wreath at the feet of the Great Emancipator, in honor of the little children of the South who attended integrated schools despite, at times, local hostility. After the reading of the Scriptures and prayer, Mahalia Jackson sang.

The program was getting off to a slow start. Randolph had asked for no applause because of the religious tone that the meeting was meant to have. But by the time Mordecai Johnson, president of Howard University, began speaking, enthusiasm mounted and handkerchiefs were waved in the air, signifying hearty approval of points he scored. There were some "amens," too. Dr. Johnson declared that the Supreme Court decision of May 17, 1954, was a second Emancipation Proclamation. An eloquent and notoriously lengthy speaker, he had trouble in holding himself down to fifteen minutes.

The Rev. William H. Borders of Atlanta, the Rev. C. K. Steele of

Tallahassee, the Rev. F. L. Shuttlesworth of Birmingham and the Rev. A. L. Davis of New Orleans were successively presented as "freedom fighters of the South." They recounted dramatically their contests—mostly with Jim Crow buses.

Then came Roy Wilkins, who extended himself in co-operating with the spirit of the occasion. As suave as he is, he preached a little sermonette, taking for his text a verse from Paul's letter to the Ephesians: "Put on the whole armour of God. . . . For we wrestle not against flesh and blood, but against principalities." With deep sincerity he advanced his political ideas in religious terms. The assault upon the NAACP, the deathlike silence of federal legislators, the new spate of segregation laws in the hard-core resistance states were all painted as "spiritual blindness in high places." He ended as he began, by quoting Paul: "We are troubled . . . yet not distressed; we are perplexed, but not in despair; persecuted but not forsaken; cast down, but not destroyed. . . ."

While Wilkins was speaking, a helicopter appeared to buzz the crowd, making hearing difficult—and then abruptly disappeared. Wilkins quipped: "Senator Eastland must be up there."

Mahalia Jackson sang once more. This time she let herself go with "I've Been 'Buked; I've Been Scorned." The level of emotion was rising. Congressman Charles Diggs raised it a bit more by declaring that singing and praying were all right but that Negroes must demand political action of both parties.

Then came Adam Clayton Powell. He and his fellow Congressman Diggs, he said jokingly, had called their offices and through them had made the helicopter leave. Some of the crowd, misunderstanding Powell's jest, thought he said that Senator Eastland was in the helicopter and that he and Diggs had chased Eastland away. This loosened up the audience, which laughed uproariously and thereafter began to cheer and applaud whenever it felt like doing so. "We are here in front of the Lincoln Memorial," Powell went on, "because we are getting more from a dead Republican than we are getting from live Democrats and live Republicans." He called for a "third force—nonpartisan but political" that would move forward with courage and strength. Based on passive resistance, this force would utilize "boycott, mass demonstrations, picket lines and, above all, political unity."

A racially mixed chorus from the Philadelphia Friendship House sang; after which, A. Philip Randolph said, "I give you Martin Luther King!"

The crowd arose. This was what the people had been waiting for. The program had been going for three hours. Mordecai Johnson and

Adam Clayton Powell were as accomplished speakers as the nation afforded and many of the others had been impressive. But it was clear that many were there because of the "Little Fellow," as some of the New Yorkers called King. They gave him an ovation even before he started.

This time King had a manuscript; there was too much excitement to depend upon memory. He started slowly, deliberately, clearly. His voice carried well and the richness of it was retained by the microphones even in the open air. The crowd hung on his every word, until he reached the climax:

> Give us the ballot . . . and we will no longer plead to the Federal government for passage for an anti-lynching law. . . .
> Give us the ballot . . . and we will transform the salient misdeeds of blood-thirsty mobs into the abiding good deeds of orderly citizens.
> Give us the ballot . . . and we will fill our legislative halls with men of good will. . . .

"Give us the ballot . . ." and at this point the audience picked up the words and repeated, "Give us the ballot" and then waited for King to add "and we will place judges on the benches of the South who will 'do justly and love mercy.'

"Give us the ballot"—again the crowd chanted back the words—"and we will quietly and nonviolently, without rancor or bitterness implement the Supreme Court's decision of May 17, 1954. . . ."

The response of the audience had been altogether spontaneous.

When King finished, the crowd gave him another ovation. It was indeed a moment of reality.

The audience stood and sang "America" and remained standing for the benediction. It was over. The pilgrimage had passed into history.

Epilogue

The big meeting got a good press; the networks and wire services reported it; the Negro papers were filled with it. The police department reported that the pilgrimage was one of the most orderly crowds of its size that Washington had seen. Edward P. Morgan for the American Broadcasting Company added, "Nobody was incited or inclined to violence. No Senator Eastland was hanged in effigy."

There was a chorus of praise for the restraint of the pilgrims, although most journalists from the North and many from the South felt, on second thought, that the meeting, despite its great success, had fallen short of its possibilities. Publications as different as the New York *Times, National Guardian, New Leader* and *Nation* said as much. In the words of New York City Councilman Earl Brown: "You can't exorcise the devil with prayer alone." William G. Nunn of the Pittsburgh *Courier* concluded that the pilgrimage was "the philosophy of Montgomery, Alabama, expanded to the national level."

Obviously, King himself emerged from the pilgrimage with greatly increased national prestige. Miss Ethel Payne, writing in the Chicago *Defender* for May 25 said: "Those who a few months ago thought of young King as a brilliant comet shooting across the sky never to be seen again, came away from the rally with a firmer conviction than ever of his mature, wise leadership. . . ."

James L. Hicks, *l'enfant terrible* editor of the *Amsterdam News,* was much more forthright. In his edition of June 1 he said that Martin Luther King had "emerged from the Prayer Pilgrimage to Washington as the number one leader of sixteen million Negroes in the United States. . . . At this point in his career, the people will follow him anywhere."

And, as if not content with that provocation, Hicks went on to charge that Wilkins and Randolph had "dragged their feet" during the promotion preceding the mass gathering.

Randolph, as was customary with him, did not answer Hicks. But the Rev. Mr. Kilgore, pilgrimage director, and Roy Wilkins did. They gave the editor a thorough drubbing in their rejoinders, quoting facts and figures to the effect that but for the financial and organizational support of the NAACP there would have been no promotion of the pilgrimage worth mentioning. Wilkins was angry. He wrote: "Mr. Hicks's article is an effort to destroy unity by planting suspicion, jealousy and rivalry."

Hicks held his peace for a while, waiting several weeks in quiet. Then he sprang forth with a whole series of articles, criticizing "Negro leadership." These weekly pieces stirred up furious discussion. Perhaps this was what Hicks and his publisher wanted most. After the series had drawn counterthrusts continuously, Hicks wrote:

I'm catching Hell. . . .

These "leaders" are ganging up on me nine ways from Sunday. They are holding meetings and caucusing about the articles and filing reports and making motions and just plain raising Hell.

But you know something—we are going to keep right on writing the series and we are going to continue to write straight down the middle as we have been.

At the least, everybody seemed to agree positively that the next step, the follow-up to the Washington "prayer meeting," had to be political action.

XII - Of Men and Evil

FOR his share in the big "next step," King decided that the time had come to pick up the bid that Vice-President Nixon had extended to him in Ghana. Such a meeting would have Eisenhower's blessings, for Sherman Adams had written to King that "the President . . . is pleased to know that you will be meeting with the Vice-President. . . ."

Nixon was a good man to see. For one thing, the newspapers had him at various times as "Acting President" and "heir apparent." For another thing, his report on his good-will tour of Africa had been widely quoted and praised in the Negro press as well as in the American press in general. "We in the United States," he urged, "must come to know, to understand and to find common ground with the peoples of this great continent." Nixon called for economic and technical assistance to the Africans and a firm policy of nondiscrimination. On this he said, "We cannot talk equality to the peoples of Africa and Asia and practice inequality. in the United States." This was what Negro leaders had been saying all along. They were pleased that the nation's number two man was standing with them on the relationship of foreign and domestic racial practice.

King could have seen Nixon alone; instead, he took along his "right arm," Abernathy. The two boycott veterans trudged up Capitol Hill on Thursday afternoon, June 13. Nixon, accompanied by James P. Mitchell, Secretary of Labor, met them at the Formal Room of the

Capitol. It was 3:25 P.M. Some seventy-odd pressmen were there waiting. While photographs were being taken, Nixon, easy and informal, kidded King that the picture would look better if Coretta were there. This done, the photographers hurried away, but the newsmen said that they would wait until the interview was over and get statements.

With the preliminary public relations out of the way, the four conferees retired to the Vice-President's office. The conference was scheduled to last for an hour, but Nixon said immediately, "Take plenty of time; there is no rush," and invited everybody to draw up his chair a little closer.

Abernathy and King had worked out some points that they intended to make. Some of their friends had also given them some briefing, warning them to beware of Nixon's "noncommittal charm."

With Nixon

King started things off. He began to describe the situation in the South, for he and his colleagues had said repeatedly that Washington surely would do more, if it but knew. He told of the bombings, intimidations, disfranchisement, corruption of the legal system and the various pressures put upon those who would be courageous.

Then Abernathy picked up the discussion and characteristically described the conflict situation more bluntly. He said that Negroes were resolute and so were white segregationists; Negroes meant to have their rights *now* and would not be hoodwinked or frightened from them. At the same time, he continued, their opponents were equally determined "that the house that they have ruled for so long will not pass from under their control." In between these two active and opposing groups, Abernathy explained, were most white Southerners. They were not members of the White Citizens Councils or the Ku Klux Klan. Perhaps they preferred segregation but would go along with the law, if those in authority made it clear that the law really meant "desegregate." Abernathy said that he was sure that the President did not realize what the situation was or else he would have spoken out, adding with a smile that the Vice-President had spoken out more clearly than had the President.

Nixon smiled, too, but came to the President's defense, quietly and pleasantly. The President, he pointed out, was not making as many speeches as was the Vice-President and thus did not get around to all of the subjects. Moreover, the President had called together the Republican members of Congress and told them that he did not believe in platform hypocrisy and that civil rights was in the Republican platform.

The discussion then moved directly to the civil rights debate then raging in Congress. Nixon thought that a civil rights bill would pass the House and had a fifty-fifty chance of getting through the Senate.

When King said that neither party had done much to push the bill, Nixon referred to insincere legislators who played politics by introducing civil rights bills that they knew had no chance of passing, just so they could say back home, "You see, I'm for civil rights." He praised the President and the Republicans for favoring a bill that had some reality about it that had a chance of becoming law.

Nixon then went back to the subject of the South, asking about the co-operation that came from white preachers there. King and Abernathy answered that privately many of them endorsed the Supreme Court's decision but feared to do so publicly; more would come out and take a stand if the President and Vice-President would speak up strongly for the court decrees.

Then King put the concrete proposition up to the Vice-President: What about coming south and making a speech for law and order? Nixon agreed that the general idea was good but had questions about the best way to carry it out. If he came south at the request of Negroes, he said, he would be speaking to Negroes. This reasoning seemed odd, but King and Abernathy let the point pass. Nixon thought that perhaps he could come south naturally in connection with the work of the Committee on Government Contracts that he had worked with for a long while.

Mitchell then took over and gave a rather lengthy description of the committee's operations and the way it sought to persuade concerns that held contracts with the federal government to abide by the clauses prohibiting discrimination in employment on the basis of color, creed or national origin.

Mitchell said that the committee had difficulty whenever it tried to break new ground. It was, for instance, hard to get Negroes into the "air industry." Stewardesses had to go through a lengthy training period before they were assigned, and a pilot had to work his way up from training school to co-pilot first. A Negro had to be not merely good but excellent before the airlines would agree to let him fly a plane.

Then the conversation faded back to Nixon's personally coming along with the committee on its schedule of hearings in the South.

Later, Abernathy said that he felt like interrupting at this point and suggesting that Nixon either come south and make a report to the President as he did on the Hungarian refugees or come south and make a good-will tour as he had done abroad. But Abernathy held himself back. He did not wish to break up the interview by pressing too hard. After all, he reminded himself, he was really an extra at the conference.

Nixon asked where in the South it would be most appropriate for him to appear if he could make just one stop. King suggested Atlanta or New Orleans. Atlanta seemed a good choice to both the Vice-President and the Secretary of Labor, for the Committee on Government Contracts would be there soon.

Finally, the conversation came back to the question of the President. What would he do? Nixon thought that maybe Mr. Eisenhower himself would like to hear first hand about conditions in the South. Accordingly, Nixon suggested that it might be well to wait until the civil rights fight in Congress was concluded and then if King would send him a memorandum on it, he would help arrange a meeting for him and others with the President.

The talk had gone on for two hours and ten minutes. Everybody had indeed taken his time. The Vice-President and the Secretary of Labor had apparently been genuinely interested. King and Abernathy felt good about the interview although they did not get all that they had wanted.

As King and Abernathy emerged from Nixon's office, a tall, brown-skinned stranger appeared suddenly and attempted to whisk them away. This man was Bayard Rustin. He hurried the two boycott leaders down a corridor and out a side door, toward a waiting automobile for a quick getaway.

But the newsmen, who had been waiting for them to emerge, caught sight of the three fast-moving figures and gave chase. But there was no stopping Rustin, who was King's public relations representative. Slamming the car door shut, he shouted that there would be no statements from King until the press conference that he was setting up for six o'clock at the Raleigh Hotel. The reporters were furious.

Later at the press conference, King spoke less about the conversation with Nixon than about his own plans, which grew only in part out of the recent interview. He said that he appealed to the Vice-President to do three things: first, come south and speak; secondly, urge all Southerners to support the law as interpreted by the Supreme Court; thirdly, call together Republicans in Congress and urge them to fight for the enactment of the civil rights bill. He then added that he was recommending to Negroes that they "hold unswervingly to non-violence in word, thought and deed," for if they did, they would win.

He got a good press on this, but there were a few journalists whom he had not enchanted. One of them, Louis Lautier of the National Negro Newspaper Publishers Association, gave King his first real roasting in the Negro press. It would not be his last.

Lautier's piece appeared in most of the Negro weeklies for June 22. The *Afro* carried it on page one, under a big picture of King and Nixon shaking hands. The three-column lead for the story read, "Was King Ready?" with the subhead: "Opportunity with Nixon Seen Missed." The first paragraphs said:

The Rev. Martin Luther King, Jr., leader of the Montgomery (Ala.) bus boycott, is an estimable young man and excellent pulpit orator, but he is not yet ready for the political big-time.

At his press conference here, after he and the Rev. Ralph D. Abernathy, another leader in the bus boycott talked with Vice President Nixon for more than two hours, he showed that he has more homework to do if he is to become a political as well as a spiritual leader.

Lautier added that King answered specific political questions with generalities, and that Secretary of Labor James P. Mitchell gave the reporters more of the meat of the Nixon conference than did King himself.

Compromise

King was so busy that he had little time to nurse his wounds from Lautier's barbs. Even while he was in Washington to see Nixon, a call had come to him from Billy Graham to come to New York. It was mid-July before the boycott leader could respond to this invitation. When he did, the great evangelist heartily said to one of his Madison Square Garden revival meetings, "A great social revolution is going on in the United States today. Rev. Martin Luther King is one of the leaders. We appreciate his taking his valuable time and coming here tonight." The Rev. Dr. King led the huge audience of twenty thousand in prayer.

He was happy about his meeting with Graham who promised to have his "Crusade for Christ" meetings in the South racially integrated wherever public officials would not force him to do otherwise. Graham had a tremendous following and was himself a native Southerner.

For Congress, the big domestic issue of the summer of 1957 was civil rights. National sentiment was so strong that something had to be done. General legislation on the subject was passed in the House rather easily, but the opposition forces in the Senate were strong enough to whittle the House bill down to the single item of the right to vote. They also attempted to write in a guarantee of a jury trial for persons who might be charged with violating such a law. For a while pro-civil rights Senators fought this provision. They realized that white juries in the South would be disinclined to convict white Southerners for interfering with Negro voters. However, as the fight bogged down, Senate leaders confided to their supporters in and out of Congress that, unless a compromise was reached, no civil rights bill at all would be passed.

The White House appeared to be opposed to a compromise. Congressman Adam Powell, though ill and off the scene during most of the summer, came out for "all or nothing"; so did the Chicago *Defender*. But as the session of Congress was coming to a close, Negro, liberal and labor leaders caucused together and decided to accept a "weak bill now and come back for more next year." Roy Wilkins and Martin Luther King, as sorely distressed as everyone else, went along with this decision.

This concession was considered a "sell-out" by those who contended for "all or nothing." The Chicago *Defender* in a front-page editorial and a cartoon elsewhere for August 31 declared:

In accepting the Senate version of the tattered civil rights bill, Roy Wilkins, executive secretary of the NAACP, and Rev. Martin Luther King of Montgomery, Ala., have committed the gravest tactical blunder that has ever been made by Negro leadership throughout the whole course of our turbulent history in America.

A week later, in his column "Dope and Data," the executive editor of the *Defender,* Louis E. Martin, who had once spoken of King as a "real charmer," expressed himself this way:

Last week I drowned my disgust with our leaders who approved the Senate version of the Civil Rights Bill . . . by attending a Broadway opening. Incidentally, the Rev. Martin Luther King's statement in Detroit was particularly unfortunate. At the very moment the fight is raging to strengthen the bill behind the scenes in Washington, he tells the nation that the Senate version of the bill is acceptable. How silly can you get?

The Pittsburgh *Courier* struck back, saying that everybody wanted a civil rights law "full of teeth; but wanting and getting are two very different things, as years of fighting in Washington proves."

King, as usual, made no reply. However, Roy Wilkins again was his own best defender, saying, "If you are digging a ditch with a teaspoon and a man comes along and offers you a spade, there is something wrong with your head if you don't take it because he didn't offer you a bulldozer!" Emory O. Jackson of the Birmingham *World* also defended King and Wilkins.

The much-compromised bill was finally passed and signed by the President. It provided for a jury trial only in cases where the fine of the judge exceeded $300. Weak as it was, this was the first civil rights legislation that the American Congress had passed in eighty-two years.

At the time, the compromise decision was a gamble. However, with the benefit of hindsight, everybody knows now that the "all or nothing" stand was wrong. The American people would have been greatly discouraged, after so much excitement, if there had been no new civil rights law. Moreover, it would have been a mistake to wait, expecting a strong civil rights bill at the next session of the Senate. It so happened that the political climate of the nation changed sharply. The Russians launched their Sputniks and the United States slid into an economic recession. Even Little Rock was driven from the front pages by the space satellites. There was not a chance in the world of getting Congress or the American people to concentrate on civil rights during the autumn and winter of 1957. King and Wilkins were right.

Meanwhile in Montgomery King had called together his fellow Southern leaders once more. Again, the name of the organization was changed, this time to the Southern Christian Leadership Conference. The word "Christian" was added, "Negro" dropped. Would the addition frighten away support from those of other religions? Would the subtraction mean that the conference would now welcome whites? In the rush of things, nobody seemed to have had time to give clear answers.

The meeting was held August 7 and 8 in Montgomery. Again attendance and spirits were high, and at the mass meeting closing out the session the orators swept everything before them. Perhaps equally eloquent was the $11,000 that the Packinghouse Workers of America contributed to the campaign of voter registration the conference was sponsoring.

Incidentally, one of the resolutions passed condemned the gerrymandering of Negro voters out of the town of Tuskegee, Alabama, and the "Gestapo-like pressures" that were being put upon leaders of the Tuskegee Civic Association. King himself had made a personal appearance at one of the Tuskegee mass meetings a few weeks before the conference, pledging support and demonstrating unity in the common cause.

Murray Kempton, whose prose style embellishes the pages of the New York *Post,* stopped in town long enough to see something of the conference and privately ventured the observation that it appeared as though the Southern white segregationist realized that he had lost his argument.

Repeated announcements on the part of the Southern Christian Leadership Conference and the NAACP of the vast number of voters that they were going to register gave the opposition a chance for heckling and counterstrokes. For example, Attorney General Eugene

Cooke of the state of Georgia told the newspapers that he suspected that the NAACP and King were at odds, both trying to work the same field. A Southern newspaperman, Stuart Culpepper III, took the point a few paragraphs further. Under the caption "Money Talks," he wrote that "the Reverend King is competing with NAACP for funds and supporters."

There was so much oral and written rumor about friction between the SCLC and NAACP that King scampered up to New York with a thousand dollars in his pocket. He met with Wilkins. Actually the two men always got on famously together. They both laughed at the efforts to pit them or their organizations against each other. Then to clinch this show of co-operation, King took out a $500 life membership in the NAACP for himself and purchased a similar certificate for the MIA. Wilkins and King then posed for pictures for the press.

Close on the long, hot civil rights summer, came the opening of school, and the capital city of the state of Arkansas leaped into the headlines. It remained there for so long that Little Rock became familiar even to semiliterate people around the globe.

The Little Rock story is very different from the Montgomery story. It poses, in effect, the constitutional question: What will the federal authority do when its judicial order is defied, even by a governor? The answer was that sufficient force would be used to execute that court order. The ordeal of the Negro schoolchildren who stuck it out at Central High School is epic, and Mrs. Daisy Bates, who directed and protected them throughout their travail, is a heroine in every way.

But the Montgomery story was not so much what the government would do as what the people would do. Specifically, what are the Negro people of the South prepared to do about their condition? The massive, sustained, nonviolent character of that response is the distinguishing feature of the Montgomery movement.

The MIA and the SCLC sent words of hope to Little Rock. In a telegram to Mrs. Bates, King said:

Urge the people of Little Rock to adhere rigorously to a way of non-violence at this time. I know this is difficult advice at a time when you are being terrorized, stoned, and threatened by ruthless mobs. But non-violence is the only way to a lasting solution of the problem. . . .

You have no alternative but to continue the struggle for integrated schools, but do it with a thorough commitment to Christian principles. . . .

King also endorsed the President's sending in of troops, telling him that "the overwhelming majority of Southerners, Negro and white, stand firmly behind your resolute action." Moreover,

In the long run, justice finally must spring from a new moral climate. Yet spiritual forces cannot emerge in a situation of mob violence . . . even the small and confused minority that oppose integration with violence will live to see that your action has been of great benefit to our nation and to the Christian traditions of fair play and brotherhood.

The President wrote back,

Thank you for sending me your comments regarding the necessity of the decision I had to make in the difficult Arkansas situation. I appreciate your thoughtful expression of the basic and compelling factors involved. I share your confidence that Americans everywhere remain devoted to our tradition of adherence to orderly processes of law.

King had also written to Nixon, thanking him "for so graciously receiving me and my colleague, Rev. Abernathy," and went on to speak of the "rich fellowship" and "fruitful discussion" of the June 13 conversations. He also thanked the Vice-President for his "assiduous labor and dauntless courage in seeking to make the Civil Rights Bill a reality." He could say with good grace that the compromise bill, of course, did not satisfy everybody but went a long way to insure the right to vote. Much, he continued, would depend upon "a sustained mass movement on the part of Negroes. This is why I am initiating in the South a crusade for citizenship."

Nixon answered: "I appreciate your generous comments with regard to my personal activities in behalf of the Civil Rights Bill . . . progress slow . . . sorry I couldn't do more . . . we are moving ahead."

Critics and Non-Co-operators

In mid-October King was paid a visit by two gentlemen representing Hollywood. Jeffrey Hayden, who had been connected with the production of movies and such TV shows as *Omnibus, TV Playhouse* and *Color Spectacular,* and John O. Killens, author of *Youngblood,* flew into town with the idea of making a movie on the Montgomery boycott. Killens would do the script and Hayden would handle the production. They gave the city quite a stir.

Killens had everybody remembering anecdotes while Hayden was convincing everyone else that the movie would be the best thing that ever happened to Montgomery. He even won the support of one of the city fathers. All that this official wanted guaranteed was that he would be shown in the film as "a complete and sincere segregationist." Hayden smiled, for this was just what he wanted. On the other side of town, the MIA voted its approval. Everybody began jockeying for position, wondering about parts and credits and profits.

When Hayden and Killens left town they said that they would be back, possibly in the spring, to begin shooting.

After a few weeks, things changed. Word got to the Montgomery city father in question that King was to be the hero of the movie and that the "sincere segregationist" would be more or less the villain, at least a foil for the leading man. So the city father wrote to Hayden, denouncing the proposed film and threatening to do everything in his power to keep it from being made—especially in Montgomery.

Perhaps this was the reason that the film project faded. Then, too, word came back from Hollywood that there really was not a sufficiently detailed biography of King for the story. At any rate, for a few months Montgomery was intrigued by the thought that it would become a movie.

About the time that the excitement of a possible King movie had subsided, along came the announcement that he would be featured on a national TV program to originate in Montgomery.

The National Broadcasting Company announced that King would appear on *Look Here,* Sunday, October 27. This was a half-hour interview program with Martin Agronsky asking the questions, which, at times, could be quite searching.

Immediately, the White Citizens Council set up a howl. The morning paper tried all it could to quiet the protesters on the grounds that the more they opposed King, the bigger he grew. The thing to do, the *Advertiser* advised, was to ignore him. "No outcry should be made. Say merely 'ho-hum' to this and all such."

But the anti-King forces, apparently, ignored the *Advertiser* instead. Quite nervous, the local TV station, WSFA, finding no valid ground for declining to co-operate with the network of which it was a part, offered to appease the opposition by giving equal time for an answer to whatever King might say.

Apparently, that was not enough for the WCC. The news went out to the rest of the country that NBC and Martin Luther King were having trouble with free speech down in Montgomery. As a slight addition to the disturbance, the *Advertiser* itself for Sunday, October 27, somehow failed to carry the *Look Here* item in its TV log for the day. Numerous calls were made to the station, inquiring about the program. Thus, as the *Advertiser* had predicted, the telecast would have one of its largest listening audiences, nationally and locally.

Even so, few suspected the lengths to which the opposition would go. About five minutes before the program was to come on, the station itself blacked out, went off the air completely.

What had happened? everybody wanted to know. Telephone lines became jammed. The police were alerted. Negroes, suspecting foul play, jumped into their cars and rushed down to the Dexter Avenue Baptist Church where the interview was to be staged.

There was considerable confusion, but after a while it was learned that a huge chain had been thrown around one of the TV transmitters, causing a short circuit and power failure. The big headline in the Monday morning paper was "TV Interview Blacked Out by Sabotage." Only the local station had been silenced; the rest of the country heard and saw the interview as scheduled.

All this, of course, was embarrassing to WSFA, which was finding it difficult to keep on good terms with NBC, the Federal Communications Commission and the White Citizens Council at the same time. After some hesitation, the announcement was made that the Montgomery station would show the film of the telecast on the following Sunday, with a rebuttal following.

Editor Grover Hall was disgusted. "Brilliant Press Agentry," he called it. "Thousands who wouldn't have listened in the first place will now glue themselves to their sets. . . . Dr. King has had nothing but the ablest promotion service from whites." So the rest of the nation heard and saw King on October 27; Montgomery, where the telecast originated, saw him a week later on November 3.

It was a normal, high-level, somewhat philosophical discussion of nonviolence, Gandhi and the positive results of the bus boycott, with not a single inflammatory word. Perhaps the climax of the King-Agronsky colloquy was a question that had been suggested by Editor Hall. He wanted Agronsky to find out from King how the philosophy of nonviolence was reconciled with the use of troops at Little Rock. King answered that he was not a pacifist, believing in nonviolence at any price or an anarchist opposing the state altogether, and that he favored the intelligent use of the nation's police power to maintain order.

When the King-Agronsky film was over, a local white Baptist minister and the city commissioner who wanted to be portrayed in the movie as a "complete and sincere segregationist," attempted to give a rebuttal. But there was little to refute. Nor were the refuters accustomed to philosophical discussion. Probably they would have served their cause best by not appearing at all. The *Advertiser* was right, King's "keenest adversaries are in fact his press agents and ablest sponsors."

Events continued to crowd each other. One development of far-reaching importance brought King again into court. When he was convicted, back in March, 1956, under the Alabama anti-boycott law, his lawyers appealed immediately. They had anticipated the possibility of an adverse verdict in the lower court and had brilliantly laid the groundwork for a review based on the constitutional issues involved. If necessary, the case could go all the way up to the Supreme Court of the United States.

In the light of the higher court's rulings for the past two decades, students of civil rights law were quite confident that the conviction of the lower court would be reversed—probably unanimously.

But the court reporter was late in completing the transcript of the verbatim record of the King trial. Delays of this kind are frequent enough when cases come faster than the clerical staff can handle them. In such an event, however, it is the responsibility of the lawyers involved to ask the appellate court to grant an extension and postpone the date of the hearing until the full transcript has been prepared.

King's attorneys forgot to do this and thus by rule of law they were not ready when the trial date came. They expected the prosecution attorneys to be "good sports" and not press the issue of the delayed transcript. But this was no game of gentlemen at tennis. Perhaps realizing that their chances of winning on the merits of the case were slight, the prosecution seized upon the technicality, charging "improper procedure." This was true. Consequently, the state Court of Appeals simply denied King's motion on *procedural grounds* and it was unlikely that the United States Supreme Court would reverse such a ruling.

And so, all the long hard nights of labor, the thumbing through musty records for precedent-setting and relevant judicial decisions; all the calculated cross-examination of witnesses; all the deft objections to the trial judge's rulings; all the suggestions from the best constitutional lawyers in the nation—all, went down the drain. King's lawyers were utterly disgusted with themselves for forgetting such an elemental item of their trade. They had missed becoming famous by a few days—the time the court clerk took to complete the transcript.

Now the best they could do was to look for the simplest settlement, pay the fine for King, and then take up another of the cases of the indicted boycott leaders.

Surprisingly, the opposition came forward with a proposal. Several white men had been apprehended who confessed to dynamiting homes and churches in the wave of bombings that woke Montgomery up before dawn on January 10, 1957. But when the first two of these men were brought to trial, their lawyers pulled out all of the stops, appealing to the violent tribal loyalties of the jurors. The men were found "not guilty" and the crowd in the courtroom cheered. The prosecution was sure that it was useless to go through with the other trials, for no Montgomery jury would find anybody guilty who was charged with bombing Negro bus boycotters.

So the "package deal" was that (1) King would pay his fine; (2) all other cases against Negro boycott leaders would be dropped; and (3) all cases against white "bombers" would be dropped.

Prosecution and defense agreed—and it was so ordered.

Those who called themselves realists accepted this as possibly the best way out of a difficult situation; it would give the city a little peace and the issues, in a sense, were somewhat stale. However, the idealists felt that this compromise was a surrender. The *Afro* asked King why he agreed to such a settlement. He replied that "it would have been a needless waste of time and money to continue the case. We decided the best thing to do was to pay the fine and move on to another phase of the battle."

A college professor from King's home town said: "If these people are serious about their talk of going to jail for their beliefs, here was their best chance."

A little later, P. L. Prattis, of the Pittsburgh *Courier,* in his searching series of articles on nonviolence, wrote in his column for December 21: "Even if the case should have been lost in the United States Supreme Court, Dr. King and the 89 other persons, mostly ministers, involved, SHOULD HAVE GONE TO JAIL AND WORKED OUT THEIR FINES."

The out-of-court settlement, obviously, was a victory for the self-styled realists rather than the idealists.

King's troubles were not over. The Asian flu epidemic, which was sweeping the country in the fall of 1957, got him, too. He was out for a week in early November.

Of greater duration—and perhaps pain—was the series of articles that Trezzvant Anderson ran in the Pittsburgh *Courier* during November and December. Unlike all of the previous writers on the Montgomery boycott for the Negro press, Anderson was looking for "sensations" and "revelations." In the natural history of social movements and personalities an exposé was overdue. As one wit put it, "After the period of acclaim, comes the period of defame."

"Roving Reporter" Anderson came to Montgomery and found his disgruntled witnesses. His big mistake was his failure to check their stories. And so his series fell apart in the middle because of inaccuracies. It was easy for those in the know to shoot holes through his charges that the condition of the ordinary Negro in Montgomery was not improving and that Mrs. Rosa Parks and E. D. Nixon had been shunted aside by King in his grab for publicity. The *Courier,* in all fairness, printed rejoinders that practically destroyed the effect of the articles that the paper was publishing.

King's woes were not over. In December the MIA attempted another institute on social change through nonviolence, celebrating the second anniversary of the boycott. It was a flop, leaving King quite distraught. Again, he wondered if he had lost his touch in Montgomery. He could feel his "non-co-operators" and "enemies" breathing down his neck.

One simple truth was that since the momentum of the Montgomery movement had inevitably slowed down, those who desired success for MIA projects would have to cultivate the arts of planning and promotion as did others elsewhere.

Another simple truth was that King himself was too much in motion. He was pulled in a hundred different directions at once—almost pulled apart. He was still trying to do what would have overwhelmed three good men. He was flying about the country, speaking almost everywhere. It was true that he had stopped accepting new engagements but he was already dated up two years ahead, and some of these appearances, like the one in St. Louis before the triennial assembly of the National Council of Churches, "just couldn't be missed." Then, too, King was the head of MIA and SCLC. And there were also his pastoral duties.

But as the new year, 1958, rolled in, King did get away for short rests and vacations. He had a hideout in Montgomery where he was inaccessible to everyone but his family and secretary. He had another in an Atlanta hotel. Between them, he was able to rest and do a little writing during December and January. He could have done more but at times, unguardedly, he would say to his friends that he was going to his hideout and even confided to a few of them where these places of refuge were. Such an open-hearted man would scarcely make a good agent for the FBI.

King did whittle down his day-to-day responsibilities with the MIA, even moving his office over to his church. There his trustees built him a new office with paneled walls, built-in bookshelves, a big glass-top desk, a bright green sofa and gold, wall-to-wall carpeting.

The MIA had tapered off its program of civic betterment. The main activity remaining was the campaign of voter registration. This was a slow, plodding expedition against the indirection of registration officials and the apathy of nonvoters.

Generally speaking, race relations had quieted down in the city. Since desegregated buses had become an accepted fact, tension, and apparently interest in social change, had eased off. The Negro community had not pressed its legal victories, hoping to win the whites over with sweet reasonableness. Even on the buses, it was the younger and educated Negro who usually sat up front. The older people and the domestic servants, riding to and from work in white neighborhoods, took seats, as before, behind the white passengers.

On their part, white bus riders, when traveling through Negro neighborhoods, sat as close to the front as possible, at times jamming themselves up behind the bus driver. Some few, however, took seats wherever they could find them. There were a few scuffles, but for the mass of human beings transported about the city each day, the percentage of clashes was infinitesimal.

In other areas of city life, interracial contacts were also more self-conscious and deliberate than before the boycott. Some of the business houses had learned from the experience of the bus company that a policy of courtesy paid off. Nothing—absolutely nothing—was being done to desegregate the schools. In general, whites and Negroes of Montgomery perhaps "loved" each other a little less but respected each other a great deal more.

Easter, 1958

The restraint of the Negroes could be misleading. Some less perceptive observers may have felt that the spirit of the boycott was past and gone forever. Easter Sunday, 1958, would show them how wrong they were.

For some six years Jeremiah Reeves had languished in Alabama jails under the shadow of death. He had been a drummer in his high school band and with local jazz combos. He was a slim, attractive youth of sixteen when he was charged with the violation of some half-dozen white women at sundry times and places. He was tried and convicted on one of these charges. The United States Supreme Court reviewed the case, found it faulty and sent it back to the lower court for correction. Reeves was again tried, and again appealed to the high court, but this time he lost.

Public opinion was much divided on Reeves. As is usually the case with sex crimes involving white and Negro, everybody seems to choose sides on the basis of color. But there were some whites—expressing themselves privately, of course—who also had doubts about the aggression that the young man had found necessary in his alleged rapes. From his prison cell, Reeves himself carried on an extensive correspondence with sympathizers. His letters were well written and he expressed hope and fortitude.

Committees were formed, petitions were submitted and the moderates, Negro and white, agreed that perhaps a long term of imprisonment would satisfy the situation reasonably. Others, however, disagreed and at 12:01 A.M., Friday, March 28, Reeves was electrocuted. This was a rude shock to those who felt that he would never receive the death penalty. The Negro community was stunned. Reeves' mother claimed her son's body, and the crowd at his funeral was so great that the little church collapsed. This was an ominous sign of evil portent, some said. It added to the weeping and anger.

So, on the morning of April 1, mimeographed leaflets, calling for collective action, appeared mysteriously all over the Negro community. The leaflets said:

Dear Negro Alabamians,
Jeremiah Reeves went to the electric chair Friday charged with rape. On the day before his execution a white man, similarly charged with raping a teen-age Negro girl, was not even arrested. Our nation is supposed to be founded upon equality before the law. But the fact is that the laws are administered around the voting power of the white people. . . .
IN ORDERLY, NON-VIOLENT PROTEST AGAINST LEGAL MISCARRIAGE OF JUSTICE WHERE NEGROES ARE CONCERNED, EVERY NEGRO FAMILY, ORGANIZATION, CHURCH, CLUB, AND INDIVIDUAL, ARE ASKED TO MEET IN FRONT OF THE CAPITOL ON SUNDAY, APRIL 6, AT 1:30 P.M. IN A CITYWIDE MEETING, THAT THE PUBLIC MAY KNOW THAT NEGROES WANT JUSTICE IN THE COURTS.
BE PRESENT AND ON TIME. COME RAIN, SHINE, SLEET OR SNOW!!!

This was the way the bus boycott had started. In many respects the pattern of December 1-5, 1955 was repeated, but this time all the players knew their lines and spoke them clearly, moving on and off stage as if by prearrangement.

The White Citizens Council also was more knowledgeable than formerly. A few hotheads were for stopping the protest in one way or another. But the WCC leaders advised by radio, TV, newspaper and direct message that "all right-thinking white citizens" should stay away from the meeting because its purpose was "to provoke violence." For the moment Editor Grover Hall was heartened that his suggestion of ignoring the "troublemakers" was catching on. Moreover, the city fathers announced that no official action would be taken to halt the Negro protesters.

And then, on the night of Good Friday, large KKK signs were stenciled on the walks and pavement of the Capitol grounds. Grover Hall was outraged. He called the unknown sign painters "klan trash" and "albino idiots" and then he labeled them as equally unwise and unrepresentative as "Dr. King" and "these misled Negro citizens" who were protesting "a rape trial so fair that the United States Supreme Court upheld the conviction."

City street cleaners had to use blow torches but they succeeded in erasing the KKK markings on Saturday.

On Easter Sunday, by 1:30 in the afternoon, some twenty-five hundred Negroes had gathered on the spacious steps and walks in front of the whitewashed Capitol and near the statue of Jefferson Davis and the very spot where he swore allegiance to the Confederacy. It was a beautiful day with a sad quietness about it. The orderly well-dressed crowd moved about with such restraint that one piercing scream of anguish might well have started hundreds to weeping, though they could not have said why they were crying.

City police were on hand, courteously directing traffic. State highway patrols were present on orders from the Governor to see that the meeting was not molested. He had assured Negro leaders privately that they were thoroughly within their rights to be there. It was Easter and everybody appeared to be moderate and decorous.

At 2:10 about fifteen Negro ministers, in black robes, marched the short block from the Dexter Avenue Baptist Church to the Capitol steps. Then the program began. The crowd repeated a pledge that was read by the Rev. S. W. Shultz, affirming "the fatherhood of God and the brotherhood of all mankind," faith in democracy and a plea that "all Americans . . . join us . . . to eradicate racial and religious prejudices."

"America" was sung. The Rev. Mr. Abernathy prayed—at length. The Rev. R. E. DuBose, Jr., led the reading of "A Litany of Freedom," which had been originally prepared for the Washington pilgrimage. The only speech of the afternoon was made by the Rev. Dr. King. It was a short Easter sermon. He began by paraphrasing the ideas of the leaflet in religious terms:

We assemble here this afternoon on the steps of this beautiful Capitol building in an act of public repentance for our community for committing a tragic and unsavory injustice. A young man, Jeremiah Reeves, who was little more than a child when he was first arrested, died in the electric chair for the charge of rape. Whether or not he was guilty of this crime is a question that none of us can answer. But the issue before us now is not the innocence or guilt of Jeremiah Reeves. Even if he were guilty, it is the severity and inequality of the penalty that constitutes the injustice. Full grown white men committing comparable crimes against Negro girls are rarely ever punished, and are never given the death penalty or even a life sentence. . . .

We are here to repent for the constant miscarriage of justice that we confront every day in our courts. . . .

We appeal this afternoon to our white brothers, whether they are private citizens or public officials, to courageously meet this problem. This is not a political issue; it is ultimately a moral issue. It is a question of the dignity of man. . . .

. . . Man has separated from God and . . . from his brother. . . . God is in Christ seeking to reconcile the world unto himself . . .

King and the others spoke through a portable loud-speaker. Those on the fringes of the crowd did not hear all the words, but they knew what to expect.

Again, there was a prayer. Then a hymn, "Leaning on the Everlasting Arms." Finally, the benediction by the Rev. Ralph Hilson. That was all.

The crowd dispersed as quietly as it had assembled. There were no incidents. A few curious whites had stood in the distance, looking at what went on. A single carload of white youths, flying the Confederate flag and with their radio playing loudly, circled the assemblage and then disappeared.

Once King had preached a sermon entitled "The Death of Evil on the Seashore." That might come later, but for one Easter afternoon at least, evil had been driven from the city by the air of decency of citizens and preachers and policemen at the steps of the Capitol.

The morning *Advertiser* congratulated Montgomery for behaving like "an old pro," concluding with the usual thrust: "*Life* magazine happened to have been in town Sunday on a political assignment and went to the Capitol, lens cocked. The photographers went away disappointed, for the whites had refused to make any news."

There were, however, other Montgomerians who felt that their fellow Negro citizens should not be permitted to score such a clean propaganda victory by default. Accordingly, some thirty white ministers and three hundred lay churchmen issued a statement to the press, denouncing the Easter mass meeting and defending the justice of Southern courts. This group proposed that mass gatherings that "build race hatred and the heightening of tensions" be supplanted by "conversations among responsible leaders. . . ."

The Rev. Dr. King and his colleagues responded immediately: "We are pleased . . . to accept the invitation" for such conversations and asked the white ministers to suggest "a date and a place of meeting."

The next day the newspapers reported: "Clerics Cold to Talks Bid," the white ministers saying that "We have extended no invitation to Dr. King or his committee." King and his colleagues came right back, asking the ministers to name the "responsible leaders" to whom their invitation was, in fact, directed. There was no reply to this and no further exchange and no meeting. Grover Hall was right. Perhaps it was best to say "ho-hum" and pass on.

Mississippi to Washington

As King became less tied down by the MIA he became more and more involved in the program of SCLC. This furnished a broad base for activating the whole South and an appropriate platform from which any national action that he thought necessary could be taken.

The SCLC still dreamed the great dream of registering millions of dark-skinned Southerners and had ready ideas as to how this could be done. But the implementation came more slowly. Big conferences and mass meetings were easier.

The SCLC met in Memphis in mid-November of 1957, but it was December before the central office was opened, and then with only a temporary commitment from Miss Ella Baker as director. Bayard Rustin would lend a hand in an emergency but afterward he would be off, following his star to another great cause in some corner of the world. For example, on the morning of April 4, 1958, CBS in its *World News Roundup,* reporting on a mass march on Trafalgar Square, London, in protest against nuclear bomb tests, said, "And the leader of the parade is an American Negro, Bayard Rustin."

King called his SCLC board together in Atlanta in January, 1958, urging full attendance, for "this will be our last meeting before the mammoth kick-off for the Citizenship Crusade on Wednesday, February 12."

And so, last-minute plans were made. Leaflets were printed; news releases issued; and instructions were sent out to local committees. The big idea was to have giant mass meetings in twenty Southern cities—all on Lincoln's birthday.

When February 12 came, the pulpit orators had their audiences singing and shouting. If the SCLC had only the setup to crystallize the enthusiasm! The general morale effect was good but actually the names of few new voters would get on the books during the next month or so. The crusade, however, did stimulate local groups that already had workers in the field.

On April 30, the SCLC board met again. The long search for an executive director was ended. The Rev. John L. Tilley, who had done a splendid job of voter registration in Baltimore, made plans to move into the Atlanta office with Miss Baker, who was now designated as associate director.

The board also set plans for an open conference in Mississippi for May 29. This was daring, for to many Negroes and their friends "Mississippi" has an evil sound, with loud echoes of plantations and white man bosses and the painful cries of Emmet Till and his brothers. Moreover, in 1956 the Governor of Mississippi had warned King to stay away.

In due course May 29 came and the conference was held as scheduled. Actually, some of the conferees who had thought that going into Mississippi was an act of bravery afterward were loud in their praises of the deportment of the police, newsmen and white Mississippians they encountered. The news stories on the activities of the conference deserve to be described as "objective" and no case of the expected brutality of local or state "peace" officers was reported. Governor Coleman did not interfere with Dr. King, and Mississippi Negro leaders came out to the meeting in force. The bulletin of the SCLC described the Clarksdale assembly as "best meeting yet—in attendance, enthusiasm and sense of direction." This was the most "down-to-earth" conference the SCLC had ever held; there were fewer speeches, more field reports and analysis. At last it seemed that the organization had "found" itself.

In terms of national affairs, the conference shot a single arrow into the air. It scored a direct hit. Its target was the White House. This was a letter to President Eisenhower saying:

Amid continued violence in the South and the dreadful prospect that some areas may close schools rather than obey Federal Court Orders to desegregate in September we urgently renew our request that you grant an immediate conference to Negro leaders in an effort to resolve these problems. . . . Since quite some time ago you promised to meet with Negro leaders and because the present climate of lawless defiance threatens to produce incidents that will shame America at home and abroad when school opens in September, we respectfully request an immediate audience.

About a week later, the answer came back. It was a telephone call from the White House: Yes, the President did find it possible to see Dr. King and a few others. Please come to Washington so that the particulars of the conference could be worked out.

This was great news! King would be in Washington on June 9. On the way, he stopped to receive two more honorary degrees: Doctor of Laws from Morgan State College, Baltimore, Maryland, and Doctor of Humane Letters from Central State College, Xenia, Ohio.

Mrs. King continued to match strides, so to speak, with her husband, making "Woman's Day" talks at churches in Denver and Dayton, and singing at Birmingham.

In Washington, King met with White House aides Rocco Siciliano and E. Frederic Morrow and a member of the staff of the United States Attorney General. At this preliminary meeting, the date for the White House session was set at June 23, 11:15 A.M. King got the impression that the interview with the President would last for fifteen minutes.

The next question was, who should come? King's first thought had been to suggest the names of his top colleagues of SCLC, for the White House bid had come in response to that organization's requests. But he felt that the conference might be so significant that a national rather than a strictly Southern representation should be made. So King suggested his fellow co-chairman of the Washington pilgrimage, A. Philip Randolph and Roy Wilkins.

Randolph was acceptable but there was some objection to Wilkins from the White House representatives on the grounds that perhaps the President would not want to talk with anyone who had spoken of him the way Wilkins had at the Negro "summit" conference. This was a meeting of some four hundred heads of organizations, scholars and others, that the National Negro Publishers Association had held in Washington on May 12 and 13. Almost every Negro leader had been there except Martin Luther King. And he was absent because he had a long-standing commitment to the American Jewish Congress which was meeting at the same time in Miami.

President Eisenhower spoke to the publishers and their guests for twelve minutes. First, he urged his mutual security, defense and foreign aid program. Then he came to civil rights, saying:

. . . every American, if we are to be true to our Constitutional heritage, must have respect for the law. He must know that he is equal before the law. He must have respect for the courts.

He must have respect for others. He must make perfectly certain that he can, in every single kind of circumstance, respect himself.

In such problems as this, there are no revolutionary cures. They are evolutionary. I started in the Army in 1911. I have lived to see the time come when in none of the Armed Services is practiced any kind of discrimination because of race, religion or color.

In the Federal Government this same truth holds steady. . . . But I do believe that as long as there are human problems . . . we must have patience and forbearance.

I do not decry laws, for they are necessary. But I say that laws themselves will never solve problems that have their roots in the human heart and in the human emotions.

The "patience and forbearance" advice did not go down easily with the delegates. For one, Roy Wilkins said:

I understand the President of the United States gave you some startling advice this afternoon. I guess from where he sits, this makes sense. If you were President, you would want everything to go smoothly. You wouldn't want anyone to kick up a fuss—labor, Democrats, the Negro. If you could convince the Negro that he was being impatient, I guess you would do so. From where Mr. Eisenhower sits, I suppose this makes sense. I don't sit there.

This was mild in comparison with comments of others. Almost every Negro newspaper that editorialized on the conference, rejected "patience and forbearance."

King asked the White House men if they had seen his criticism of the President. They said that they had. King had called Eisenhower's words "potentially dangerous," adding that they would only "encourage those who have defied the Supreme Court decisions and who have created the climate of tension and crisis culminating across the South." Then he indicated in his indirect way that if Wilkins did not come he himself would not come. So Wilkins was declared acceptable.

Then the aides brought up the name of Lester B. Granger, who was thought to be a rather conservative liberal and perhaps a Republican. He was thoroughly acceptable to King, who remembered him from the celebration in Ghana and had occasionally encountered him in and about New York before and since.

The preliminaries concluded, King notified Randolph, Wilkins and Granger that they would be receiving invitations from the White House. Everybody was delighted and agreed that the four of them should put their heads together before going in to talk with the President. The best day for this would be June 22, the Sunday before the Monday of the White House visit.

Meanwhile the news leaked out that Eisenhower would meet with several Negro leaders. Congressman Adam Powell assumed that this was the meeting that he had been promised by the White House as far back as the time when the Little Rock issue first flared. Powell made an announcement to the press and actually named the persons that he felt should compose the delegation. The White House promptly let it be known that this was not Powell's meeting and that Powell himself would not be in the group, though King, Randolph, Wilkins and Granger would.

Back in Montgomery, King and his advisors went to work. This time there would be no charge of homework undone. Accordingly, a six-page memorandum was put together and sent airmail to Randolph, Wilkins and Granger. In turn these three prepared memoranda supplementing and correcting King's and brought them along to the planning session of Sunday, June 22, at the headquarters of the Washington NAACP. King arrived at 9 P.M. and found the other three already there. It was a real work session, lasting until 4 A.M.

At first, Wilkins was a little reluctant to have things cut-and-dried. He himself was a master at improvisation and naturally favored feeling out the situation, sensing the flow of things as the conversation with the President proceeded, pushing wherever possible, retreating wherever necessary. In this way, he felt, more would be gained. But the others thought that a set plan should be drawn; however, if the talk took a special direction of its own, then the plan might be thrown aside and the topic of the moment followed. Thus agreed, the men then laid out their memos on the table. King had also a dozen telegrams from various other persons whom he had asked for suggestions. So, far into the early morning hours the men talked, wrote and rewrote until they had hammered out a seven-page statement. Later Granger would say everybody had agreed to every word of it.

The men also determined the procedure they would follow in talking with the President. Randolph would lead off, making the opening statement; then King, Wilkins and Granger would each discuss three of the nine points of the joint memorandum. Copies of the document would be made available to the President and the press.

Feeling that they had done a good night's work, the men separated, dashing off to catch a few hours of sleep. As King went away, he felt satisfied with the evening's labor, for everyone had got along well together. He had expected this from his two old pilgrimage colleagues, Randolph and Wilkins. He was delighted to find that it was also true of Granger; for this was the first time that King had had close contact with him.

Lester Blackwell Granger was a social welfare expert. His name was synonymous with the National Urban League, of which he was executive secretary. Until a few years ago, almost all of Granger's problems seemed to dissolve when confronted by his ability and charm. He was a success as a tennis champion, an artillery lieutenant in the First World War and a social worker. He had attended mixed schools for most of his education, and while at Dartmouth was a schoolmate of James V. Forrestal, later Secretary of the Navy and Secretary of Defense.

It was Granger, more than any other single individual, who gave expert advice on the integration of Negro and white servicemen in the Navy under Forrestal. Everybody in Washington who knew Granger liked him, as did his fellow social workers all over the country, who elected him president of the National Conference of Social Work.

But ten years ago, Granger's good fortune deserted him—at least temporarily. He was stricken with cancer and about the same time began having trouble with his board of directors at the National Urban League. Only his close friends knew about his illness but the revolt of his board finally broke into the newspapers. Some of his most prominent Negro members—such as Kenneth Clark, the psychologist, and Ted Brown, AFL-CIO research specialist—issued public statements and resigned. Their charges were that the League's board was self-perpetuating and undemocratic and that this made it easy for a clique of wealthy men—some of whom were in real estate—to sabotage any real programs of integration, especially in the housing field.

Miraculously, Granger survived both of these attacks. He is today one of those fortunates who have been cured of cancer because it was detected early. Granger also regrouped his board and projected a harder-hitting program for the League.

In June of 1958 he was sixty-one, balding and graying. His step was no longer spry. A line or two marked the Granger smile. But he was still very much himself—sincere and affable, and not wanting people to mistake his pleasantness for conservatism.

With Ike

The conferees met on time: 10:30, June 23, in the outer office reception room of the White House. There was ample time (forty-five minutes) for the exchange of stray thoughts that had come to them since they had parted. They were told that they would have thirty minutes with the President. They agreed that they would not quote him directly afterward, leaving him free to make his own statement in words of his own choosing. Morrow, Siciliano and Attorney General William P. Rogers came in. Everybody was chatting amicably when the signal came (11:15) that "Gentlemen, the President will see you now."

The conferees took seats fanning out from the President's big desk in a broken circle, King sitting directly opposite the Chief Executive. After the preliminaries were over, Randolph, according to plan, began. He was completely at ease; his first White House conference had taken place back in the days when he was with a delegation, led by the fiery Monroe Trotter, during the Coolidge administration. Randolph, omitting the preamble of the joint statement, read aloud the nine points:

1. The President of the United States should declare in a nationwide pronouncement, prior to September, that the law will be vigorously upheld with the total resources at his command.
2. Much emphasis has been laid on the need for restoring communication between white and colored Southerners who are troubled by a common fear of reaction. The President can well set the example in this matter by convoking a White House Conference of constructive leadership to discuss ways and means of complying peaceably with the Court's rulings.
3. Information, resources, and advice of the appropriate government agencies addressed to the problems of integration should be made available to all officials and community groups seeking to work out a program of education and action.
4. The President should request both parties to lay aside partisanship so that the Congress can enact a civil rights bill which will include Part III originally in the 1957 bill, in order that constitutional rights other than voting rights may be enforced by the United States At-

torney General. Lack of adequate and clear statutory authority has made the Federal Government a mere spectator in the disgraceful maneuverings at Little Rock.

5. We urge the President to direct the Department of Justice to give all legal assistance possible under the law, including the filing of a brief as a friend of the court and appearance of counsel, in the appeal from the [Judge Harry] Lemley decision in the Little Rock case.

6. The President of the United States should direct the Department of Justice to act now to protect the right of citizens to register and vote. In the nine months since the enactment of the 1957 Civil Rights Act, overt acts have been committed against prospective Negro registrants in some areas and numerous complaints have been submitted to the Department, but to date, not a single case has reached a court of law. Unless immediate action is undertaken, thousands of Negro citizens will be denied the right to cast a ballot in the 1958 elections.

7. The President should direct the Department of Justice to act under existing statutes in the wave of bombings of churches, synagogues, homes, and community centers; also in the murderous brutality directed against Negro citizens in Dawson, Georgia, and other communities.

8. In order to counteract the deliberate hamstringing of the new Civil Rights Commission, the President should recommend to the Congress the extension of its life for at least a full year beyond its present expiration date.

9. The President should make it clear both in statement and in act that he believes in the principle that federal money should not be used to underwrite segregation in violation of the federal constitutional rights of millions of Negro citizens, and that this principle should be applied whether in matters of federal aid to education, hospitals, housing, or any other grants-in-aid to state and local government. In support of national policy, the Federal Government should finance continuation of public schools where state funds are withdrawn because of integration.

The President seemed to listen intently. Then, each man, on cue from Randolph, took up a section of the document, elaborating and explaining. The President followed them closely, occasionally frowning or smiling and asking a question here or there as the exposition went along.

King observed that the conference with the President seemed to transform the personalities of two of his colleagues. Wilkins, the man whom the administration shrank from meeting because he personified that horned devil NAACP, turned out to be the most moderate of the conferees. On the other hand, Granger was the most aggressive. Apparently, he was not going to have anybody think that he was holding back or being soft. In his column in the *Amsterdam News* for May 24, he had written: "President Eisenhower's 'Patience and Forbearance' message to Negro leadership assembled at Washington, D.C., could not have been more poorly timed, from the standpoint of the government and our Afro-American population." Granger repeated this to the President, who flushed for a moment, then recovered his composure.

King was also surprised to find that the President did not know that Negroes were greatly displeased with his administration for not supporting the Supreme Court's integration decrees more strongly. King wondered what the President's advisors had told him on this score.

The President spoke generally, saying in broad terms that he believed in law and order and that all Americans should have their rights. But he would not be drawn into any definite commitment as to what he would do. He would not even comment on the current Little Rock situation.

The President spoke briefly of some of the things that his administration had done for the benefit of all Americans, including Negroes. Attorney General Rogers took over at this point, extending the President's remarks.

By this time, thirty minutes for the interview had stretched into fifty. As the group was breaking up to leave, the President again expressed faith and optimism. At a moment when King was near him, Mr. Eisenhower said with a sigh, "Reverend, there are so many problems . . . Lebanon, Algeria . . ."

The presidential aides preferred that the Negro leaders not release their nine-point statement to the press, but they did. Wilkins was designated as spokesman to the waiting journalists, photographers and TV men. According to protocol, he concentrated upon what the Negro leaders had said rather than on what the President had said to them. Wilkins expressed encouragement from the talk. But the reporters would not be put off with generalities. One of them asked: "Did you come away with the impression that the President would do anything about your suggestions?" Wilkins' answer was that if the President had immediately agreed to the requests of the four leaders they would not have thought that he meant it.

Then the newsmen turned to Randolph, who said:

The conference has put a new hope into the hearts of colored people, that as a part of the great American family they have greater assurance of belonging to this family as equals in order that they may utilize their gifts, talents and genius to make America great and strong.

Some of the papers merely used this quote and let it gc at that. But the *Afro* commented editorially: "Come, come, Philip. You can talk plainer than that. What did the man say?"

King talked about re-establishing communication between Negroes and whites of the South. Granger said next to nothing at this time.

The *Amsterdam News* ran the headline: "Successful Meeting: Ike Says 'Nothing.' " The *Courier* expressed mixed emotions:

The question therefore arises as to what this conference accomplished except to possibly re-emphasize what is on the whole country's mind; which is all to the good, of course, but how much good? Even the most skeptical persons, however, will agree that it was better to have had it than not to have had it, because conceivably something good may come out of it.

Under the caption "Did Ike Charm Negro Leaders?" Louis Lautier wrote that

The President apparently turned on the Eisenhower charm and pacified four top colored leaders who conferred with him at the White House, Monday. After the conference none of the quartet uttered a single word in criticism of Mr. Eisenhower. Particularly noticeable was the about-face attitude of Roy Wilkins, executive secretary of the NAACP, and the Rev. Martin Luther King, leader of the Montgomery, Ala., bus boycott movement.

Earl Brown, Democrat, in his column in the *Amsterdam News* for July 5, concluded that "the conference was so meaningless that it may have been better if it had not been held at all."

Brown's fellow *Amsterdam News* columnist, Lester B. Granger, gave his estimate of the meeting he had attended: "People . . . are still asking—by phone, letters or in casual encounters—was the meeting worthwhile? The answer is still the same, 'It depends on what you were expecting.' " Granger then went on to say that no "realist" should have looked for "definite commitments" from the President. However, the "plain-talking, face-to-face" discussion with the President demonstrated the unity of Negro leaders on civil rights. "Perhaps this will be the most lasting effect. . . ."

Back in Montgomery, King looked over his press clippings. From coast to coast the daily as well as the weekly newspapers had featured the June 23 interview. One of the curious and perhaps revealing contrasts in the treatment of the story was furnished by the New York *Times* and the Montgomery *Advertiser*. Both papers of June 24 ran the story on page 1. But in the very spot—top, left of center—where the *Times* placed the photograph of the President and the Negro leaders, the *Advertiser* placed a picture of a handcuffed Negro criminal suspect. This was not a story of local origin but came in from New York. The *Advertiser* put the picture of Eisenhower and the Negro leaders at the bottom of its second page, a good place to hide almost anything. The *Times* story had the lead: "4 Negro Leaders See Eisenhower," the *Advertiser*: "Ike Silent on Negroes' Plea." Students of the influence of the social environment on the treatment of news—and vice versa—may find these contrasts worthy of study. However, they should know that Lester Granger cursed both papers for he was, no doubt inadvertently, left off the AP wirephoto that both the *Times* and the *Advertiser* used.

A week or so after June 23, King was asked to give his considered evaluation of the White House talk. He spoke of two positive results: First, the excellent press that gave the nine points to the nation. The American people thus got a chance to learn what was on the minds of Negro Americans and what they expect of their government; secondly, the President learned this, too. Whatever he might do or not do immediately or in the future could no longer be explained or explained away by the charitable consideration that perhaps "Ike just didn't know."

Looking back, even Wilkins agreed that it was a stroke of wisdom that the Negro leaders did prepare a document that they could present to the White House—and to the world.

Danger of Limb . . .

And so the Rev. Dr. Martin Luther King reached a climactic point in his career. To share a conference with the President of the United States on one of the great problems of the nation is no mean achievement for a young man under thirty.

Ordinarily this biography would stop at this point. But it cannot end on this note of triumph, with the White House fading away in the distance behind the bright young face turned toward the future. Two incidents that occurred during the month of September, 1958, added a frightening reminder of the insecurities of our time and the dangers of public prominence and fame. One of the incidents almost ended King's life itself.

On the morning of September 3, Dr. King decided to accompany his friend, the Rev. Mr. Abernathy, who was to appear in court that morning to testify in the case of a man being tried for an assault on Abernathy a few days previously. There were indications that this attack might have been part of a plan to discredit the Negro leadership of the Montgomery movement, since wild and irresponsible charges against Abernathy emerged during the trial. As the Rev. Mr. and Mrs. Abernathy and Dr. and Mrs. King arrived at the door of the municipal court, the guard there rudely announced that no more seats were available inside. Abernathy informed him that he was a party to one of the cases being heard and then added, "This is my wife here with me." The guard, in a less than civil manner, told Mrs. Abernathy that unless she had a subpoena she could not go in.

At this moment, the Kings, who were a few paces behind the Abernathys, came up and Dr. King asked what the trouble was. Mrs. Abernathy answered that the guard would not let her in. King, feeling that maybe an attorney in the court could get the group admitted, asked the guard if he could speak to Fred Gray, his lawyer, who was also representing Abernathy. The guard replied: "Boy, if you don't get the hell away from here, you will need a lawyer yourself." At that moment and before anything more could be said, two policemen dashed up from behind the Abernathys and the Kings and one of them said: "Boy, you done done it; let's go." Then, grabbing King and twisting his arm, they hustled him to the police department which was just around the corner, in the same building.

Everyone was taken aback but Mrs. King hurriedly followed the officers who were whisking her husband away. They looked over their shoulders at her, one of them saying: "Gal, you want to go, too? Just nod your head." King pleaded, "Don't say anything, darling."

In a few moments they had him inside the police station, still twisting his arms while asking for the keys to the cells. "Put him in the hole," the desk officer yelled, tossing out the keys.

Nobody seemed to be mindful that a photographer was snapping pictures all the while.

Another policeman roared: "Everybody clear out. You, too, gal"— meaning Mrs. King, who was with a few other Negroes who had followed the commotion from the court steps.

When they got King to the cell they told him to raise his hands above his head, frisking him and kneeing him. Then, they seized him by the throat, spun him around and kicked him as he was thrust into the cell and the door locked.

In about ten minutes the officers returned for him. It was apparent that something had happened at a higher level, for these same policemen were now almost courteous in their silence and restraint. Obviously, the colossal blunder had been discovered by someone in authority who damned the policemen for their "dumbness" rather than praising them as they expected for "roughing up" the "chief agitator."

At the desk, King was permitted to sign his own bond in an atmosphere of deference.

The news distributing agencies soon had the story on their wires, and the late afternoon and next morning's papers all over the nation carried the account. The accompanying pictures graphically answered the question of whether there had been any "police brutality." The Commissioner of Public Safety, in charge of the city's law enforcement agencies, was quoted as saying that the treatment of Dr. King was not different from that of others. This was probably true—at least for Negroes.

King's trial was set for the following Friday morning. Between the Wednesday of the arrest and the trial date, messages and advice poured into his office and home from many parts of the country. The MIA board went into special session. Roy Wilkins of the NAACP sent a telegram to the White House, asking the President to condemn what had happened. King told his friends that, since he had not violated any law, if the court found him guilty, he would not pay a fine but would go to jail instead.

Meanwhile, the opposition forces were also consulting together and planning. It was realized that arresting King had put the police department in a jam. As a way out, the commissioner could apologize, even privately, drop the charge against the clergyman and thus end the matter. But for the commissioner, who was a member of the White Citizens Council and who desired to be known as a "complete and sincere segregationist," to apologize to Martin Luther King was unthinkable. As an alternative, the judge of the court where King would appear could dismiss the case. But this would mean that the whites were yielding to the blacks.

And so the court of September 5, 1958, made the same mistake as the court of December 5, 1955, when Mrs. Rosa Parks stood before it. In each instance, prudence and charity would have recommended a verdict of "not guilty." But the best that the court could do both times was to find the defendants guilty and then let them off with a light fine. The judgment of guilt was precisely what was unacceptable to both Mrs. Parks and Dr. King. The penalty was $10 "and costs of court," totaling $14 or fourteen days in jail. Incidentally, the charge was changed from loitering to refusing to obey a policeman.

Attorney Fred Gray told the court that his client would serve out the time. King himself said: "Your Honor . . . I could not in all good conscience pay a fine for an act that I did not commit and above all for brutal treatment that I did not deserve." A full statement of his position was handed to the judge in writing and copies were passed by Abernathy to the newsmen present.

Visibly, the court was upset. King was then taken to a detention room, where he met and made friends with Negroes and whites waiting to be tried or transported to the city jail. He attempted to get on the police wagon taking a load of prisoners to the jail but was told that there was no more room on the vehicle.

In the meantime, since the police were not allowing King's sympathizers inside, a crowd had gathered outside the courtroom. Some 150 to 200 persons were crowding the walks on both sides of the street in front of the municipal building. Logically, the police could have made wholesale arrests for loitering. But this was, apparently, not the time for any more blunders. And 150 "loiterers" might precipitate as big a scandal as had the roundup of the boycott leaders in February, 1955. What is more, protests were already pouring into the state and American embassies abroad about the scheduled execution of a fifty-five-year-old Alabama Negro, Jimmy Wilson, for the crime of robbing a white woman of $1.95, a sentence later commuted by the Governor.

After King's trial was over, the crowd was disappointed in not seeing him come out of the courtroom when his wife, his lawyer and his chief witness, Abernathy, emerged. Somebody announced that their leader was voluntarily going to jail. The police stopped Abernathy from making a speech but he did get to say, "Let's walk to Dexter." The deliberate gesture of not riding the seven blocks to the Dexter Avenue Baptist Church reminded everyone of the days when, as Professor Norman Walton put it, Montgomery was the "walking city."

At the church a meeting was held with prayers and testimonials, including one by Mrs. King. It was decided that a constant vigil would be kept outside the jail house, with singing and praying all day and all night, as long as Dr. King was serving out his sentence there. The "watchers" would come and go in relays.

While this was taking place, King at the municipal building was told that somebody had paid his fine. He tried to determine who had done this, but even the clerk who receipted court fines pretended not to know. King then went back to see the judge who had tried his case. They talked together in the judicial chambers. When King protested the payment of his fine, the judge remarked in a fatherly tone that there was nothing that could be done about it. He sought to wash his hands of prejudice against Negroes, submitting that one reason he remained on the bench when he could retire was to avoid being succeeded by some rabid, anti-Negro jurist.

Freed, King started walking to the Dexter Avenue Baptist Church. A passerby in an automobile insisted upon giving him a lift, but by the time King arrived his sympathizers had left. They had gone halfway to the city jail before word reached them that King was out.

When they returned to the church, King spoke to them. Later that night, he spoke to a crowded mass meeting. He said:

Today, in many parts of the South, the brutality inflicted upon Negroes has become America's shame. . . . Something must happen to awaken the dozing conscience of America before it is too late. . . . Somewhere the Negro must come to the point of refusing to co-operate with evil. . . . But you must go out of here with love and nonviolence. I have no malice toward anyone, not even the white policemen who almost broke my arm, who choked me and kicked me. Let there be no malice among you.

Before the day was over, the identity of the person who paid the fine was discovered: it was the Commissioner of Public Safety. He professed to have done it to save the city the cost of King's board and keep for fourteen days and to foil a "publicity stunt." Perhaps he saw that the moral victory would grow each day that King served his sentence and that the world would see as Thoreau had said of his jailers a hundred years ago: "They plainly did not know how to treat me. . . ."

. . . And Life

Ever since the bus boycott had ended, Martin Luther King had wanted to write a book based on his memories of that great experience. On September 17, 1958, this memoir, *Stride Toward Freedom,* was published. As part of the sales promotion for the book, the author began a series of radio, TV and personal appearances that would take him over the country.

On Saturday afternoon, September 20, King sat at a desk in Blumstein's department store on 125th Street in Harlem, autographing copies of his book, shaking hands and chatting with the crowd of men, women and children who had come for the occasion. Among them, a dark-skinned woman, after assuring herself of his identity, came up to him, startlingly uttered a few wrathful phrases, and then, suddenly lunging forward, plunged an eight-inch Japanese letter opener into King's chest. She at once attempted to escape, but Walter Pettiford of the *Amsterdam News,* who happened to be present, caught her and turned her over to the authorities, who found that she also carried a loaded revolver.

In the resultant tumult and confusion, King, with the letter opener protruding from his chest, appeared to be the least excited person present. Shortly afterward, he was taken to Harlem Hospital, where Dr. Aubre Maynard and an interracial surgical team removed one of King's ribs and part of the breastbone. King's doctors say that he was within "a sneeze" of losing his life, for the blade of the letter opener had penetrated to within a fraction of an inch of the aorta, and a cough, sneeze or twist of the body might have resulted in the puncture of this artery.

News of the stabbing spread to the nation. Telephone lines in New York, Montgomery and Atlanta were swamped. New York's Governor Averell Harriman hurried to King's bedside. The stricken man's wife, relatives and friends, including Abernathy and Bob Williams, flew up from Montgomery and Atlanta. Crowds gathered in the streets in front of Harlem Hospital.

After the operation, hourly bulletins on King's condition were carried by TV and radio networks. A wave of deep emotion swept over the Negro community of Montgomery, and prayer services were held for King's recovery. An indication of the depth of concern felt by the community is found in the comparison made by a prominent clergyman in one of the main services: "The Lord giveth and taketh away. . . . Even his only begotten son was also suffered to bear the cross of Calvary while yet a young man. . . ." Following a decline on the second day, King rallied and continued to gain steadily. After ten days, he was released, the doctors predicting that his recovery would be complete.

Messages of sympathy came in by the hundreds, including letters from the President's staff and Vice-President Nixon. There were none from the public officials of Montgomery. Nor was there an editorial for King in the Montgomery *Advertiser,* though there was one in the New York *Post.*

There were some hate letters, however, and several threats that the hospital would be bombed. A few places in the South even sent congratulations and small monetary contributions to King's assailant.

The stabbing of Martin Luther King has a nightmarish irrationality about it. On the surface, there is no reason in the world why Mrs. Izola Ware Curry should have wanted to kill this man. A European, unfamiliar with American affairs, might ask: Why should *anyone* want to kill a man who is an advocate of love and nonviolence? But those who know the King story know that opponents of the cause he represents have continually abused him; have attempted to dynamite his home.

Even Americans might ask the second question: Why should any *Negro* want to kill a champion of his own cause? The answer is that King is not a hero to *all* Negroes. There are some who totally disagree with him and reject his counsel. They repose no confidence, as he does, in the good faith of white people. They feel that interracial co-operation is a snare, the campaign for racial integration a delusion.

Their immediate hope for a tolerable life in America rests in the doctrine of Negro cohesiveness—Negro businesses, Negro social organizations and Negro standards of culture and physical beauty. Their ultimate hope lies in actual or vicarious migration "back to Africa," where the black man will once again govern himself under his own flag and fig tree.

These "Negro Nationalists" or "Black Zionists" feel that the Rev. Dr. King is "soft" on the "white enemy" and that he weakens and dilutes "Negro integrity." There were scattered boos for him at a Harlem rally where he said: "Black supremacy is just as bad as white supremacy." That he should autograph his book in a "white" store and not in a Negro store of Harlem brought forth picket lines in front of Blumstein's on the eve of the fateful Saturday.

Thus, out of either white or black racialism could come the impulse to assassinate Martin Luther King. We remember that Gandhi was slain by a fellow Indian—a "nationalist" outraged by the Mahatma's moderation.

And there are yet others who sincerely regard King as a menace. Lest we forget, there are some few Negro servants as well as many more white employers who feel that the struggle for desegregation is destroying the genteel tradition that they once knew, when white and black trusted each other and paternal favors were exchanged for services and loyalty. Social revolutions often crush such private worlds. To say that the casualties are expendable in the light of progress toward the larger good for the much greater number is not to forget the resentment of those who experience the personal tragedy of losing what was dear to them.

Even in Montgomery, where King is presumably a hero of heroes, there are Negroes who still commiserate together with their white friends over the good old days before "that terrible bus boycott." To them the name King is Satan.

As for Mrs. Izola Ware Curry, it is not necessary to establish her definite connection with white or black extremist groups in order to understand her motivation. Born on a Southern plantation, child of a broken home, unsuccessful in marriage and work, a rootless wanderer —she is, in her own person, a symptom of the frustrations of our day. Perhaps quite properly she has been committed to an institution for the mentally ill, but, as everybody knows, that does not rectify the circumstances that produce her type. In our "civilization" unhappiness is widespread, the struggle for security unremitting and the hunger for the golden living that the screens of our movies and TV's parade before us is largely unsatisfied.

And while these desires are burning within us, along comes a man who galvanizes public attention, who speaks with a voice that is heard, who moves in the councils of the mighty. The troubled mind fastens upon such an influential figure as the answer to life's woes: "If the Great Man would but hear me, if I could but tell my troubles to him, he could say what I should do; he could speak to the President about me. Perhaps he himself would help me through his own generosity. . . ."

And so, thousands of letters are written to Dr. King about all manner of personal difficulties and projects. Devices of every conceivable sort are concocted by persons fiercely anxious to meet him, to talk with him.

But if such efforts should fail, if King or some assistant of his should appear to turn away, rebuffing the suppliant, then adoration turns to scorn—or worse.

King himself seems to sense all of these possibilities when he says that "a climate of hatred and bitterness so permeates our nation that inevitably deeds of extreme violence must erupt."

And Now

The crisis that came near ending the life of Martin Luther King appears to have been a natural turning point in his life. It gave him an opportunity to make a thoughtful reordering of the inner as well as the outer pattern of his activities. Only time will tell if this has been done.

If measures of personal security are not considered he is almost certain to be killed. Those who live by the sword are not the only ones who perish by it. The social pressures, both positive and negative, are increasing, and if King's enemies do not destroy him, his admirers will. For example, when he was released from Harlem Hospital, several hundred persons were there in the streets to meet and cheer him. In their enthusiasm to touch him or shake his hand, these well-wishers would have overrun his family and attendants and unintentionally crushed him but for the police escort that was present.

It is not a happy thought that from now on every woman who moves toward King with a bouquet of flowers or a handbag or even a book for his autograph will be suspect. However, the alternative is an even less happy anticipation.

But while these external measures are being taken, what about Martin Luther King himself? How is he faring? What are his great decisions on his future course?

Is he, for example, yet ready to give full commitment to the ideals that he projects? Is he prepared to follow Gandhi not only in nonviolence but in the discipline of meditation and restraint and the renunciation of worldly goods?

Moreover, as a leader has he at last accepted the hard necessity of planning ahead and co-operatively sharing the tasks and rewards that this involves?

King's great initial triumph, we recall, had about it an element of chance. The bus boycott was not premeditated; it happened. King did not create it; he was at first its creature and later merely its guide. The man and his environment met in beautiful and fruitful harmony by grace of good fortune.

But now that the charismatic leader is heading an organized operation, should the future be left to individual improvisation? There are, of course, intellectuals, organizers and experts of every kind who would willingly contribute their talents to such an idealistic movement, if they could be sure that it is indeed what it seems to be. Perhaps the technical competencies are what the crusades for social justice need most just now. This, King is realizing.

In a sense, he, like others, is but a product of his environment. His rearing has been middle class—no hunger or fuel-less nights or begging for jobs. His was a happy, wholesome childhood and from adolescence he slipped easily into manhood; a good life, reminiscent of our Age of Innocence. His college taught him to succeed.

Neither by experience nor reading is King a political radical. There is not a Marxist bone in his body. He accepts his society save where injustice and violence defile it. In the classic phrase, Martin Luther King is a bourgeois leader of the masses.

However, he cannot be explained fully by environmental determinism. Where did he learn nonviolence? Surely not from his father or brother or schoolroom or playground or the way of life of his region or social order. His sensitive spirit found its own direction in spite of so many examples to the contrary. He transcended his immediate environment even as a child, long before he could appreciate Gandhi or Thoreau or Christ intellectually. That he has risen above the society that bore him and shaped him is part of the extraordinary quality of his personality.

By any yardstick, his has been a remarkable life. The fact that it could happen in America, even in the South, is heartening in a day when the great American Dream appears to be receding and shrinking before a specter from the East.

Looked at impersonally, Martin Luther King is a national asset, a human resource that is worth more to the United States than, say, the Grand Coulee Dam. He symbolizes an idea that meets a fundamental need of our times. His way is needed in the painful transition through which the South is presently passing, and his way is needed by the American nation in a divided world. He could be a real ambassador of good will abroad but we ourselves must accept what we, through him, would offer to others.

Nonviolent resistance is an alternative to war as well as to domestic conflict. Each nation is frightened of fighting but dares not lay down its arms, fearing attack from its neighbor. But here is a voice that says: "See, we will not harm you; our hands are clean and empty. Let us be brothers."

Not all but at least some of the people of the earth are willing to listen to such a plea, to contemplate a possible destiny other than the utter ruin of mankind through bombs and missiles and strontium 90. Perhaps the harassed and hesitant heart will listen to this message, if it comes with no hollow sound and is thoughtful and sincere.

Montgomery has given Martin Luther King to all men everywhere. Someday *all* of Montgomery will be proud of him. At thirty, with international recognition, he should have decades of usefulness ahead. We should all want this promise to be realized, for perhaps he and others like him may be able to help us survive the days of anguish that are upon us. Even in a mad world, the spirit of man may yet prevail.

How This Book Was Written

ALMOST by chance, I attended that first, huge mass meeting of December 5, 1955, that converted the day-old bus boycott into the year-long Montgomery mass movement. Although I was baffled by much that I saw and heard that evening, I was at least able to realize that something socially significant was happening. Accordingly, I took copious notes then and continued to do so until integrated buses became a legal fact on December 21, 1956.

During this period, from December to December, I also saved clippings from the daily white press and the weekly Negro press, recorded anecdotes and talked frequently with members of the board of the Montgomery Improvement Association and others who seemed to be playing leading roles in what was going on. My colleagues and students helped, too, reporting incidents and bringing in leaflets that I would probably have missed. This was very true of Professors Norman W. Walton, Joseph M. Brittain and William Gibson. Apparently, everybody wished to assist me in taking advantage of the unusual opportunity, for a student of history is seldom so lucky as to be a participant-observer of the life drama that he would write about.

While the boycott was in progress, I talked with Dr. King from time to time. But because he was so rushed, I did not get a chance to do depth interviewing of him until the summer of 1957. Then, as we talked about some of the more intimate relations of the movement and his own personal history, it soon became clear that here was a story of the rise of a charismatic leader of the people that deserved immediate and somewhat independent treatment. It would also illuminate the history of the movement itself, which could come later.

235

Since I had lived and worked in Atlanta for nine years, I was fairly familiar with the world that Martin Luther King was born into and remained in for the first nineteen years of his life. Before coming to Montgomery, I had known him, his family and his college.

Dr. King co-operated fully in the preparation of this biography. Our practice was to divide the time we would spend together, giving the first half of it over to discussing his ideas, outlines and drafts for his own memoirs and the last half to my questions.

Mrs. King, too, took an active interest in the undertaking. I visited her home in Perry County, Alabama just outside the town of Marion and found her family and childhood friends there quite eager to talk about and "tell on" Coretta.

Many helped me find pictures, Mrs. Alberta King once calling me up at midnight when she uncovered a rare snapshot of her son.

The whole King clan seemed to like the sections of the story involving their own lives that I would read aloud to them from time to time. Martin and Coretta went through the whole manuscript.

Beyond the family circles, numerous other persons supplied information. Mrs. Maude L. Ballou, secretary to the MIA, was wonderfully helpful. After the Board voted to give me access to the files of the organization, her exact knowledge of them saved me many hours of searching. Mrs. Thelma B. Archer checked through the pages of the *Maroon Tiger*, student paper of Morehouse College, for me. Dr. Frank Forbes submitted the records of intercollegiate athletics at Morehouse, 1944-48, while young King was attending there. Gerone Taylor dug out academic reports and student enrollments for this same period. My sister, Mrs. Fan M. Diaz, helped gather information on the stabbing of Dr. King in New York. Miss Ollie Brown and her staff at the library of Alabama State College let me have the run of the place.

I was quite fortunate, also, in the three critics who were good enough to read the manuscript.

1. Leonard R. Ballou and I have been tearing apart each other's writings for years. He is professionally a musician and music teacher, who is writing the story of the Negro composer in America. But Ballou reads widely and is well informed on the history of the Negro in Africa and America. Moreover, he has a sharp eye for dangling participles and other indelicacies. Ballou would read the second drafts as they came from the typewriter and took such an interest in the biography that he seemed to be genuinely sorry when he read the last sentence of the last chapter.

2. Lewis Wade Jones has been running red marks through my compositions ever since I first submitted stories and poems to him when he was editor of the *Fisk Herald*, back in the good old undergraduate days. Jones even then was a right-hand assistant to Charles S. Johnson, the great social scientist, and is now, himself, a Columbia University Ph.D. and a sociologist at Tuskegee Institute, just forty miles down the road from Montgomery. Dr. Jones read the next-to-the-final draft of the manuscript, looking down with olympian contempt upon any departures from

what he considers to be sound concepts of leaders and mass movements.

3. My wife, Ruth, quite humorously, would burlesque so effectively scenes and characters as they were described in the various chapters that often a portrait had to be retouched in order to give it a more rounded and authentic look.

The ever-willing Mrs. Ballou typed three of the thirteen chapters. However, the bulk of the seemingly never-ending labor of typing and retyping, first draft, second draft, next-to-the-final draft and then final copy fell upon my two student secretaries, Miss Annie Laura Powell and Miss Bertha Cornelia DeRamus. They were marvelous: technically competent, conscientious and quietly cheerful throughout.

The advice of my publishers has made this a better publication than it would otherwise have been.

In sum, this book is indeed a group rather than an individual product. Martin Luther King lived the life and the Negro community put on the boycott. I merely wrote about what they did and in doing that I had greater and more generous support than I had any reason to expect.

L.D.R.

Index